QUEERING CONFLICT

For my mum Mary and my brother Del

Queering Conflict

Examining Lesbian and Gay Experiences of
Homophobia in Northern Ireland

MARIAN DUGGAN
Sheffield Hallam University, UK

ASHGATE

Published by
Ashgate Publishing Limited
Wey Court East
Union Road
Farnham
Surrey, GU9 7PT
England

Ashgate Publishing Company
Suite 420
101 Cherry Street
Burlington
VT 05401-4405
USA

www.ashgate.com

British Library Cataloguing in Publication Data
Duggan, Marian.
   Queering Conflict: Examining Lesbian and Gay Experiences of homophobia in
   Northern Ireland.
   1. Homophobia – Northern Ireland – History – 20th century. 2. Heterosexism –
   Northern Ireland – History – 20th century. 3. Gays – Northern Ireland – Social
   conditions – 20th century. 4. Gays – Legal status, laws, etc. – Northern
   Ireland – History – 20th century. I. Title
   306.7'66'09416'09045-dc22

Library of Congress Cataloging-in-Publication Data
Duggan, Marian.
   Queering Conflict: Examining Lesbian and Gay Experiences of Homophobia in
   Northern Ireland / by Marian Duggan.
     p.   cm.
   Includes bibliographical references and index.
   1. Homophobia – Northern Ireland. 2. Homosexuality – Northern Ireland. 3. Hate
   crimes – Northern Ireland. 4. Gays – Northern Ireland – Social conditions.
   5. Lesbians – Northern Ireland – Social conditions. I. Title.
   HQ76.45.G72N673 2011
   306.76'609416–dc23   2011030391

ISBN   9781409420163 (hbk)
ISBN   9781409420170 (ebk)

Printed and bound in Great Britain by
TJ International Ltd, Padstow, Cornwall.

Contents

List of Tables and Figures

Table

Figure

List of Abbreviations

ASA	Advertising Standards Authority
CAI	Changing Attitude Ireland
CPS	Crown Prosecution Service
DUP	Democratic Unionist Party
ECtHR	European Court of Human Rights
FPC	Free Presbyterian Church
ICR	Institute for Conflict Research
IRA	Irish Republican Army
LASI	Lesbian Advocacy Services Initiative
LGB	Lesbian, Gay and Bisexual
LGB&T	Lesbian, Gay, Bisexual and Transgender
LVF	Loyalist Volunteer Force
MLA	Member of the Legislative Assembly
MSM	Men who have sex with men
MP	Member of Parliament
NI	Northern Ireland
NIGRA	Northern Ireland Gay Rights Association
NILT	Northern Ireland Life and Times
NIO	Northern Ireland Office
RUC	Royal Ulster Constabulary
PRONI	Public Records Office of Northern Ireland
PSNI	Police Service of Northern Ireland
PUP	Progressive Unionist Party
SACHR	Standing Advisory Commission on Human Rights
SDLP	Social Democratic Labour Party
STP	Stop the Parade
TRP	The Rainbow Project
UDA	Ulster Defence Association
UUP	Ulster Unionist Party
UVF	Ulster Volunteer Force

Acknowledgements

This book is the result of a long and arduous journey that was made all the better as a result of some truly great people. First and foremost I am indebted to Professor Shadd Maruna and Ms Eileen Fegan. Their valuable insights and guidance gave me much needed moments of clarity in my work, but their friendship, advice and support gave me the confidence to feel I could achieve what often felt like a task beyond my ability. Similarly, my thanks go to Professor Phil Scraton, Professor Adrian Howe, Dr Karen Corteen and Dr David Scott. You each played such an important part in making me who I am today – personally and professionally – and I can't possibly thank you all enough.

My deepest thanks go to the lesbians and gay men who shared their life stories with me and whose experiences provided the foundations of this book. I am hugely indebted to each of you. Additionally, this study would have been much more difficult without the unwavering assistance provided by several community and voluntary organisations: LASI, The Rainbow Project, Causeway LGBT, Strabane LGBT, GLYNI and NIGRA. Thank you so much for all your help and input and I hope your vital work continues to be recognised for the positive impact it is having for lesbians and gay men in Northern Ireland.

Every researcher needs time out, so massive thanks must go to all of you who kept me in beer and giggles, particularly Claire McCann, Yassin M'Boge, Smita Kheria, Lisa White, Sharon McCaffrey, Nathan Emmerich, Diarmaid Elder, Marie Thorley, Joanna Stansfield, Geraldine Murphy, Kavita Mirpuri, Gail Kersey and the rest of you lovely lads and ladies. My sincerest gratitude to Dave Moxon and Jozef Sen for commenting on drafts of chapters at incredibly short notice; I owe you both, big time!

This book is dedicated to my family who have provided all the love, support and inspiration any person would need to achieve their aspirations. My mum Mary's endless offers of cups of tea or a listening ear at the end of the phone were always welcomed. My brother Del might have been on the other side of the world for the duration of the book, but his adventurous spirit, intrigue for new experiences and lust for life have inspired me nonetheless. Thank you both so much for being fantastic throughout.

I would like to acknowledge the Economic and Social Research Council for funding my doctoral studies and the Institute of Criminology and Criminal Justice in the School of Law at Queen's University Belfast for providing excellent training and operational facilities which aided my research immensely. Finally, I have tried to represent the experiences and information shared with me during this project to the best of my ability, but of course any mistakes and misrepresentations are entirely my own.

MARIAN DUGGAN
May 2011

Introduction

In 2008 Iris Robinson, a former Democratic Unionist Party (DUP) MLA and MP, made a series of statements about homosexuality live on BBC Radio Ulster which caused a widely publicised furore that resonated far beyond her Northern Ireland audience. Mrs Robinson, wife of the First Minister Peter Robinson, stated that she felt homosexuality was an 'abomination' and that it 'nauseated' her. She also suggested that homosexuals could be 'cured' with psychiatric treatment and promoted the services of a 'very nice' psychiatrist she knew who could help to 're-orientate' homosexuals back to heterosexuality (Young 2008). She defended these statements by claiming that she believed it was the 'duty of Government to uphold God's law' (*Belfast Telegraph* 18 July 2008). These assertions proved inflammatory to many regardless of their sexual orientation across Northern Ireland and the rest of the UK. It soon emerged however that this was not the first time Mrs Robinson had expressed her repulsion towards homosexuality. As well as having compared homosexuals to murderers (Henry 2008), Hansard transcripts released in the midst of the furore showed that Mrs Robinson had also declared that 'there can be no viler act, apart from homosexuality and sodomy, than sexually abusing innocent children' (*Belfast Telegraph* 21 July 2008). Homosexuality, she believed, was worse than paedophilia.

As will be seen later in this book, Iris Robinson was not the first high–profile public minister to make disparaging comments about homosexuality in Northern Ireland. What made this particular event so notorious was that at the time of her statements, she was Chair of the Stormont Health Committee. In this role, Mrs Robinson was ultimately responsible for overseeing the delegation of funding for strategies and interventions designed to address the myriad mental health problems incurred by lesbian, gay, bisexual and transgender (LGB&T[1]) people affected by everyday experiences of homophobia. Her comments called into question her impartiality as a leader in this role, yet she remained in post. Mrs Robinson also evaded criminal action; after an investigation lasting a year the Police Service of

---

1   Hereafter, the acronym LGB&T will be used. A common complaint with this label is that including the 'T' can be tokenistic and more damaging for trans communities who, quite rightly, do not see their gender–based victimisation as the same as sexual identity victimisation. While transpeople can be lesbian, gay or bisexual, their victimisation is perhaps best analysed from a specific, gender–bias perspective. In Northern Ireland, the trans community is often included with lesbian and gay organisations (which also cover bisexuality too) although there are several smaller organisations which have their own identity. The research which informs this book derives solely from the experiences of lesbians and gay men who identify as the gender assigned to them at birth.

Northern Ireland (PSNI) stated that no action would be taken against her for any of the public statements she had made as they believed that she had done nothing wrong (Gordon 2009). Not content with this, calls for some form of comment from Westminster led to the then–Prime Minister Gordon Brown reiterating his reluctance to get involved, citing it as a matter for the Northern Ireland Assembly to resolve. Mrs Robinson remained in post until early 2010, her resignation from public office being prompted by revelations about her personal life and accusations of improper conduct. Mrs Robinson was alleged to have failed to follow procedure when involved in granting a licence to, and investing in, a restaurant owned by teenager Kirk McCambly, who she had been engaged in an extra–marital affair with at the time.[2]

These events, though interesting in their own right, indicate Northern Ireland's anomalous identity. To some, it appears to be a community rooted in the past, where moral objections to homosexuality result in it being religiously and publicly denounced alongside other forms of perceived sexual deviancy (although objections to such deviancy do not appear to extend to Catholic priests' physical and sexual abuse of children which for decades was overlooked and denied by the Catholic Church). To others, Northern Ireland is progressively moving away from its troubled past to celebrate inclusion and recognise that societies and social attitudes have changed significantly. Either way, there has most certainly been an increase in the visibility afforded to people who identify as lesbian, gay, bisexual and/or transgender in Northern Ireland, most notably over the past decade. However, despite debates about the rights and wrongs of homosexuality occupying a prominent position in social and political discourses in Northern Ireland, research and theory concerning Northern Irish lesbian and gay lives remains significantly underdeveloped compared to the rest of the UK.

This book focuses on Northern Ireland without recourse to comparisons to the Republic of Ireland or Great Britain, although at times some similarities are evident. This is because Northern Ireland offers a unique mix of British and Irish heritage which has interwoven to produce distinctive responses to particular social and political issues, several of which are discussed in later chapters. The cultural difference demarcating Northern Ireland from the rest of the UK is perhaps best introduced in the words of one of the gay male interviewees. At the time of interviewing, Rob had been in a relationship with Mack for over thirty years. Rob was from a Protestant background and Mack had a Catholic upbringing. They met in the 1970s while Rob was working in a factory, where his sexuality had become common knowledge as a result of a colleague telling people without Rob's permission. Rob's colleagues discovered that his partner was not only male, but a Catholic. What follows was, as Rob points out, an exchange that could only have happened in Northern Ireland:

---

2   In 2011, Mrs Robinson was eventually cleared of any wrongdoing in relation to the financing of Mr McCambly's business.

> This woman comes up to me one day and she says, 'You know, it's not you being gay that's the problem, but couldn't you have met a nice Protestant boy?" Now, that's a very typical Northern Ireland response; they didn't care that I was gay, but they knew he was Catholic, so it is a very Northern Ireland sort of thing. Nowhere else in the world would it really matter I suppose.

This exchange is enlightening in that it appears as if homosexuality was a more favourable social transgression than being in a cross–community relationship. This may well have been the case given the timing of the incident, which took place at the height of Northern Ireland's violent ethno–political conflict. The complexities surrounding attitudes towards homosexuality and sexual minorities in Northern Ireland, and the impacts of these on the lesbians and gay men exposed to such attitudes are focused upon in this book to draw out how homophobia has been informed and sustained. There are several different themes which are drawn upon throughout this analysis: issues of identity (including religious, political, national, sexual, gender, class and geographical), ideological constructs of 'homosexuality' and what this represents, the position of lesbians and gay men during the ongoing ethno–political conflict in Northern Ireland and the politicising of a sexual minority identity to attain recognition, rights and responsibilities.

Purpose and Structure of this Book

This book aims to account for the ways in which homophobia has become normalised in facets of Northern Irish social and political cultures to the detriment of those affected by it. It also addresses what this state of affairs may mean in terms of effecting purposeful social, legal and political change. Analyses of homophobia in Northern Ireland must be based within the particular social, moral and political perspectives relevant to that society. Such an approach links to other contemporary analyses of prejudices which suggest grounding these investigations in their culturally specific environments (Bowling 1993, Perry 2001, 2003). There has been considerable research into LGB&T people's experiences of homophobia and violence in England the past few decades and to a lesser degree Scotland and Wales. The findings from such studies have ensured that sexual orientation was eventually included in legislation addressing what has become known as 'hate crime' in Great Britain. However, these studies cannot be said to be truly representative of the UK as they often make little reference to Northern Ireland, or in some cases exclude it altogether (see Duggan 2008a, 2010a, 2010b). Some theoretical analyses which address homophobia in Northern Ireland make passing reference to existing cultural differences although few ground these examinations in empirical research with LGB&T communities. Alternatively, fact–finding studies into the nature and prevalence of homophobic discrimination or victimisation have focused on highlighting negative experiences and their impact, but have done little to assess what causes or sustains these prejudices in Northern Ireland.

The culturally specific analysis of homophobia undertaken in this book is coupled with suggestions that responding to homophobic hate crimes in Northern Ireland requires a similarly culturally specific response. This is not to say that initiatives currently in place elsewhere in the UK are not relevant or useful, but rather suggests that additional answers may be found in Northern Ireland's socio–political history. The study also hopes to show that understanding competing responses to sexual identities in Northern Ireland is integral to recognising and challenging different facets of homophobia. Existing policies which aim to address homophobia may not take into account the differing reasons why a person holds such prejudices if these are linked to religious or national backgrounds. Similarly, they may also fail to recognise homophobia which differs as a result of a prejudiced person's gender, race, class, ability, faith and so forth. Therefore, there are myriad ways in which homophobia can be addressed and engaged with to challenge the specific factors informing this prejudice.

As well as exploring how political and religious philosophies are imparted and operate to regulate sexualised identities, the chapters assess the type of victimisation experienced by lesbians and gay men, the impact of this on their lives and the methods employed to overcome sexual oppression and move closer towards visibility, recognition and acceptance. The analyses offer a historical perspective on factors informing contemporary homophobia in Northern Ireland. They suggest that if such factors remain unchallenged they will continue to sustain negative ideologies. Distinctions are made between urban and rural areas, men and women, older and younger interviewees and occasionally between Northern Ireland and comparable UK cities when this comparison is of particular note. The focus remains on exploring and explaining this prejudice within its unique Northern Irish socio–political history with a view to providing culturally informed recommendations to address the root causes of this particular prejudice.

Methodological Approach

What started out as an investigative study into contemporary homophobia soon ground to a halt when it appeared that there was very little literary LGB&T history specific to Northern Ireland to draw upon as a theoretical basis.[3] The research soon morphed into a much broader social, political and historical study of how contemporary homophobia has been informed and sustained in Northern Ireland. Much of the knowledge concerning Northern Irish LGB&T lives still resides with the often marginalised people living there, although some documents are archived in historical collections held at the Public Records Office and the Linen Hall Library in Belfast. These histories which provide testament to the struggles, progress and positive developments concerning LGB&T lives, have proved invaluable to

---

3   The research findings which inform this book arose from a doctoral project undertaken at Queen's University Belfast.

understanding not only how and why contemporary forms of homophobia exist in Northern Ireland, but why this form of prejudice remains largely unchallenged in social and political spheres.

As is the norm with exploratory analyses, this book is intended to supplement existing knowledge on homophobia, victimisation, the nature and impact of homophobic hate crime and responses to these issues. Unlike other areas of hate crime research, there is a marked absence of comparable Northern Irish research and literature within which to situate this knowledge. Looking into histories of homosexuality and homophobia in England, it becomes clear that these are not immediately transferrable when trying to evaluate similar histories in Northern Ireland. Furthermore, it is Northern Ireland's specific history of conflict that in part facilitated the perceived invisibility of LGB&T communities there. Therefore, this book proposes several starting points for further study into homophobic victimisation that are informed by historical readings of nationality, identity, community formation and political conflict which can be compared to similar postcolonial, post conflict societies.

Information was gathered through the following methods: documentary analyses; participant observation in various LGB&T community events and organisations; several focus groups held with lesbians and gay men in different parts of Northern Ireland; email contact with participants; online interviews and surveys, forum discussions, and questionnaires; attendance at several community or LGB&T public meetings; and, most significantly, two dozen recorded, in–depth, life history interviews with a selection of lesbians and gay men from across Northern Ireland who 'came of age' during the worst years of the political conflict. The documentary element is particularly significant when exploring the struggle for homosexual decriminalisation (discussed in Chapter 3). However, the oral testimonies given by the interviewees involved in the research form the majority of the book's focus and evidential base.

Life history interviewing is a popular method for exploring and understanding lesbian and gay lives (Porter and Weeks 1991; Nardi, Sanders and Mermor 1994; Diamond 2008). This popularity stems from the ability of life histories to provide insights into 'the complex, varied and uneven fashion' by which lesbians and gay men made sense of their 'needs and desires, and fashioned for themselves manageable social, and sexual ways of life' (Porter and Weeks 1991: viii). Similarly, 'coming out' stories have highlighted important themes of 'suffering, surviving and surpassing' in the lives of lesbians and gay men (Plummer 1995: 15). Life history, or biographical, research methods utilise people's subjective reconstruction of lived experiences to produce or enhance knowledge. It reintroduces the subject into sociology and privileges the experiences of people who are immersed in social relations. Roberts (2002: 3) differentiates between the life history and the life story stating that the life story 'is commonly applied to the narrated story by the author while the life history infers the later interpretive, presentational work of the researcher.' Faraday and Plummer suggest that life history research offers a subjective perspective onto historical knowledge: '[w]hen one conducts a life history interview, the findings become alive in terms of historical processes and structural constraints' (1979: 256). The individual's life is understood within the social context, but at the same time their narratives may shed light on the influence of that social situation on those experiences. In this manner, life history research is a process for understanding both the self and society (Bertaux 1996).

In the chapters which follow, the interviewees are referred to by their chosen pseudonyms as well as their age at the time of the interview. Their gender is rendered evident through their sexual orientation, as some pseudonyms may appear ambiguous. At times, these experiences are contextualised with reference to other studies of a quantitative nature, or other theories relating to homophobia, heterosexism or hate crime generally. Overall, however, it is the interviewees' experiences which provide the insight used to analyse, assess and account for the ways in which homophobia has been experienced and responded to in Northern Ireland. Therefore, references to 'the interviewees' relates to the lesbians and gay men interviewed in the course of the research which informs the empirical and theoretical foundations of *this* book.

In addition to the interviews, an online survey of women's experiences of being lesbian in Northern Ireland was conducted. This was sent out electronically via the Lesbian Advocacy Services Initiative (or LASI, a Northern Irish lesbian and bisexual women's organisation) to ask women specific issues about themes which arose from the interviews. These included: gendered experiences of homophobia, growing up lesbian in Northern Ireland, coming out as lesbian in later life, levels of engagement with LGB&T communities and organisations, managing family relationships and the impact of the ethno–political conflict and the peace process on LGB&T communities. Forty–one women responded to this anonymous survey and their answers were used to elicit more information about issues affecting women who were less likely to be 'out' about their sexuality (discussed in Chapter 5).

Outlining the benefits of involvement in a survey can be difficult, especially if there is often no direct advantage for the individual respondent. Wright (2006) indicates that researchers who offer to share the information they obtain with the community involved can foster a harmonious relationship and potentially increase the number of responses. He suggests creating a report whereby the most interesting results are communicated to those interested, either electronically or otherwise, to inform as well as bring the communication to an end. In keeping with Wright's (2006) suggestion, some of the preliminary findings were disseminated via several feature articles for the Northern Ireland feminist publication *Women's News* (Duggan 2008b, 2008c, 2008d, 2008e). Copies of these articles were provided to LASI to forward on to the respondents via the organisation's mailing list (which was how the survey had been distributed). Although only a small gesture, ensuring that people see the worth of their involvement is a necessary part of community research and helps break down the barriers between academic and non–academic stakeholders.

As with all research, this study has its limitations. The views of the interviewees are not representative of all lesbians and gay men who grew up in Northern Ireland, nor are they meant to be. However, they do offer an important insight into experiences which, as a result of the underlying moral conservatism evident in Northern Ireland's history and the dominance of the ethno–political conflict, have otherwise been overlooked in academic research.

Chapter Outline

Chapter 1 offers an overview of particular events in Northern Ireland's socio–political history which can be seen as impacting on lesbians' and gay men's lives. Embedded in this chapter is a history of the Troubles and the events leading up to this thirty–year period of violent division and heightened security. Interestingly, there are facets of this history which evidence the tactical use of sexual denigration in Ireland at a time when the legal suppression of same–sex activities was being enhanced. This analysis develops into a wider exploration of homophobia, heterosexism and hate crimes in order to set the scene for the culturally specific examination to follow.

Chapter 2 provides an in–depth look at homophobia and hate crime in Northern Ireland as it currently stands. Using official and unofficial statistics, prosecution figures, existing research and several of the interviewees' experiences, attitudes towards homosexuality are theorised using a framework of power, identity constructs and acceptable forms of victimisation. An examination of several barriers to reporting victimisation leads on to a consideration of the influence of paramilitary opposition to homosexuality in local communities. Finally, the chapter concludes by outlining the measures some lesbians and gay men continue to take to negotiate and resist these forms of sexual regulation in their day–to–day lives.

Chapter 3 focuses on politics and politicising sexual identities in Northern Ireland. Starting with an outline of the struggle for, and opposition to, legislation decriminalising homosexuality in Northern Ireland, the analysis indicates the necessary politicisation of the burgeoning LGB&T community during a time of heightened political conflict. Enhanced security measures are shown to have advantaged some lesbians and gay men in terms of visibility, space and freedom from sexual persecution due to the desertedness of the city in the evenings. Implicit in this chapter is the theme of resilience and resistance to social and political forms of identity persecution, particularly in light of the comments made by several prominent Northern Irish politicians in recent years.

Chapter 4 looks at the underlying level of moral conservatism which permeates Northern Irish society and interrogates its impact on both the lives of lesbians and gay men and the attitudes of others towards them. Issues such as addressing the 'lifestyle choice' debate, reorientation ideologies and attempting to reconcile sexual and spiritual selves indicate the myriad difficulties negotiated by many lesbians and gay men growing up in a culture where religious rhetoric dictated the life course. The chapter also provides an evaluation of the current controversies surrounding the picketing of the annual gay pride parade by Evangelical opponents and the importance of this event to sustain LGB&T visibility in a largely invisible society.

Chapter 5 provides a gender–specific focus by looking solely at women's experiences of being lesbian in Northern Ireland. Although lesbian women were not legally persecuted in the same was as gay men, several social and political constraints were evident in the women's stories. In covering issues such as managing family relationships, parenting and vulnerability to victimisation, it is clear that the additional aspect of gender difference impacted on some women's social and sexual regulation in a manner not experienced by gay men. Also addressed in this chapter is the importance of activism to the women involved in this research and the effect of women's politicisation on developing and sustaining lesbian visibility in Northern Ireland.

Chapter 6 addresses the personal impact of homophobia. The focus is on some of the less visible impacts of homophobia and negative coping strategies employed by people. These ranged from denial, isolation, migration and substance misuse through to contemplating more drastic measures. In addition, and to reflect the tenacity of those who overcame these challenges, the chapter also illustrates the freedom gained through undergoing personal 'coming out' journeys.

Finally, the conclusion offers an overall analysis of the central themes evident in lesbians' and gay men's experiences of homophobia in Northern Ireland, indicating how these can form the basis for change. Taking the core tenets of political imperatives, cultural conservatism and community interventions, the chapter suggests alternative measures of dealing with homophobia and hate crime in Northern Ireland which draw on the unique environment, history and identity inherent to this society.

Chapter 1

Contextualising Prejudice and 'Hate' in Northern Ireland

Much of the extensive academic coverage of Northern Ireland has concentrated largely on the three decades of ethno–political conflict known as 'the Troubles'. This focus has been described as being discernibly disproportionate to the actual size and scale of the issue (see, for example, Bell 1991, Whyte and FitzGerald 1991, Ruane and Todd 1996, Fay et al. 1999, McKittrick and McVea 2001). As a result, it can also be seen as having pushed other social, political and legal issues to the margins. Instead, the national and social divides routinely discussed indicate the importance of demarcating identity: Republican or Loyalist, nationalist or unionist, Catholic or Protestant, Irish or British (Whyte and FitzGerald 1991). In reality these are rarely neat divides: unionists usually align more with a Northern Irish or a British identity, but not always; myriad identities are to be found under the label 'Protestant'; and nationalists may range from favouring a somewhat limited amount of British intervention to none whatsoever (Whyte and FitzGerald 1991).

This chapter outlines the most pertinent aspects of Northern Ireland's history to provide a cultural backdrop and necessary context for the forthcoming narratives which were often situated in, and refer to, this significant time. Upon doing so, the chapter shifts focus to concentrate on locating LGB&T communities within what is perceived to be a 'new' Northern Ireland, one moving towards a post–conflict identity. Here, the examination indicates how histories of homophobia can be linked to the formation of this political entity. The ways in which homosexuality is understood by the two dominant religious doctrines in Northern Ireland – Catholicism and Protestantism – is also addressed.

Following on from this, the chapter explores the concepts of homophobia, heterosexism and hate crimes. Here, the justification for situating analyses of sexual prejudice within their specific cultural frameworks is exemplified. Understanding and challenging homophobia in Northern Ireland necessarily requires a focus on Northern Irish politics, morality and society before comparisons can be made with places such as Great Britain or the Republic of Ireland. Therefore, although theories of homophobia and heterosexism are part used to understand prejudice against sexual minorities, the following chapters aim to discern if and how these theories may not be as applicable to lesbian and gay experiences in Northern Ireland. Similarly, political shifts towards addressing hate crime indicates the limitations of this move in situating prejudice within the pathologised individual rather than addressing wider social factors. Theories which have arisen in relation to this developing field indicate the need to culturally locate such prejudice within its specific environment. Therefore, in addressing these, a more holistic analysis is provided of the factors informing homophobic ideologies and sustaining homophobic prejudice in Northern Ireland.

A Society in Transition

During the prolonged period of conflict in Northern Ireland, identity and spatial struggles between nationalist and unionist groups overshadowed other minorities, rendering them politically invisible (Kitchin and Lysaght 2003, 2004). As a result, identification within this sectarian currency was often required before individuals and groups claimed access to a politically–recognized 'self' (Conrad 1999: 55). This situation remains evident in the devolved Northern Ireland Assembly where MLAs must assign themselves to one of three options: 'Nationalist', 'Unionist' or 'Other'. Nevertheless, Northern Ireland is very much a society going through a significant period of transition. The ongoing and relatively successful peace process and the predominant stereotypical Irish temperament of welcoming hospitality have helped shift attention away from these past troubles and towards a more modern image of inclusivity and cultural richness. Indeed, Derry/Londonderry's[1] success in being chosen as the inaugural UK Capital of Culture for 2013 indicates the progress made in Northern Ireland since the late 1990s. Although peace is to be welcomed, it does not mean that the past can be forgotten; the drive for stability is very much an ongoing process in Northern Ireland as has been demonstrated with the dissident Republican events of 2011. The murder of Police Constable Ronan Kerr coupled with the discoveries of several explosive devices in and around Belfast indicates the small but significant threat to the peace process by those who reject the progress which has been made so far. Therefore, an exploration of Northern Ireland's socio–political history provides some context through which to understand these issues and the reasons for this ongoing sectarian concern.

Implicit in many analyses of life in Northern Ireland are the themes of politics, religion, nationality, identity and conflict. The language used to depict tensions often situates these along religious lines, but while religion may have played some part in segregating communities the crux of the conflict was political and based on national identity (Mitchell 2006). Part of ensuring community stability requires recognising how the intersectionality of several linked elements goes back further than the events of the 20th century. A brief summary of key events is necessary to indicate the complexities to what is commonly referred to as 'the Northern Ireland question'.

---

1   This city will be referred to using both names to recognise the continued dual identities it holds to the people of Northern Ireland and to avoid any inference of a particular allegiance.

The creation of Northern Ireland as a political entity is less than a century old – the result of a long and drawn–out process of partition from what eventually became the Republic of Ireland. Prior to the plantation period of the 16th and 17th centuries, the island of Ireland was an autonomous, largely agricultural, Catholic country, where religious adherence bound otherwise rural, isolated communities (Ruane and Todd 1996). Ulster, in the uppermost north–east of the island, is one of the four provinces which historically (and geographically) comprise of nine counties.[2] British Protestant settlers who arrived in the country primarily inhabited this well–positioned north–east area, taking ownership of land possessed by the native Irish then forcing them to rent it back. Many of these Protestant settlers were Scottish, bringing with them the Presbyterian religion: an increasingly puritan form of Protestantism that was more regimented than Catholicism (Connolly 1995).[3] The struggle for control of Ireland led to the Battle of the Boyne in 1690, where the Protestant King William of Orange defeated the Catholic King James II, deposing him of the British crown and effectively establishing Protestantism in Ireland.

The Descent into Conflict

In the decades that followed, the industrial revolution prompted an expanding linen, shipbuilding and engineering industry with much of the production being located in Ulster. Therefore, most of the incoming wealth was harnessed by the increasingly Protestant north–eastern part of Ireland (Hayes and McAllister 2001). By the time of the Act of Union 1800, which created the United Kingdom of Great Britain and Ireland, a quarter of Ireland's four million population were descendents of the Protestant settlers. The following year Westminster abolished the Irish parliament, taking complete control of Irish affairs. Opposition to this Act was both political and physical, with a principal organisation being the Repeal Association founded by Daniel O'Connell in 1840 and a splinter group, the Young Ireland movement forming from this and commencing physical action in 1848.

Few benefits of this revolution were felt by the native Catholic Irish. Their hostility towards British rule intensified following the 1845–1849 famine years in which the failure of the staple potato crops meant that thousands of poorer Catholic Irish people starved or migrated. The British Government refused to intervene financially, fearing that the money may be used to arm the increasingly unsettled Irish. As a result, Irish Catholics put forth a series of motions for what became a succession of Home Rule Bills. Their aims included removing the British from

---

2   The other provinces are Leinster, Munster and Connacht. The counties are Antrim, Armagh, Down, Fermanagh, Londonderry, Tyrone, Cavan, Donegal, and Monaghan. The latter three form part of the Republic of Ireland.

3   For example, practices such as transubstantiation, confession and the sacramental offerings were removed from Protestant religious services.

Dublin Castle, where they were currently overseeing the Irish administration. Unsurprisingly, the Protestant minority opposed these Bills, fearing religious and political oppression as well as a diminishment of their growing wealth (Amstutz 2004). Finally, in 1920 The Government of Ireland Act split the island of Ireland, enacting Home Rule in 26 largely southern counties while governing the remaining six – Fermanagh, Armagh, Tyrone, Derry/Londonderry, Antrim and Down – directly from Westminster. The Anglo–Irish Agreement of December 1921 created the Irish Free State a year later, eventually to be renamed the Republic of Ireland. Opposition to this partition was intense amongst those who sought a united Ireland facilitated by the British Government's withdrawal.

The new political state of Northern Ireland was christened by violence; 428 people were killed in the two–year period that followed partition, two–thirds of them Catholic (McKittrick and McVea 2001). The Royal Ulster Constabulary (RUC) was established in 1922 to quell tensions. However, with the majority of its 3,500 members being derived from Protestant communities, many Catholics were sceptical of the RUC's ability to be impartial. As World War Two broke out, tensions abated somewhat with communities becoming more integrated, especially in larger urban areas (Feldman 1991). The post–war period was also relatively calm, remaining that way until the mid–1960s when tensions again began to mount as a result of perceived unfair treatment towards Catholics by the predominantly Protestant/unionist government. A succession of peaceful demonstrations, marches and protests aimed at highlighting this discrimination tapped into similar civil rights movements taking shape in England and America, most notably the black civil rights uprisings. A series of events in the late 1960s and early 1970s – including Bloody Sunday, a report about which recently decreed that those shot and killed by British servicemen were indeed innocent after a 12 year investigation into the event – led to the worst period of sustained combat in Northern Ireland's short history.

From 1968 to 1998, social and political life in Northern Ireland was dominated by often violent sectarian struggles (see O'Hearn 1983, Feldman 1991, McKittrick et al. 1999, Hayes and McAllister 2001, McKittrick and McVea 2001, Amstutz 2004). The high number of casualties during this period illustrates the severity of the Troubles. Estimates suggest that almost 40,000 people were injured and more than 3,500 people were killed (Fay, Morrisey and Smyth 1999). These are significant figures when contrasted against Northern Ireland's population, which currently stands at just 1.7 million. It is evident, then, that ethno–political tensions have dominated life in Northern Ireland for a significant period of time. Although progress has been made with regards to peace and stability, the events of the past cannot be overlooked when analysing interpersonal or political relationships. Additionally, these events were so predominant in society that other socially progressive, cultural developments occurred far later (if at all in some cases) in Northern Ireland than elsewhere in the UK.

The Belfast (Good Friday) Agreement 1998 signalled an end to the worst years of the Troubles and the start of the current peace process. This new era was characterized by several amendments to policing and legislation which arose as part of the post–Patten era of institutional change in the police service. The Patten Report, published following the signing of the 1998 Agreement, recommended changes designed to harmonise traditionally divided members of Northern Ireland's communities. Negative connotations associated with the RUC centred on the inherent British ethos and suggestions of brutality towards members of Catholic communities. As part of the measures brought in to address this, the RUC was renamed the Police Service of Northern Ireland (PSNI). Changes to recruitment meant that Catholics, women, ethnic minorities and members of the LGB&T community were actively targeted to diversify membership. The enactment of various laws and policies enshrining equality and promoting good relations, trust and mutual respect was rolled out beyond the PSNI. This has set the scene for Northern Ireland currently being at its most culturally diverse, benefitting largely from migration as a result of a growing European Union. These values were also outlined in the first of the *Programme for Government* documents, which offered guidelines to embed these values in the 'new' Northern Ireland.

Following the 1998 Agreement, a wealth of specific laws aimed at enhancing LGB&T rights, equality and protection from discrimination and victimisation were introduced to Northern Ireland. The key organisations tasked with implementing equality and combating hostility included the Office of the First Minister and Deputy First Minister (OFMDFM), based at the Northern Ireland Assembly (NIA). Here, politicians are known as Members of the Legislative Assembly (MLAs). Responsibility also resided to a lesser degree with the Northern Ireland Office (NIO), based at Westminster (CJINI 2007). Northern Ireland was in a period of 'direct rule' (governed from Westminster), so much of this legislation was implemented by the Labour government and not domestically. Although advantageous to members of LGB&T communities in Northern Ireland, it appeared that Northern Irish politicians, if left to their own devices, would be less willing enact such laws. The failure to implement this legislation through domestic channels meant that underlying social and political prejudices towards homosexuality were not engaged with, challenged or addressed. Northern Irish politicians opposed to homosexuality were not made to state this on the record in the same way as many have openly objected to extending the 1967 Abortion Act to Northern Ireland. This may have been a crucial opportunity that was lost for Northern Irish LGB&T communities to confront negative ideologies and rectify problematic prejudices.

Histories of Homophobia in Northern Ireland

Several important historical events can be seen as informing contemporary representations of homophobia in Northern Ireland. These events indicate the ways in which homosexuality has been constructed as foreign (not naturally occurring in Ireland) and, perhaps most importantly, as British. Homosexuality may have been used by the Irish as a weapon against the British to undermine their dominance during the conflict over who ruled Ireland. Towards the end of the 19th century, a scandal broke of alleged homosexuality between elite members of the British establishment governing at Dublin Castle and criminal justice bodies. Hyde (1955: 133) provides an in–depth account and analysis of the numerous Irish men charged with sexual offences under the different criminal law Acts imposed by the British Government, claiming that '[t]he widespread belief that homosexual 'vice' was rampant in official circles in Ireland did much to discredit Gladstone's Liberal administration at this time'.

The activities were brought to light by two Irish nationalists who were also staunch supporters of the Home Rule Bills which were passing through Westminster during this period. The resulting prosecutions occurred just prior to the amendments made to the 1885 Criminal Law (Amendment) Act, which widened the scope of the criminal law to include any unspecified sexual acts between men that could be termed 'gross indecency'. Alluding to the simultaneous timing of these events, Rose (1994: 6) indicates that there may be some importance in the fact that 'Irish nationalist ideology developed during such a homophobic period in European history'. The Irish effectively employed homosexuality as the 'alien other, linked to conspiracy, recruitment, opposition to the nation, and ultimately a threat to civilisation', in doing so instigating early dichotomous divisions between identities in Ireland (Stychin 1998: 9).

At the heart of the Irish Catholic identity was the 'heterosexual, procreative, patriarchal family' upon which the success and survival of the Church depended in such desperate times (Martin 1997: 96). These families were characteristically large in number, owing to the strict teaching of the Roman Catholic Church against any form of birth control. Sexuality was seen to be a gift from God to be used only for procreation. In uncertain times, the family offered a form of stability, recognition and security for both the individual and the community. Drawing on Foucault's (1976) concept of the family cell as regulating normative heterosexuality against the deviant 'other', Conrad argues that, 'the centrality of the family cell to social, economic, and political organization defines and limits not only acceptable sexuality but also the contours of the private sphere, the public sphere, and the nation itself' (2004: 4). In other words, the primacy and continuation of the family cell was central to Irish national identity, homogeneity and community. The ideology of the family is not just heterosexual and procreative, but also alludes to history, continuity, regularity and the familiar. Homosexuality, on the other hand, is perceived to be on the negative end of this dichotomy. Conrad (2004: 25) claims that it was perceptions of homosexuality as 'flexible' and 'unstable' which caused concern for British and Irish societies, stirring up wider fears over control:

> The concept of the homosexual as a foreign body, an infectious agent in the family cell, thus reveals a profound anxiety not only about sexual identity but also about the stability of the nation and state and the security of their borders.

This early implication of homosexuality as 'a tool in the hands of the Irish nationalists' was employed in a manner which made it impossible to 'equate homosexuality with the nationalist ideal of Irishness' (Hanafin 2000: 54). Indeed, Hanafin argues that 'the Irish self that was posited by the postcolonial elite was pure and clean, expelling what it considered to be 'impure' elements' (2000: 51).

Analyses of the trial and execution of Sir Roger Casement, a British revolutionary and Irish nationalist sympathiser involved in the failed Easter Rising of 1916, indicate how homosexuality was used to cast aspersions on one's integrity by both sides in the Irish conflict. During his trial, Sir Casement's diaries were seized and made public. These apparently indicated that he was homosexual, a fact which was referred to repeatedly in court (Hyde 1955, Dudgeon 2002, Conrad 2001, 2004). Although it was his political actions which sealed his fate, the employment of his diaries to illustrate his seemingly deviant sexual exploits, though entirely unrelated, effectively enhanced the allegations made against him. The links between sexual deviancy and general deceit had been strongly forged. Conrad (2001: 129) notes how the treatment of Roger Casement illustrates the importance placed upon dividing sexual and national identity at the time:

> Both the British and the Irish made his sexuality foreign, either by denying it and accepting his patriotism (the Irish Nationalist response), or by accepting both his Irish nationalism and his sexuality as evidence of the same problem.

While for the British fears of homosexuality may have centred upon treason and blackmail, for the Irish fears of homosexuality tended towards invasion of difference and the onset of change. In both cases, the breach of borders could be seen as physical and metaphorical, yet comprising of very real fears for both sides. Expanding on this, Stychin (1998: 194) indicates that defining homosexuality through colonial discourses implies change, difference, unpredictability and unknowing:

> This use of homosexuality has been exemplified by the colonial contamination model. In this guise, same sex acts and identities are seen through the lens of colonialism, and homosexuality becomes a symbol of modernity, contrasted to a 'traditional" way of life based on heterosexual marriage and strict gender roles that existed before the perversion of the colonial encounter.

Stychin's discussion of modernity and marriage is further reinforced by the Christian dominance which continues to inform Northern Irish society. Importantly, differences in understanding and responding to homosexuality shape the ways in which lesbians and gay men have been, and continue to be, perceived and responded to by Catholics and Protestants in Northern Ireland.

Demarcating Key Differences between Catholicism and Protestantism

Northern Ireland is a Christian society, with Catholicism and Protestantism comprising the dominant doctrines. Several core social and political themes can be identified to differentiate between Catholic and Protestant ideologies. While Catholicism remains strongest in social and institutional spheres (including within education sectors in Northern Ireland) Protestantism is more dominant politically as a result of strong and voracious ideologies (Mitchell 2006). Social identities divided along these lines often, but not always, indicate nationality and political preference. Importantly, what sets Northern Ireland apart from the rest of the UK is the way in which religion functions both top–down in a political sense and bottom–up in a community sense (Mitchell 2006). Although overshadowed by political tensions in the conflict, religion continues to greatly influence social and cultural differences in modern–day Northern Ireland.

The social and cultural dominance of Catholicism remains an important part of life for many living in Northern Ireland, from involvement in the education system through to shaping and underpinning smaller, rural communities linked by their local church (Mitchell 2006). This dominance may be due to the unified nature of this religious perspective. Contrastingly, Protestantism is a more diverse and fragmented theological position and comprises of several denominations including Presbyterian, Church of Ireland, Methodists, Brethrens, Baptists and the Free Presbyterian Church. Interestingly, it is this latter, smaller denomination, comprising of approximately one per cent of Protestants in Northern Ireland (Northern Ireland Census 2001) which has had the most impact on lesbians' and gay men's lives over the past four decades. The founder of this church, the Reverend Ian Paisley, also founded of one of the current power–sharing political parties, the Democratic Unionist Party (DUP). Both organisations have routinely and publically demonstrated their oppositional moral stance against homosexuality.

Protestant perceptions of homosexuality routinely separate the 'sin' from the 'sinner', intimating that heterosexuality can be somehow 'restored' with the correct treatment. Therefore, they are not attacking the person as such, but the 'evil' that they see as residing within them. Catholic views on homosexuality differ in that they see the homosexual element of a person's identity as being part of their holistic self, but this can be accepted so long as they do not act upon their desires but instead live with their situation. Therefore, the person is to be loved and supported so that they do not succumb to temptation as with other forms of sin. However, as will be indicated throughout this book, the strong links between religion and politics in Northern Ireland mean that the loudest and most vociferous negative responses to homosexuality and homosexuals are often the view of a well placed, politically powerful minority who dictate from a strong theological position. As a result, anti–homosexual sentiment appears frequently within this routine denigration of supposed 'sinners'.

Understanding Homophobia, Heterosexism and 'Hate Crimes'

Prejudice against homosexuality or people labelled as 'homosexuals' has a long and drawn out history in the UK. The legal persecution of sexual acts defined as socially deviant dates back as far as 1533 with the introduction of the Buggery Act (Plummer 1975). The medicalised 'homosexual' label was eventually coined in 1869 by Dr Karoly Benkert. Constructing the homosexual label proved to be a key turning point for male same–sex desire, as it moved from being perceived as a sexual act to constituting a sexual identity (Weeks 1986). To a degree, this paved the way for changes in social understandings of homosexuality and responses to oppressive laws regulating this form of behaviour. Nonetheless, medical theories of homosexuality have informed various approaches designed to 'cure', contain or control same–sex desire, in turn constructing the homosexual as a patient, a criminal or a deviant (Kinsman 1996, Moran 1996). Biological ideologies have informed, and been informed by, genetic testing of homosexuals (see De Cecco and Elia 1993), investigations into twins (one or both who may have been homosexual) (see Bearman and Brückner 2001), and spawned numerous other laboratory based tests designed to examine whether homosexuality is rooted in nature as opposed to nurture (see Satinover 1997).

What many now recognise is that the sexuality is not the problem; it is the social response to this sexuality which requires attention. In the early 1970s the term 'homophobia' was first used by psychologist Dr George Weinberg to define the fear of and hatred felt towards people classified as 'homosexuals' (see Weinberg 1972). Weinberg (cited in Herek 2004: 7) described the term's origins as follows:

> I coined the word homophobia to mean it was a phobia about homosexuals … It was a fear of homosexuals which seemed to be associated with a fear of contagion, a fear of reducing the things one fought for – home and family. It was a religious fear and it had led to a great brutality as fear always does.

Weinberg's motivation was to shift the concerns of the scientific community away from the challenging or accounting for homosexuality, and instead focus on factors informing a *heterosexual* intolerance of homosexuality. In this model the origins or cause of homophobia were not to be found in the behaviour of the homosexual; rather, it was the negative 'social constructions' of homosexuality which gave rise to such fear or hatred. Weinberg identified these social constructions as emanating from the family, the Church and hegemonic masculinity (1972). The notion of 'the family', influenced to a large degree by Church doctrine, promoted and reinforced normative heterosexuality so that homosexuality was rendered other to this 'natural' state of sexuality. Weinberg argued that this fear was essentially based upon perceptions of what homosexuality may usurp, and hence could lead to forms of social control that identified homosexuals as acceptable targets of prejudice. However, as few 'cures' or treatments for homophobia (as opposed to homosexuality) have been developed, 'homophobia' may in fact be a misnomer.

The term is meant to describe value judgements and prejudices as opposed to a treatable 'fear' in the conventional sense:

> When a phobia incapacitates a person from engaging in activities considered decent by society, the person himself is the sufferer... But here the phobia appears as antagonism directly toward a particular group of people. Inevitably, it leads to disdain toward the people themselves and to mistreatment of them. The phobia in operation is a prejudice, and this means we can widen our understanding by considering the phobia from the point of view of its being a prejudice and then uncovering its motives. (Weinberg 1972: 8)

Weinberg's central point is that homophobia is less of a traditional 'phobia' in that the social and cultural responses to those who demonstrate homophobia do not emulate other phobias. For example, people rarely 'join in' when a person is experiencing a fear of heights, water or arachnids. Research focused, and continues to focus, on the homosexuals rather than people's reasons for hostility towards them. Similarly, acknowledging that prejudice, discrimination and victimisation are real and harmful threats to some lesbians and gay men, fears of homophobic victimisation are often marginalised within mainstream victimology research (Moran et al. 2003).

The Impact of Cultural Heterosexism

Theories of homophobia since Weinberg's conceptualisation of the problem have tended to develop his original hypothesis by looking to the factors in society which cast the homosexual as 'other', rather than locating the problem in homosexual individuals themselves. They also seek to look outside the prejudiced individual in order to explore where this prejudice may be stemming from. Such theories have concentrated on the family, religion and hegemonic masculinity in their discussions and analyses of this particular form of intolerance (Plummer 1975, Comstock 1991, Kinsman 1996, Mason and Tomsen 1997, 2001). Homophobia, like many prejudices, rarely occurs in a social or political vacuum (Perry 2001). The culture of negative ideologies informing homophobia was labelled 'heterosexism' by Morin and Garfinkle (1978). Contemporary displays of homophobia may be perceived as being at the far end of a continuum of normalised heterosexism, defined by Mason as being 'the belief system that allows homosexuality to be stigmatised, denigrated or ignored' (1993: 2). While the actual commission of violence is an extreme manifestation of a form of heterosexism, everyday, heterosexual privilege is 'sustained and perpetuated though societal customs, institutions and individuals' attitudes and behaviour' (Mason 1993: 2).

Questioning processes of heterosexism allows the focus to broaden out from the homophobic incident and consider wider social factors implicit in this form of prejudice (Herek 1992, 2004). Therefore, although a distinction is made between cultural heterosexism and homophobic statements, sentiments and acts, the presence of one is normally dependent on the existence of the other. As Kinsman (1996: 25) states, a culturally relative reading of homophobia and violence is not only useful to explain how homophobia has been informed and sustained, but also may develop its potential for change:

> Examining historical experiences and practices can help us understand from where lesbian and gay oppression and, more generally, oppressive sexual regulation has come, where it may be going, and the possibilities for transformation.

Theories of homophobic violence may overlook the wider issue of heterosexism, or the belief systems informing sexual prejudice in a society, in order to focus on the individual's experience. As Kinsman indicates, these experiences may differ across time and space. This difference has been indicated in studies conducted in western societies which have evoked notions of 'hegemonic masculinity' and how this may account for anti–gay violence (Connell 1987, 1995, Messerschmidt 1993). Jefferson (2001: 138) describes hegemonic masculinity as 'the set of ideas, values, representations and practices associated with "being male" which is commonly accepted as the dominant position in gender relations in a society at a particular historical moment.' Some American and Australian investigations into homophobia have exposed perpetrators' prejudices as being rooted in ideologies of gender roles and deviation from heteronormative masculinity (Comstock 1991, Herek 1991, Herek and Berrill 1992, Mason and Tomsen 1997). In many of the cases outlined by Comstock, the gay male victim was being punished for being different from socially perceived 'norms' of masculinity. Comstock's research also indicated how concepts of hegemonic masculinity held amongst young men were used as the rationale to commit randomised acts of violence as a form of group bonding. The perpetrators forged their group identities through their violent acts whilst also situating their masculinity against the perceived femininity of their male victims. Seemingly, the perpetrators' understandings of gender roles (and gender deviations) formed part of the wider culture of misogyny and heterosexism to which they had been exposed.

Recognising that reasons for homosexual victimisation differ across time and space has led some theorists to suggest locating this prejudice within individual socio–political contexts (Perry 2001, Hall 2005, Iganski 2008). In other words, what may be informing homophobia in one society may not be the reason for its existence in another, despite the fact that other similarities exist between such societies. More will be understood about the nature and impact of homophobia if the culturally specific factors informing the heterosexist prejudice specific to that society are exposed. Perry (2001, 2003) promotes this more in–depth exploration, claiming that the commission of homophobic violence can be seen as perpetrators 'doing difference' by aligning to dominant social norms about sexual and gender roles. By this, she suggests that such violence is an extreme manifestation of normalised human behaviour against those marked as 'different' that in turn demonstrates the social structures of labour, power, sexuality and culture.

Targeting particular members of minority groups is also predicated upon 'structural exclusions and cultural imaging [which] leave minority members vulnerable to systemic violence and especially ethnoviolence' (Perry 2003: 17). This positioning makes members of minority communities simultaneously vulnerable to victimisation and 'acceptable' targets of such treatment. Perry suggests examining the connections between cultural oppression (such as heterosexism) and personal experiences of violence (such as homophobia) through exploring how certain minority groups have been constructed in a given society. These retrospective analyses are as important for understanding contemporary prejudices as the proposed initiatives designed to address them. Therefore, these social structures must first be understood in order to examine how they impact on power relations and oppression. Examining the denigration of homosexual identities may go some way to exposing oppressive social structures which inform and sustain heterosexist and homophobic ideologies. Differentiating between 'homophobia' and 'heterosexism' provides ideological understandings of individualized harms and their social roots, but this may not prove beneficial to those actually experiencing such harms.

Taking the victim's perspective further, Iganski (2008), has explored the notion of 'social harms' incurred by survivors of prejudicial violence. Iganski illustrates the impact of prejudice on the minority community and the attitudes towards the community held in wider society. In doing so, he highlights the complicated dynamics which set prejudicial violence apart from non–prejudiced violence (where the victim's racial, sexual or religious identity, for example, is not the motivating factor). Importantly, Iganski demonstrates how survivors (and potential victims) make sense of and adapt to belonging to a community targeted for prejudice. Assessing this phenomenon from a largely victimological perspective, Iganski questions the effect that this situation has on people's sense of safety and security. His analyses have added an important 'view from below' to contemporary understandings of prejudicial violence, or 'hate crime', which seeks to account for the impact on both the individual and the wider community. In doing so, he has translated how negative constructions of minority communities impact on their feelings of fear, whether or not they incur victimisation as a result of these constructions.

'Hate Crimes': A Useful Concept of Analysis?

Social responses to identity based discrimination, victimisation and violence and laws surrounding these acts have led to a growth in discourses concerning 'hate crimes'. Theories on identity based prejudice and hate initially developed in America following a number of high profile racial and homophobic murders which were characterised by their severity and brutality (Jacobs and Potter 1998).

The fact that it was the victim's identity which accounted for their selection and the subsequent severity of the violence prompted campaigns to recognise the implications this had for social interaction and minority groups' fears. The concept gained currency in the UK following the death of black teenager Stephen Lawrence in 1993 and the subsequent McPherson report into institutional racism in the police service, published in 1999 (Ray and Smith 2002, Hall 2005).

As with 'mugging' (see Hall et al. 1978) hate crime is a social construction arising out of a change in social perspectives to violence, victims and motivations. No new criminal offence is committed, but rather the prejudicial motivations behind an existing offence are demarcated and may be additionally punished (Jacobs and Potter 1998, Hall 2005). The Association of Chief Police Officers (ACPO) defines hate incidents in the UK as: 'Any incident, which may or may not constitute a criminal offence, which is perceived by the victim or any other person, as being motivated by prejudice or hate' and hate crimes as: 'Any incident, which constitutes a criminal offence, perceived by the victim or any other person, as being motivated by prejudice or hate' (ACPO 2005). In other words, the factors which make a crime a 'hate' crime in the UK are currently determined by the subjective interpretation of the victim or a third party to the incident. This subjective element means that concepts like 'hate' and 'hate crimes' remain intentionally vague. This definition has been incorporated by the PSNI as a working template to address hate crime in Northern Ireland.

Debates concerning the additional tariffs afforded to hate crimes have unearthed several problematic issues, not only defining qualifying 'hated groups', but also demarcating which prejudices turn supposedly ordinary crimes into hate crimes (Jacobs and Potter 1998, Perry 2001, 2003, Hall 2005, Iganski 2008). These discussions have also questioned whether all variations of hate crime should be punished equally as harshly (with increased tariffs designed to reflect the additional prejudicial motivation) regardless of the level of violence involved. For example, it has been argued that an assault deemed to be motivated by prejudice which resulted in a medium level of physical injury could incur a harsher sentence than one without the prejudicial element but with a greater level of physical injury. Arguments in favour of this include the perspective that there is a need to punish crimes motivated by prejudice more severely due to the message that they send to the victim's wider community and the increased levels of emotional harm incurred as a result of being singled out (Iganski 2008). Conversely, arguments opposing this suggest that the creation of a victim hierarchy may be inevitable if crimes against some people are seen to hurt less as a result of assumptions made on the basis of their identity.

There are some issues regarding the vagueness of the term 'hate crime' and the cultural implications it may have. While there are demarcated minority identities – such as ethnic minorities, LGB&T persons or disabled people – cases such as the murder of Sophie Lancaster have demonstrated that the application of the label 'hate crime' is not necessarily limited to those groups outlined in UK law. In 2007, Sophie Lancaster and her boyfriend Robert Maltby were violently attacked while walking through a park in Lancashire, England. Sophie fell into a coma and died almost two weeks later when her life support was switched off after it became clear that she would not recover from her injuries. At the trial the prosecution suggested that Sophie and Robert were targeted because their style of dress indicated that they conformed to a goth (gothic) subculture. Witness accounts of the language used by the accused – referring to the couple as 'moshers' – supported these claims. In an unprecedented move, not only did the trial judge Anthony Russell QC agree that a prejudicial motivation was present, he used the term 'hate crime' to describe the attack, stating that Sophie and Robert were targeted because their appearance was different. In effect, this opened up the hate debate to consider what the true basis of a hate crime might be. As Weinberg indicated when he coined the term 'homophobia', speaking of a phobia as being based on fear or hate implies an intense dislike and suggests active avoidance rather than an interaction with the hated subject (Herek 2004). Conversely, in hate crime scenarios, interaction is often predicated on selecting a person who represents the hated identity and engaging with them in a volatile manner. Taking this as a basis, much football rivalry could be seen as a hate crime.

Jacobs and Potter (1998) argue that a paradox exists when social cultures overlook, allow or even publicly condone prejudices against certain minority groups yet enforce harsher punishments for those who act on these prejudices. Perry (2001) questions the fairness of this additional tariff if people are acting on prejudices which they have absorbed through social ideologies – in effect 'doing difference' – but recognises the impact that crimes motivated by prejudice can have on the victim. Similarly, Iganski (2008) argues that hate crimes are not committed by certain individuals set apart from the rest of society but by ordinary people within the context of their ordinary lives. Therefore, there needs to be some form of recognition that it is their prejudices, and not the minority groups, which are wrong.

Examining how societies sustain prejudices which may feed into violent acts, Mason (1993) asserts that, 'violence will fail to serve a function for the perpetrators if the prejudicial attitudes undergirding such violence are no longer supported by societal norms or by religious, legal and political doctrines', suggesting that the failure to condemn homophobic attitudes 'promotes an atmosphere that condones violence against gay men and lesbians' (1993: 6). Already in Northern Ireland, situations have occurred whereby homophobia is both condoned and condemned in the same political breath. This indicates that understanding the nature, prevalence and effects of homophobia and violence may be crucial to accounting for discrepancies between the perceived and actual acceptance of homosexuality.

Summary

Pathologisation is a key concept inherent to understanding homophobia. This has shifted from medical discourse's need to identify and treat the homosexual individual, through to a grass-roots resistance movement which seeks to expose and question heterosexual privilege. George Weinberg's central thesis is that homophobia stems from a fear of what the socially constructed homosexual identity may usurp: family stability. Seeking to account for acts of prejudice against sexual minorities in a society such as Northern Ireland, where the family is paramount may require a fundamental re-engagement with the concept of homophobia. In other words, what are the *actual* fears currently informing feelings of homophobic prejudice? Discovering these, making people account for what it is that they feel threatened by as opposed to presuming these fears are the same as Weinberg's assertions made four decades ago, may provide answers which help address sexual minority prejudice in Northern Ireland as a result of looking at this within a culturally specific framework.

Homophobia has been demonstrated as having a unique history in Northern Ireland, yet the impact of this on contemporary prejudice towards lesbians and gay men remains relatively under–explored. Several social, political and historical differences set Northern Ireland apart from comparable areas of the UK as a result of its post-colonial and post-conflict background. If acts of prejudice towards sexual minorities are rooted in a wider feeling of alienation or ostracism, or a need for community cohesion and a strong identity, then these factors are outside of the control of LGB&T communities alone. These same issues may be evident in other forms of minority persecution, not just against lesbians and gay men. If so, then this is something which goes to the heart of people in Northern Ireland and requires engagement on a much broader level if such sentiments are to be addressed in light of the shift to the 'new' inclusive, diverse and integrated Northern Ireland.

The following chapter examines how lesbians and gay men become victims of victimisation and violence. The analysis explores the impact of legal regulation of same–sex acts on social prejudice. It also questions how symbolic this legal shift from persecution to protection might be on social interactions. Additionally, the chapter demonstrates the resistant tactics employed by lesbians and gay men confronted with sexual regulation and the efforts taken by people to ensure their own and others' safety and security.

Chapter 2
Constructing 'Acceptable Victims': Violence, Regulation and Resistance

Like lesbians and gay men elsewhere in the UK, those living in Northern Ireland face similar challenges to their sexual identities, lives and relationships. This chapter explores homophobic prejudice and sexual regulation, focusing on several culturally specific themes which operate to control sexual minority freedoms in Northern Ireland. The analysis of existing research, data and statistics is juxtaposed with the personal narratives of the interviewees. The exploration of violence, regulation and resistance illustrates how fears of victimisation may be perceived and managed, regardless of the actual likelihood of these fears materialising. An overview of the laws enacted to recognise and respond to homophobically motivated incidents and crimes in the UK indicates the significant, yet relatively recent, move from sexual minority persecution to legal protection. However, such laws will remain ineffectual if barriers to recognizing, reporting, recording and in some cases prosecuting such prejudice continue to exist unchallenged. In the context of Northern Ireland, these barriers are often linked to the unique nature and composition of community interaction, paramilitary regulation and a historical wariness of trusting criminal justice representatives.

Techniques of resistance to actual or perceived dangers in Northern Ireland illustrate much about the wider society in which this management occurs. Scholarly attention which has concentrated on deconstructing the 'hate' element within hate crimes often overlooks the complex social dynamics of prejudice–based victimisation (Craig 2002). One such dynamic are assumptions about who commits hate crimes. Popular conceptions that hate crimes usually involve strangers have been challenged by research indicating that frequently there exists some degree of familiarity or relationship between the perpetrator and the victim, particularly in incidents involving homophobic prejudice (Mason 2005a, 2005b, Moran 2007). In smaller or closer–knit communities, this may mean that the psychological harm incurred by the victim as a result of a hate incident is increased as they are familiar with their persecutor(s) (Mason 2005a). The analysis of victimisation in this chapter demonstrates how the nature of community relationships in Northern Ireland impacted on the decisions taken by some of the interviewees around relationship disclosures, cohabiting arrangements and modifying behaviours or appearances. To some, these are small steps to take in order to deflect potential hostility, informing larger social and spatial safety mapping measures. Others, however, perceive the legacy of Northern Ireland's 'Troubles' to have made such measures unavoidable seeing as minority groups may be recast as more acceptable targets of violence in the wake of sectarian abatement (Knox 2002, Steenkamp 2005).

Attitudes toward Homosexuality in Northern Ireland

A useful source of information on attitudes towards homosexuality is the Northern Ireland Life and Times (NILT) survey. This survey was established in 1998 and asks a selection of questions on social, political and religious issues. It is facilitated by the ARK research project and is impartial insofar as it is not commissioned by any particular government organisation. It is designed to provide information on various areas of Northern Irish life without any ulterior social, legal or political agenda. Occasionally, the NILT survey includes questions relating to homosexuality. These questions may be repeated verbatim over the course of a number of years to chart longitudinal changes in social responses. These changes can then be analysed within the wider socio-political context in which they have occurred to show what significant developments may be taking place, both overtly and covertly within communities.

In relation to questions on homosexuality, one asks the respondent to grade sexual relations between two adults of the same sex, with the options being: 'always wrong', 'almost always wrong', 'wrong only sometimes', 'not wrong at all' or 'can't choose'. In the 1998 survey, when the question was asked for the first time, 58 per cent of respondents chose the 'always wrong' option while 15 per cent chose 'not wrong at all' (NILT 1998). At the time of this question LGB&T visibility, politics, equality and protection legislation and social space was less developed than it is currently. In 2004, when the question was asked for the second time the percentage choosing 'always wrong' had reduced to 44 per cent (NILT 2004). In the interim 6 years significant developments had been made by both LGB&T groups and equalities organisations, improving sexual minority visibility in Northern Ireland and information relating to prejudice and discrimination faced by members of these communities. However, by 2008, the third time this same question arose the percentage answering 'always wrong' had not altered but the number of people choosing the 'not wrong at all' option had risen slightly from 21 per cent to 24 per cent (NILT 2008). Interpretations of this change could relate to general negative responses to increased levels of LGB&T recognition and visibility. In the interim period between 2004 and 2008, several disparaging comments about perceptions of LGB&T culture as homogenous and harmful had been made by several Unionist politicians (see Chapter 3). It is possible that these sentiments had resonated with those taking part in the study.

A more nuanced investigation of the respondents' demographics may shed some light on the backgrounds of those answering this question. The NILT survey provides information on the gender, age and religious affiliation of the respondents. One consistent trend throughout each time this particular question arose was the different views held between Catholics and Protestants. A greater number of

Protestants consistently answered that sexual relations between two adults of the same sex was 'always wrong' (1998: 67 per cent; 2004: 56 per cent; 2008: 58 per cent) than Catholics (50 per cent; 32 per cent; 31 per cent respectively). From these statistics it appears that a consistent third of Catholic respondents disapprove of same–sex relations compared to two-thirds of Protestant respondents. Unsurprisingly then, fewer Protestants answered 'not wrong at all' to this question (10 per cent; 13 per cent; 14 per cent respectively) than Catholics (17 per cent; 19 per cent; 31 per cent respectively). Although the Protestant response to this question remained fairly consistent, the percentage of Catholics changing their minds to adopt a more accepting approach to same-sex sexual relations among adults almost doubled. This could indicate that there is something about Catholic interpretations of homosexuality which are more liberal than, or appear more liberal in comparison to, Protestant interpretations. If this is the case, then it may prove beneficial to investigate Catholic perceptions of homosexuality with a view to understanding how identity differences can be integrated better into society.

Other studies conducted into attitudes towards homosexuality can also be used to show an ever–changing picture of acceptance of diverse sexual orientations in Northern Ireland. The Lesbian Advocacy Services Initiative (LASI), an organisation dedicated to improving the lives of lesbian and bisexual women in Northern Ireland and their families, surveyed over a thousand people on their attitudes to lesbians and gay men (LASI 2006). The study found that 88 per cent of the people questioned were supportive of the principle that lesbian and gay people should not be discriminated against. However, two-thirds recognised that sexual minorities were 'not very' or 'not at all' accepted in Northern Ireland generally. Although it is apparent that lesbians and gay men were not as well regarded, the analysis refrained from speculating why this might have been the case (LASI 2006). Similarly, in a larger research project into Western bigotry conducted the following year, over a third of the Northern Irish respondents in the study said they would not want gay people as neighbours (Borooah and Mangan 2007). The results of this survey demonstrated that out of the 23 countries and 32,000 people surveyed, Northern Ireland (tied with Greece) was the most homophobic country involved in the research. A report produced by the Equality Commission in 2009 found similar levels of prejudice continued to be demonstrated towards LGB&T communities but, as before, did not indicate where these prejudices may be emanating from (Equality Commission 2009).

The impact of this prejudice has also been made clear. A recent study into homophobia in the workplace indicated that despite the swathe of equality and anti–discrimination legislation which is now in force, many LGB&T workers hide their sexual orientation from colleagues where possible (McDermott 2011). In the private sector, 40 per cent of the 752 respondents claimed that colleagues had made derogatory comments about homosexuality. Here, as with the public sector, one in four workers chose not to disclose personal details about their intimate relationships. Homophobia was less pronounced in the community and voluntary sector yet derogatory attitudes were still reported by 31 per cent of respondents.

One in five felt that their sexual orientation may have a negative effect on their career progression (McDermott 2011: 10). An encouraging 75 per cent of the participants in the survey said they did not hide their sexuality at work. However, in a very Northern Irish–specific context, some describe being preached to by Christian colleagues attempting to educate them about the sin they were living in. Of those in the study who had made a complaint about experiencing prejudice, 70 per cent were dissatisfied with the outcome. Several cited the existence of a 'put up and shut up' culture operating for some who chose to be open about their sexuality at work. As well as highlighting the personal impact of such negative environments on workers, the study indicated the economic cost to employers and the community as a result of employees taking time off through stress arising from such situations (McDermott 2011).

Surveys which depict the generalised attitudes of people are helpful indicators of popular opinion yet remain underused in Northern Ireland, despite holding potential clues as to how homophobic prejudice can be most effectively addressed. They allow a 'bigger picture' perspective and may illustrate the extent of what Perry (2001) calls 'doing difference': accounting for the rate at which individuals act upon a socially sanctioned prejudice in society. Observers have argued that interventions designed to tackle prejudice need to focus on societal attitudes at large, not just on the perpetrator of the crime (see e.g. Moutzos and Thompson 2000). However, current laws pertaining to crimes motivated by a person's prejudice do exactly that.

The Move from Persecution to Protection

It has taken a long time for the law to recognise that lesbians and gay men need their victimisation and experiences of violence recognised, responded to and remedied. The violence experienced by gay men in England has been increasingly reported in the mainstream media since the violent murders of David Morley in 2004, Jody Dobrowski in 2005 and Ian Baynham in 2009. In larger cities, the increased likelihood of randomised assaults can constitute a serious threat to visible sexual minorities. Doug Janoff, whose analysis of homophobic violence opens with a list of the names of the hundred–plus victims to whom his book is dedicated, suggests that violence against lesbians and gay men exists 'as a way of keeping us in our place' (2005: 35). Alluding to a similar point, albeit in a less dramatic manner, Ruthchild (1997: 1) states that 'the homophobia which finds expression in violence against individual lesbians and gay men is an individual response to signals which exist throughout our society and which are universally understood'. In other words, homophobic violence can be argued as constituting a form of symbolism working to ensure compliance or regulation to heterosexual norms. In some cases, this regulation can be excessively vicious.

Berrill (1992: 25) notes that the severity of some homophobic attacks against gay men, described as 'heinous and brutal', frequently involved 'torture, cutting, mutilation and beating, and showed the absolute intent to rub out the human being because of his [sexual] preference'. In the early 1990s, the court trials of young men accused of murdering older gay men in Australia illustrated the significant levels of violence whereby the victims were not just murdered, but were frequently mutilated and strangled after death (Johnston 1996, Howe 1997, Mouzos and Thompson 2000, Janoff 2005). The National Lesbian and Gay Task Force (NLGTF) illustrated this 'overkill' in the murders of gay men stating that in more than 60 per cent of cases extraordinary violence was demonstrated (NGLTF 1995). Howe (1997) suggests that the symbolism or message in such crimes is contained in the manner in which they are carried out. In other words, she suggests, the medium is the message.

Prior to the recognition of homophobia as a hate crime, those who levied their own form of social justice through the violent regulation of homosexuality may have thought that they had both legal and social backing. Indeed, transcripts of several of these Australian court trials of young male defendants charged with killing older men indicate that they might have been right to some extent (Mison 1992, Johnson 1996, Howe 1997). Pleading provocation as a defence in such murder cases resulted in a narrative whereby the deceased's identity was posthumously reconstructed as a dangerous sexual predator who was culpable in his own demise (Howe 1997, Lunny 2003). Similarly, Janoff (2005) found the most common accusations levied at gay men in his study included being labelled unnatural, sick, sexually aggressive, too visible in society, or a predatory threat to children and young people (2005: 58–59). Commenting on this secondary victimisation and unchecked dangerous imagery, Johnston (1996) questions that if such murders are enabled, or even condoned, by prevailing negative legal attitudes towards homosexuality, then what message is sent out to others who similarly victimise on the basis of sexual identity?

Thankfully, such serious forms of violence appear rare. However, fears or experiences of less serious forms of persecution can be just as debilitating (Moran and Skeggs 2001). Indeed, these may be at the lower end of a 'continuum' upon which, in a similar manner to sexual violence, homophobic violence can be assessed (Kelly 1988). Although there are commonly held, or generic, fears of crime in any given society (Croall 1998, Ditton and Farrall 2000), specific fears of incurring victimisation on the basis of identity 'is just as important in people's lives, if not more so, than actual experience of victimisation' (Goodey 2005: 66). Victim survey research illustrates how victimisation can be an everyday experience for sexual minorities yet this research has consistently failed to adequately document fear of crime relating to lesbians and gay men (Moran et al. 2001). Furthermore, Ruthchild (1997: 4) illustrates how 'violence may be effective at maintaining social control, but it is not necessary for all, or even a majority, of lesbians and gay men to experience attack, because the fear of violence helps to keep people in line'. This effect does not necessarily reside solely with the victim of harassment, as Johnston (1996: 1190, his emphasis) indicates:

> The efficacy of homophobic violence is the message it sends to those who are not its direct recipients, that at any time, anywhere, if you are (noticeably) gay, or even an 'effeminate' heterosexual, you *could* be attacked, you are *always* a potential victim.

Therefore, even seemingly 'low level' violence such as harassment proves powerful in its implication of potential escalation (Mason 1997).

Given its lengthy history of persecuting same–sex acts, the legal protection of lesbians and gay men from discrimination, victimisation and violence is a relatively recent development in the UK. In England and Wales, section 146 of the Criminal Justice Act 2003 introduced tougher sentences for offences motivated by the victim's sexual orientation. Although this aggravating factor must be taken into account by the court during sentencing for the base crime (i.e. assault, criminal damage), actual recognition of the offence as being motivated by prejudice still only applies to cases involving a racial or religious element (CPS Hate Crime Report 2008). In other words, perpetrators of racially and religiously motivated hate crimes can be charged by the police with specific offences such as racially or religiously aggravated harassment or assault; perpetrators of homophobic hate crimes cannot be charged with a specific offence of homophobically motivated harassment. Instead they are charged with an existing offence and the homophobic motivation, if recognised, is taken into account during sentencing. The additional tariff is discretionary as the Criminal Justice Act 2003 does not specify the amount by which sentences should be increased where sexual orientation is an aggravating factor. Available statistics indicate that in the three years ending March 2008, over 2,400 defendants were prosecuted for homophobic or transphobic crimes in England and Wales with three quarters being convicted (CPS Hate Crime Report 2008: 4). In almost 90 per cent of the cases the defendant was male, with the most common offences being those against the person. In Scotland, statistics are yet to be produced given that the Offences (Aggravation by Prejudice) (Scotland) Act, which accounts for offences motivated by a homophobic or transphobic prejudice, was only passed in 2009.

Further reinforcement of legislation addressing homophobic motivation came in the form of section 74 and schedule 16 of the Criminal Justice and Immigration Act 2008. These additions amended the Public Order Act 1986, creating new offences in England and Wales of stirring up hatred on the grounds of sexual orientation. These amendments covered conduct – namely words or behaviour – or material which is threatening in nature and which is intended to stir up hatred against a group of people who are defined by their sexual orientation. In 2008, Conservative peer Lord Waddington added a late amendment to the Bill as it went through Parliament. This cited that discussions or criticisms of homosexual conduct or practices, as well as encouraging people to refrain from or modify such conduct, is not enough to be considered threatening or intent to stir up hatred. In response, voting ensued on 'Clause 61', which was designed to overturn this late amendment. It was defeated in the House of Lords in 2009, keeping the religious exemptions in place. Therefore, a person voicing temperate opposition to same–sex relationships or expressing an opinion on same–sex adoption within the remit of their religious beliefs would not risk prosecution under these incitement laws. Anyone else prosecuted under this law faces a maximum punishment of seven years imprisonment or a fine. In 2011, a group of five people were the first to be charged under this law after distributing leaflets which suggested that homosexuals should face the death penalty. These leaflets had been handed out at mosques in Derby and posted through letterboxes in and around the area (*BBC News* 2011b).[1]

Homophobically motivated crime in Northern Ireland is covered by the Criminal Justice (No. 2) (Northern Ireland) Act 2004. Like similar legislation in England and Wales this aggravating factor is taken into account by the court during sentencing. However, whereas lengthy debates took place in England and Wales as to whether or not to extend laws to cover incitement to hatred on the basis of sexual orientation, in Northern Ireland this issue was resolved some years earlier. The Criminal Justice (Northern Ireland) Order 2004 amended the Public Order (Northern Ireland) Order 1987 to include sexual orientation in the categories covered by incitement to hatred. This Order specifies that hatred can be incited 'against a group of persons' or that a person can be charged with 'arousing fear' or 'fear of persons'. This Order supersedes the equivalent Act in Great Britain on two grounds. First, the additional inclusion of the 'arousing fear' element theoretically affords greater protection to members of LGB&T communities in Northern Ireland. Second, unlike comparable legislation in England and Wales, there is no requirement to prove 'intent' for a successful prosecution. Instead, the Order states: 'having regard to all the circumstances hatred is likely to be stirred up or fear is likely to be aroused thereby'. However, this law remains yet to be implemented and, as demonstrated by the inaction following Iris Robinson's comments, confusion surrounds when, how and against whom this 'incitement to hatred' law can or will be implemented.

Homophobic Victimisation Trends

The first large study into LGB&T harassment in Northern Ireland in 1996 demonstrated that over a third (39 per cent) of respondents had experienced homophobic violence, a similar number encountered homophobic harassment (36 per cent) and over two thirds (67 per cent) had been verbally abused (Mason and Palmer 1996: 106). The level of violence uncovered within Northern Ireland rendered it the area with the highest rate of homophobic victimisation and violence in the UK–wide study. This finding was supported by a study undertaken by the Institute for Conflict Research (ICR) in 2003 which stated that 'the percentage of people who have experienced violence and harassment was higher than indicated

---

1   As this case was ongoing at the time of writing, whether or not they use the religious clause to defend their actions remains to be seen.

by comparable studies in Great Britain and Ireland' (Jarman and Tennant 2003: 6). Some of the respondents in the ICR study also noted that within homophobic harassment 'there [is] now a greater use of violence and a greater propensity to use violence in such attacks' (Jarman and Tennant 2003: 65). This issue has been raised by representatives of LGB&T groups who warned of both the increasing frequency and ferocity of attacks, particularly on gay men (*BBC News* 2004a). In several murder cases, namely Warren 'Aaron' McCauley, Ian Flanagan (*BBC News* 2004b) and Shaun Fitzpatrick (*BBC News* 2010), significant levels of violence preceded the fatal outcome. Other attacks on gay men in areas outside of Belfast have attracted a similar level of media interest as a result of the violence involved. One gay male victim lost several teeth and required numerous stitches to his face after a particularly vicious attack (*BBC News* 2004c). Another young gay man sustained severe physical injuries and almost lost an eye in an attack involving an attempted gouging (*BBC News* 2006).

Hate crimes continue to account for 2 per cent of the annual number of recorded crimes in Northern Ireland (2,000 out of 100,000). Sectarian motivated crimes comprise of 50 per cent of recorded hate crimes, making it the most dominant form of identity victimisation in Northern Ireland (CJINI 2010: 9). Racism accounts for 39 per cent and homophobia seven percent with the remaining four per cent comprising of faith, disability and transphobic motivations (CJINI 2010). Between 2000 and 2004, on average 50 homophobic *incidents* were reported to the PSNI each year. Following the implementation of the Criminal Justice (No. 2) (Northern Ireland) Order 2004, the PSNI began separately recording homophobically motivated *crimes*. By 2006, of the 148 crimes reported to the PSNI over two thirds of these (68 per cent) involved a violent physical assault. This indicated that interpersonal violence towards lesbians and gay men remained a significant problem a decade after the first major study into this area (Mason and Palmer 1996). Despite a reduction in the number of crimes recorded, the percentage of violent assaults remained constant over this period. The PSNI recorded 114 homophobically motivated crimes in 2008, 34 fewer than two years previously, yet two thirds (68 per cent) of these still involved a violent assault (PSNI 2008). An annual overview of the number of PSNI recorded incidents and crimes motivated by the victim's actual or perceived sexual orientation over the previous decade are indicated in Table 2.1 and Figure 2.1:

Table 2.1   PSNI Recorded incidents and crimes with a homophobic motivation 2000 – 2010

Year	00/01	01/02	02/03	03/04	04/05	05/06	06/07	07/08	08/09	09/10
Total incidents	57	40	35	71	196	220	155	160	179	175
Total crimes	–	–	–	–	151	148	117	114	134	112

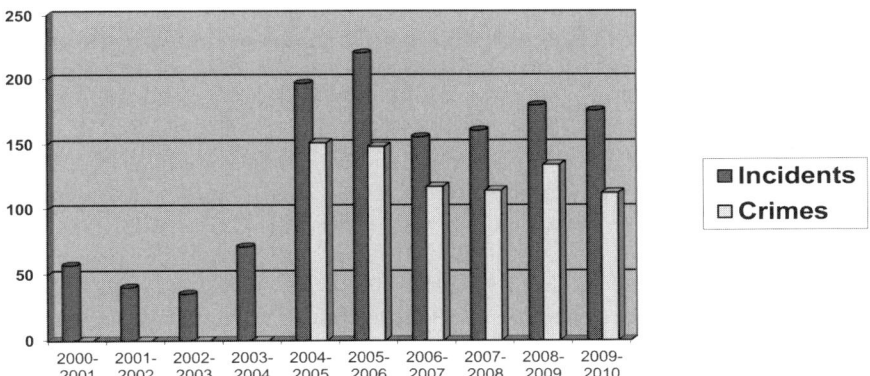

Figure 2.1   Total reported incidents and crimes with a homophobic motivation 2000 – 2010

Source: PSNI (2010)

In comparison to major English cities with urban LGB&T populations such as London or Manchester, these figures appear quite low. Taken in their wider cultural context and against a backdrop of Northern Ireland's population of fewer than 2 million, a different picture becomes evident. This is particularly so given the smaller nature of LGB&T communities and lesser visibility of sexual minorities there. Images of same–sex couples holding hands or embracing which many be popular in cities such as Brighton or Manchester are markedly absent in Belfast or Derry/Londonderry. Additionally, some lesbians and gay men living in Northern Ireland may take measures to ensure that their sexual identities are not identifiable. Carefully constructed mannerisms may be employed which allow them to blend in with wider society, or appear to 'pass' as heterosexual. Therefore, a complex situation arises: members of LGB&T communities in Northern Ireland believe that their demure conduct is 'natural' given their particular environment (although it may not be), and this conduct reinforces the ideology that LGB&T identities are largely invisible in Northern Ireland. As a result of these constructed mannerisms and general LGB&T invisibility, it is possible that hate crime statistics account for repeat incidents of victimisation against fewer people who are more discernable as lesbian or gay. Nevertheless, it is estimated that as many as 60 per cent of homophobic incidents go unreported on an annual basis (O'Doherty 2009).

Barriers to Reporting Victimisation and Violence

There are many reasons why lesbians and gay men may not report their victimisation. Incidents may not be recognised by the victim as criminal or as having a homophobic motivation, or not recognised as having taken place at all. The victim may not wish to report recognised crimes to an authority figure for myriad reasons, or if they do, they may find that the crime is not pursued. Should this happen, it is likely to discourage the future reporting of crimes if levels of confidence in the police have diminished.

In Northern Ireland, as policing became more diverse and community orientated, new forms of prejudice and discrimination emerged which were seen as impacting on relationships between the police and LGB&T communities. Studies conducted in the wake of these changes illustrated the levels of institutionalised homophobia experienced not only by LGB&T citizens who were coming into contact with PSNI officers, but also lesbian and gay officers within this service too (Jarman and Tennant 2003, Radford et al. 2006). This prejudicial culture was highlighted as affecting the reporting and investigation of homophobic incidents and crimes which in turn was having a knock–on effect on LGB&T communities' faith in the PSNI to take homophobic victimisation and violence seriously. Similar disillusionment was cited by lesbian, gay and bisexual (LGB) police officers themselves (Radford et al. 2006). Claims of workplace discrimination were perceived as illustrative of the wider culture of racism, sexism and general prejudice (Radford et al. 2006). If this was the way colleagues were interacting with one another, serious doubts were cast by the researchers on how such a service could adequately understand, meet and address the needs of the wider LGB&T communities in Northern Ireland:

> [LGB police officers'] experiences are of a police service that mirrors the conservatism and homophobia they experience in the wider community. They consider it one where only a very few are confident enough to be 'out' about their sexual orientation to colleagues, due to a distinctly homophobic atmosphere. … It is obvious from the experiences of LGB PSNI personnel that there is an issue to be addressed within the PSNI. If homophobic attitudes are allowed at any level, particularly senior levels within PSNI, it will appear to all ranks that homophobia is acceptable. Where training may address the problem to an extent,

only a clear and consistent approach will provide the message to all officers that homophobic attitudes and behaviour are unacceptable. (Radford et al. 2006: 20)

The research indicated that over a third of the non–police LGB respondents in the study thought that the PSNI remained a homophobic institution, despite the much publicised reforms. This number had reduced to one–fifth in O'Doherty's (2009: 42) study, but those who held criticisms about the police reiterated the same issues as before. Incidents of police harassment were also noted in both reports. Respondents in Radford et al.'s research claimed that they felt as though the police were directing undue attention towards them, leading the authors to conclude that 'due to some activities engaged in by gay males that contravene norms, the police are still seen as targeting rather than protecting gay males in particular' (2006: 7). O'Doherty's study also indicated that one in five respondents, mostly males, had experienced police harassment and/or claims of 'misbehaviour' which they linked to hostility towards their sexual identity (2009: 39).

A more pressing issue highlighted in these two key studies was the potential further danger that already vulnerable people were being placed in through having their sexual identities revealed to others. Radford et al. (2006) document cases of police disclosing the sexual orientation of assault victims to their families without consideration of the potential impact this might have. O'Doherty (2009: 41) found that one in ten of his respondents cited their failure to involve the police in incidents as being based on their fear that their sexual orientation would be made public knowledge. For some, this meant ostracism from friends, colleagues or family members while others indicated a fear that information would filter through to paramilitary group members who may disapprove of homosexuality (Jarman and Tennant 2003, Radford et al. 2006). The culturally specific nature of this finding was particularly pertinent in rural areas in Northern Ireland where paramilitary control was seen to be more ingrained than in urban areas and had not diminished despite the progression of the peace process.

Paramilitary Regulation of Homosexuality

Paramilitary condemnation of homosexuality has been described as a covert but real problem in Northern Ireland (Jarman and Tennant 2003, Kitchin and Lysaght 2003, Hutton 2005). Kitchin (2002: 215) explains how sexual minorities form part of the wider 'social malaise' (along with youth delinquency and drugs cultures) which some community organisations indicate as in need of eradication:

> Sexual dissidence had been seen by certain organizations, operating within some localities, to represent anti–social activity. Those who have been rumoured, or proven to be gay … have come under pressure to leave tightly knit, local communities, and in many cases forcibly evicted.

Kitchin (2002) asserts that members of paramilitary organisations have also been known to target individuals and venues in a manner which sends signals out to the wider community that homosexuality will not be tolerated. In an example of this, one young gay man who chose to speak out about being targeted depicted the severity of his victimisation in a national newspaper (Hutton 2005). He had left his community after a series of attacks by a group of men claiming to represent the IRA. This was not the first time he had been attacked and seemingly this assault was a reprisal following the victim's prior involvement of the police. The men told the young man during the attack that it was 'only a taster [sic] of what you're going to get' if he reported the abuse, threatening specifically that he 'would have two less legs to walk on' in the future (Hutton 2005). The escalation in violence towards this victim was indicated through his statement that he had accepted the 'usual abuse' before, but this particular incident had left him in fear of his life.

Fears of paramilitary reprisal and leaks from the police to members of such community regulatory organisations are a key factor setting homophobic victimisation in Northern Ireland apart from comparable areas of the UK (Jarman and Tennant 2003, Radford et al. 2006). In the 2003 ICR study, one young woman claimed that her failure report homophobic abuse was due to fearing that her family would be targeted in revenge attacks as her abusers had been affiliated to paramilitary groups in the area (Jarman and Tennant 2003: 57). This fear was corroborated by a respondent in Radford et al.'s study who claimed: 'I report homophobic attacks reluctantly not because of my politics, but because I'm not sure what the paramilitary response might be in my area and how that information would ripple out' (2006: 59). The fact that it is the victimised and not the victimisers who are in fear of further repercussions in some areas of Northern Ireland indicates the differential perspectives afforded to homosexuality and homophobia. In some of the respondents' comments it appeared that many felt that members of their community would be more willing to understand and perhaps condone the victimisation or violence meted out towards them for being homosexual, regardless of the fact that they had done nothing to deserve this 'punishment' in the first place.

Although paramilitary groups date back to the formation of Northern Ireland, it was during the Troubles period that a clear demarcation was established between what constituted legitimate forms of 'political' violence and 'criminal' violence (Hillyard 1985, Sluka 1989, Silke 1998). Depending on the intent of the actors or the chosen victims, similar acts may elicit different levels of condemnation, or escape this altogether. A 'blurring' of the purpose and severity of violent acts may have created a situation whereby in comparison to 'political' or 'serious' violence, 'a communal blind eye is often turned to other forms of [criminal] violence' (Steenkamp 2005: 262). Furthermore, Steenkamp (2002) suggests that violence towards groups deemed acceptable targets – such as sexual deviants, drug users or people seen to be a threat to a peaceful social life – are more likely to have their victimisation ignored by the community as a result of their perceived 'outsider' status. Therefore, a perpetrator of a violent assault may be regarded in more sympathetic ways within their community according to the identity of their victim if the latter has been constructed as an enemy of that community. This notion – that it is the victim's identity and not the perpetrator's action which condemns or condones acts of violence – was highlighted by one of the interviewees, Mags. She juxtaposed a mistaken yet homophobic incident with a similarly mistaken yet sectarian assault. In the former, a short–haired woman had been subjected to homophobic abuse by man who had mistaken her for a gay man. In the latter, a group of Loyalists had killed a Protestant woman who they had mistaken to be Catholic. What was significant about these two incidents was that remorse was only shown when the victim's assumed identity was proven to be mistaken; only then was the act of violence atoned for. If the intended and actual identities had matched (gay or Catholic) then the crime would be no less heinous, but the reasons for it justified by the perpetrators in terms of prejudice and the construction of a 'valid enemy' within a politically sensitive context. The fact remained that the attackers' intentions were to victimise against an identity, which they thought they were doing even though that identity was not ascribed to by the victims. Nonetheless, this regulatory message was not sufficiently challenged as the focus remained on the mistaken identity factor rather than the rationales and acts of violence expressed.

Knox (2002) locates victimisation and community regulation through violence within a framework of wider political structures. His analysis of paramilitary policing within communities questions the 'blind eye' turned by the State to particular forms of unofficial policing in order to ensure the continuance of an 'imperfect peace'. Though Knox concentrates more on punishment attacks by paramilitaries from both sides of the traditional divide, his concluding comments focus on the legitimacy of violence towards 'deserving victims', those deemed to be complicit in their own demise. Furthermore if those guilty of crimes against the community are deemed 'deserving victims', Knox (2002: 181) questions the precarious position of traditionally marginalised victims:

> This raises the wider question as to whether paramilitary violence, the by–product of a negotiated political settlement in Northern Ireland, would be tolerated as a 'price worth paying' in other areas of domestic, homophobic or racist violence.

Community monetary incentives to cease involvement in sectarian conflicts have been a large part of Northern Ireland's process of rebranding and development. Factors such as a differential attitude to violence and economic incentives to desist in sectarian violence have created fears that homophobic victimisation may be less of a priority than other forms of discrimination. Additionally, homophobia may prove less important to some politicians given cultural beliefs which suggest that lesbians and gay men may be complicit in their own victimisation. Problems may arise, therefore, when these ideologies filter down in society to feed into people's notions of who might be constructed as an 'acceptable' target of prejudice.

Deflecting Violence onto Acceptable Targets

The perspective that lesbians and gay men may be the scapegoats in a largely successful peace process was an issue raised by several of the interviewees. Steenkamp (2005) suggests that the dominance of the political conflict in Northern Ireland has rendered it a place where pre–existing 'cultures of violence' may prevail. Despite having progressed to a comparably peaceful situation, the nature of conflict may have left some form of legacy behind which may affect perceptions of acceptable violence and victims. As a result, she suggests that perhaps violence does not abate, but rather is redirected to different targets. This 'legacy' was also picked up on by one of the interviewees, Colette:

> I do think there is a legacy there; there's something about having lived through a violent conflict and the toleration of violence which that involves. ... I don't discount psychological factors [in accounting for homophobic violence]; I just think that these attitudes are partly a product of the way that we are structured. (Colette, 48, lesbian)

Those engaging in acts related to the wider 'sectarian' conflict during the height of the Troubles were young, politically minded men with a strong sense of identity and purpose. Since the signing of the Belfast Agreement in 1998, those associated with activities rooted in sectarian ideologies could be seen as either dissidents who had been cast out of larger paramilitary organisations, or disaffected young people. In a similar argument to Knox, Steenkamp suggests that the impact of violent norms and values in society may create communities where there exists 'a greater social tolerance of individuals' violent behaviour' (2005: 253–4). These issues were highlighted by several of the lesbians and gay interviewees whose fears centred on three key themes. These were the paramount importance placed on the success of the peace process, the tenuous victim status attributed to LGB&T communities in Northern Ireland and the failure to take homophobic violence seriously. In effect, many saw their victimisation as being viewed as preferable against more politically sensitive outlets:

> I think some people see themselves as having a right to hostility given the history we have here. (Mary, 59, lesbian)

> On the one hand it seems as if yes, the natural targets have changed – community activists don't want [young people] stoning the traditional targets because money has been given to them to [stop] that. On the other hand, when these [same] people say that they know who is behind [homophobic] attacks and that they'll sort it out that scares me as I don't want that to happen. (Alex, 35, lesbian)

People have been saying this for a while now, that the targets have changed and the natural enemies of sectarianism have shifted as the community groups won't allow it and I definitely think there is some truth to that. I also think there is something in this hierarchy of victims, that LGBT are somewhere lower on the scale than racist or religious crime. (Connor, 46, gay male)

However, this 'cultures of violence' theory suggests that sectarian attacks are decreasing. There were mixed feelings among the interviewees about the validity of this claim. The issue may be overlooked or played down in the popular media as part of efforts to rid Northern Ireland of violent stereotypes. As well as dissident activities which are highlighted in the news, interpersonal assaults and attacks on buildings are still regularly reported in the news, particularly in interface areas and rural communities. Nonetheless, it was recognised by some that spaces had opened up to recognise other forms of minority prejudice, and this could only be positive for those trying to get these recognised:

In Northern Ireland we don't have a society that is quite open and diverse and I think the Troubles have masked that for a long time, so it's probably only now that [homophobia] being really effectively tackled in any kind of way that's going to make a difference. (Carmel, 43, lesbian)

Examining homophobic prejudice and victimisation through those who have experienced it proves necessary until more can be gleaned from prosecution figures. However, in the case of Northern Ireland, this latter resource may prove a more arduous research task as a result of several barriers to processing homophobic hate crimes in the criminal justice system.

Difficulties in Prosecuting Hate Crime

Reports on hate crime in Northern Ireland have commended efforts to encourage greater reporting, but the significant level of under–reporting has also been noted (CJINI 2007). Complaints by members of the Public Prosecution Service (PPS) about incomplete or contradictory information being provided by the PSNI led them to query some police officers' understandings of what constitutes a hate crime for the purposes of recording incidents. The PSNI follows the Association of Chief Police Officers (ACPO) guidelines on the recording of incidents and crimes that may have been motivated by hostility towards the victim's identity or perceived community affiliation. However, the 2007 report by the Criminal Justice Inspectorate Northern Ireland suggested that three years after the implementation of hate crime legislation some officers still required training to understand the subjective perception element of hate crimes, which need not be substantiated by evidential requirements at the time of reporting (CJINI 2007). While hate crime definitions were seen to be generally understood by PSNI officers, further investigations into their application, coupled with the issue of how the incident progressed and the retention of the aggravating element, highlighted some inherent problems. Subjective perceptions by the police, together with the need to meet clearance rate targets, meant some discrepancies in how incidents were recorded on the police computer systems, which in turn affected the information being passed on for prosecution (CJINI 2007).

Prosecutions for homophobic hate crime are notoriously low in Northern Ireland. As of the 2007 report, there were just 66 prosecutions for summary offences and 27 prosecutions for indictable offences where hostility on the basis of sexual orientation was an aggravating factor. While 'aggravation' may be a difficult element to prove, it has been noted that there is a problem in tracking the course of a hate crime through the criminal justice system in order to assess exactly where the attrition is occurring (CJINI 2007). Furthermore, the level of rejections by the PPS of offences recorded as being motivated by hostility to the victim's sexual orientation was of particular note as they stood out as far higher than for any other form of prejudice in comparison.

The low level of prosecutions, coupled with the high levels of the homophobic motivation element disappearing before conviction, suggests that recognising the existence or severity of homophobic hostility in a given crime may require stronger guidelines. Although the ACPO guidelines were intended to be utilised in a manner that facilitated the incorporation of prejudice if it was felt to have shaped a particular incident or crime, the vagueness of these instructions may be having an adverse effect in a society where homophobic hostility is more visible and less challenged, as in Northern Ireland. The low number of prosecutions is problematic due to the message it appears to send out. This was an issue taken up by one interviewee, David:

> I'm aware that successful prosecutions are still very few in number. It would appear that if the attacker pleads guilty to the attack, they'll be let off having the aggravating factor added on. I've heard of the most horrendous cases where it's not gone through as a homophobic attack even though the language used made that clear. I think you're going to have to see someone murdered and 'homo' carved on their back by a Stanley knife before [homophobic violence] is taken seriously in the courts over here. (David, 43, gay male)

The effectiveness of laws designed to protect or address prejudice based incidents and crimes can be called into question for several reasons. Laws generally may be seen as being in place to punish recognised offenders rather than prevent crimes from occurring. In the case of laws and policies addressing identity based discrimination, victimisation or violence these laws may be seen as a way of placating minority communities. Nonetheless, enacting legislation as a symbolic measure indicates that it is the prejudice, not the identity, which is intolerable. Either way, in order for such legislation to work victims must feel able to report their experiences to the relevant authorities. If criminal justice agents such as the police have a historically inharmonious relationship with a particular community then it may be the case that additional efforts need to be implemented to repair these lines of communication and invest trust from both sides. Such strategies need to go far beyond mere equality and awareness training; actual integration with minority communities is the very minimum in such cases.

As a result of the issues inherent in reporting, recording and prosecuting homophobic hate incidents and crimes, many lesbians and gay men may choose to conduct themselves and their lives in a manner which deflects attention (and possible hostility). Attempts by lesbians and gay men to 'deny or disguise their sexual orientation when in public' are commonly cited as being prompted by fears of incurring homophobic abuse and intolerance (Hubbard 2001: 55). Mason (1997: 27) explains this 'double move' of homophobic violence as simultaneously marking out individual lesbian or gay bodies while ensuring general invisibility through the medium of fear. Measures taken to prevent possible victimisation can be seen as a form of victimisation in itself, in the inability to engage in ordinary interactions without fear of persecution. The ability of lesbians and gay men to 'pass' as heterosexual may lessen exposure to homophobic victimisation, but can also lead to detrimental mental, physical and emotional effects due to living double lives (Plummer 1975, 1981). This theme was pertinent in many of the interviewees' narratives but was engaged with in an almost fatalistic manner as there appeared to be no other choices in many people's cases.

Managing Fear, Safety and Security

Many lesbians and gay men in Northern Ireland have experienced 'low level' victimisation and violence at various points in their lives. In the 2003 ICR study, 83 per cent of respondents who had experienced homophobic victimisation demonstrated a fatalistic, or resigned, attitude to these and potential future experiences (Jarman and Tennant 2003). In some cases it is the fear of what might happen, rather than what has happened, which takes precedence. The potentiality for more severe violence is not uncommon in hate crime incidents, with the 'low level' forms of harassment being seen in hindsight as precursors for more serious forms of victimisation. For many lesbians and gay men, therefore, such harassment serves to heighten their fears and self–regulation.

As well as taking measures to avoid or lessen risk, active engagement in resistance techniques play a large part in many lesbians and gay men's lives. The self–policing of behaviour involves social movement, dress, demeanour, association and language (Davies 1992, Corteen 2002). Resistance tactics may involve 'passing' for heterosexual through, among other things, carefully considered mannerisms, guarded discourses or disclosures of information, lessening visible indicators such as public displays of intimacy with a same–sex partner, conforming to gender stereotypes in terms of clothing and accessories to feminise or masculinise appearances and so forth (Plummer 1975, Butler 1990,

1993, Davies 1992, Corteen 2002). The effect of such a regulatory culture on lesbians and gay men in Northern Ireland was described by Kitchin (2002: 216) as follows:

> Homophobic intimidation and violence, either perceived or real, remains a significant problem, so that all but a couple of respondents continue to be 'closeted' from different family members or wider society, using carefully orchestrated patterns of spatial behaviour to protect themselves from perceived risks.

Self–regulation in terms of space, visibility and behaviour was evident in the ICR report's findings (Jarman and Tennant 2003). Respondents reported feeling so unsafe in public places that they regularly took precautionary measures such as avoiding holding hands in public places and making efforts to alter their appearance so as to not 'appear lesbian or gay' (2003: 7). However, such measures may problematically suggest that, if the person is subjected to victimisation, they feel some degree of responsibility for not having regulated themselves enough to deflect such hostility. This was also true of the interviewees, such as Smythie:

> Sometimes it's touch and go; you play it as you see it, and if you've been gay for a long time you'll know what I mean. You'll know when and where to say it and when to keep your mouth shut. (Smythie, 39, lesbian)

One interviewee, Ryan, also lived in a relatively rural area. Rather than watching what he said, he was more conscious of what his actions may convey. He indicated that he had taken on board what his neighbours might have expected of him as a young, unattached, gay male and done his best not to feed into what prejudices they might have held:

> I think if you show people respect you're ok, my neighbours are great to me and they are there if I need them. If I was having parties or strings of men in and out of my flat, then there might be a problem but I don't so we get on fine. (Ryan, 35, gay male)

Although he was careful not to give his neighbours recourse to stereotype him, as a result he was more alert to how his actions might be interpreted. It is doubtful that he would have felt the same if he was heterosexual and had 'strings of women' in and out of his flat instead. Others, however, found it easier to avoid any confrontation at all:

> I know gay couples where I live who only go in through the back door of their house as they're too afraid with the front door being more public. As well as that, how often would you see a gay couple holding hands [in Northern Ireland]?

> There's a real fear that you'd be made to feel uncomfortable and then you'd start the endless round of moving [house]. It's just not worth it. (Scott, 49, gay male)

A potential implication from this perspective may be that in order to avoid victimisation in their homes, people resort to using other, less safe public spaces to engage in sexual intimacy. If so, then they are more likely to expose themselves to greater dangers from assaults by disapproving members of the public.

Care of the Self and Others

The safety of the home proved less convincing in some of the interviewee's experiences. Instead, this environment brought with it new security considerations. Deciding to live with a partner may involve a significant amount of discussion about various practical issues in addition to considering how such a living arrangement might be received by the neighbours. For those in long term partnerships who were likely to be living together in an area for a significant amount of time, being open about their relationships with their neighbours appeared to create a more inclusive culture, yet some reservations were still evident. Others preferred to tacitly assume that their neighbours knew and were not adverse to the relationships as nothing was said. Several interviewees recognised that their mindsets had automatically changed upon cohabitation with a partner to assume that their sexuality would be noted by others. To temper out these fears and the potential hostility incurred, behaviours were modified in ways that challenged traditional stereotypes of 'homosexuality' so as not to 'annoy' their neighbours or give them reason to comment. This regulation primarily involved censoring displays of affection outside of the home. Although these displays may merely have involved a brief embrace, care was taken to avoid what could be seen as 'flaunting' their sexuality.

Generally, the fear of incurring indirect homophobia or direct victimisation appeared to be more of a concern amongst interviewees living in rural parts of Northern Ireland. For many, there was a heightened personal awareness of their sexuality, regardless of whether or not others around them recognised this difference. This was of particular worry to one interviewee, Mark, whose concerns highlighted the sometimes unique nature of victimisation in Northern Ireland:

> At the back of your mind there's that small but severe risk that I could be targeted. If it's found out, how likely are you to get bricks through the window, petrol poured through the letterbox, or stoned, or your car vandalised? How are you supposed to sleep at night, when you're thinking that there could be people out there targeting my house, putting petrol in the letterbox to burn me out? I find it on one hand very scary .. I do worry that if I come out to my neighbours, the next time my house was targeted, would I be putting that down to us being a gay couple and how do I decipher the difference? (Mark, 32, gay male)

Several of Mark's fears, including being burnt out of his home, can be seen as being definitive to Northern Ireland. This method of intimidation has long been used against families on the basis of sectarian, racial and religious hatred both during and after the Troubles (see Hillyard 1985). Other interviewees who were aware of lesbian or gay couples intimidated in this way, particularly in more rural areas, acknowledged that this had a profound impact on their feelings of security and safety. It appeared difficult to some to be able to discern between targeted homophobic victimisation and general violence.

Some of the interviewees were involved in community roles as providers of LGB&T support or information. Within this cohort there was a recognition and careful consideration of service users' security when planning LGB&T events. In one example, Jennifer, a LGB&T community facilitator established a drop–in meeting to complement the online forum she had successfully set up. She needed to ensure that the attendees felt safe accessing the meetings as her previous attempts had been thwarted by a local religious group opposed to homosexuality. Despite trying to keep publicity about the group to a minimum, word got out about the meetings and Jennifer incurred anonymous threats which claimed that the venue would be petrol bombed if the proposed meeting went ahead. This was not the first time she had heard such warnings:

> I've heard similar from other rural groups … advertise too much and you could end up with twenty or forty people outside with placards and the like. Or petrol bombed, I've heard that too. Some years ago, a group was getting started and they ended up being threatened with having the placed petrol bombed. That was the end of that. Who in their right mind would take the chance? (Jennifer, 48, lesbian)

Such a threat has specific and particular resonance in Northern Ireland, as petrol bombing was often a method of attack during the Troubles. Jennifer could not take the risk that these may be empty threats so discontinued with her plans, seeking an alternative location instead. Her second attempt to locate a physical meeting space was more successful; the venue was close to a police station, which as a result was surrounded by high beam security lighting and covered by closed circuit television cameras (CCTV). Jennifer claimed that her attendees stated that they felt safer at these meetings due to such enhanced security measures. Although seemingly excessive to an outsider, Jennifer's story represented the wider culture in which she lived where measures were taken to offset actual or perceived threats taken on board by people over the course of their lifetimes.

Summary

The type of victimisation and violence faced by lesbians and gay men in Northern Ireland may, on the whole, prove similar to members of LGB&T communities in other parts of the UK. However, what distinguishes homophobia in Northern Ireland is the fewer options open to those who have experienced persecution as well as the potential ramifications they may incur if they choose to speak out about these events. The implications of not reporting incidents and crimes motivated by homophobic prejudice include: facilitating a culture of silence around LGB&T persecution, reinforcing negative imagery that it is the lesbian or gay person who is in the wrong and not their victimiser, creating the illusion that homophobia and hate crimes towards lesbians and gay men is not a serious issue in Northern Ireland (which in turn impacts on the allocation of funding, resources and services to LGB&T organisation trying to address these issues) and ultimately goes towards constructing a level of complacency towards such prejudice and fatalism among those affected by it.

Condemning LGB&T communities as opposed to those who persecute lesbians and gay men has the double effect of both condoning victimisation and ensuring that incidents remain under-reported through fear of reprisal or being 'outed' (people having their sexual identity or orientation made public knowledge). Creating an environment which perceives the victimised party as the instigator of their ill–treatment can have significant repercussions on the LGB&T individual and the wider community. Indeed, as has been argued, this may be as debilitating as the fear of homophobic violence itself. However, engagement with this form of prejudice requires sensitivity and care; merely drafting in equality legislation or insisting on tokenistic training may serve to increase hostility and hamper organic change among the mainstream population. Ideally, shifts in thinking need to tap into wider social change which seeks to foster a greater level of inclusivity in Northern Ireland. The structural changes are being made which should mean that LGB&T communities are drawn into the reshaping of Northern Ireland, not continuing to be cast as social pariahs or dangerous 'others'.

In the following chapter, the political struggles to recognise lesbian and gay identities as valid are outlined through an examination of the decriminalisation debate. The infamous campaign to 'Save Ulster from Sodomy' sought to mobilise public opinion against homosexuality. Yet less than a decade after decriminalisation was achieved, Northern Irish LGB&T communities fought back, holding the first gay pride parade in Belfast. As will be discussed in the following chapter, comments by some public servants in Northern Ireland have indicated their prejudice against homosexuality, yet these same public servants are responsible for enacting laws that enforce harsher penalties for those convicted of crimes motivated by homophobic hostility.

Chapter 3

Playing Sexual Politics: Overcoming Criminalisation, Conflict and Condemnation

The Northern Ireland Assembly is dominated by unionist and nationalist political affiliation, with smaller, independent parties (such as the Alliance Party) slowly being recognised but usually limited to Belfast city centre. The Assembly currently comprises of power–sharing agreement between the Democratic Unionist Party (DUP) led by Peter Robinson (currently the First Minister) and Sinn Féin led by Gerry Adams (with Martin McGuinness in the role of Deputy First Minister). This was set up as part of the Belfast (Good Friday) Agreement 1998 and made history in 2011 by completing its first full term. Importantly for LGB&T communities, these two main parties have been shown to demonstrate very different perspectives when it comes to addressing sexual minority identities, rights and freedoms in Northern Ireland. These differences can be seen as rooted in notions of equality, citizenship and, perhaps most importantly, morally informed perspectives.

Politics in Northern Ireland differs from the rest of the UK due to the dominance of a religiously–informed morality often shaping the decisions of those in power (Mitchell and Tilley 2004). In England and Wales, politicians' faith, belief or religious adherence is rarely in the public interest or evident in legal and policy decisions. This is not the case in Northern Ireland where politicians are open, and in some cases vociferous, not only about stating their particular religious denomination but indicating how it has influenced key decisions. For example, in 2010 DUP minister Nelson McCausland led an unsuccessful public campaign to have exhibitions on creationism included in the Ulster Museum, claiming that their exclusion violated human rights (McDonald 2010). His belief that it was in the public interest may have been founded on a study published in the preceding year which indicated that a quarter of those questioned in Northern Ireland believed in creationism or at least 'hedged their bets' that there may be some truth in it (*BBC News* 2009). Such issues are unlikely to resonate in Great Britain.

In this chapter, the politicisation of sexuality and sexual identity is explored in relation to the struggle for homosexual decriminalisation which took place in Northern Ireland from the late 1960s through to the early 1980s. This was originally resisted on the basis of moral objections and political discourses which cast homosexuals as dangerous, predatory and harmful. Nonetheless, fuelled by gay and civil rights movements occurring elsewhere in the UK, lesbians and gay men in Northern Ireland began to organise socially and politically to campaign for the extension of the Sexual Offences Act 1967. In an interesting turn of events, these groups were able to capitalise on the ongoing ethno–political conflict. For example, many lesbians and gay men took advantage of the deserted city spaces which had opened up to them as a result of curfews imposed after dark in the wake of the heightened security situation. In these spaces, people who were ordinarily divided on the basis of religious or political identity came together under shared experiences of sexual oppression.

The examination of political dimensions in Northern Irish lesbians' and gay men's lives contained within this chapter draws on various sources of information to supplement the interviewees' accounts. These include documents archived by the Northern Ireland Gay Rights Association (NIGRA) and a collection of lesbian life stories published independently and anonymously under the title *Threads*. These additional sources help to construct a more nuanced understanding of the oppressive environment surrounding the campaign for homosexual decriminalisation. The final section of analysis in the chapter indicates that these battles are ongoing for some. The comments made by Iris Robinson against homosexuality were just the latest in a long line of Unionist politicians' harmful and accusatory statements which publicly denounced sexual minorities. An exploration of this continued and measured persecution illustrates the tactical language used which renders this form of political prejudice a 'safe' outlet, unlikely to incur disciplinary or criminal penalty as a result of Northern Ireland's unique moral fabric.

Constructing the Sexual 'Other'

In 1960s Great Britain, several social shifts had occurred which made the partial decriminalisation of homosexuality inevitable. Western attitudes towards homosexuality had begun to slowly drift towards a consensus which viewed homosexuality as more common than previously realised (Kinsey et al. 1948). Theories were also developing which led to understandings of the homosexual as constituting a 'social role', challenging popular biological presumptions of sexuality 'abnormalities' (McIntosh 1968). As these theories gained popularity, legal interference into the private sexual activities of homosexual men came into question. Civil rights discourses and media representations aided this growing concern that homosexual men were being treated in an unjust and persecutory manner. In the 1961 film '*Victim*' (Director: B. Dearden), Dirk Bogarde portrayed a closeted homosexual subjected to blackmail but refusing to comply at a time where many men chose suicide over social exposure. In a classic example of art mimicking life, the film touched on the ways in which legal regulation was causing social problems for some men. The prohibition of acts of 'gross indecency' under the Criminal Law (Amendment) Act 1885 had effectively been functioning as a 'blackmailer's charter' against men of social status. Many were being threatened by blackmailers (and in some cases the police) with public humiliation on the basis that their sexual activities would be exposed and their reputations tarnished. Sometimes, this accompanied police interrogations about sexual acquaintances following raids of licensed premises known to be frequented by homosexuals

(Jeffrey–Poulter 1991). From 1938 to 1952, prosecutions for the offences of sodomy and gross indecency rose from 134 to 670 and 320 to 1,686 respectively, whilst prosecutions for the less specific 'unnatural offences' rose from 822 to 3,087 (Hyde 1955: 212–213). Therefore, many men had grounds to be worried about potential legal repercussions and their impact.

The trials of Lord Montague and *Daily Mail* journalist Peter Wildeblood in the 1950s prompted increasing public sympathy towards such men who were seen as being hounded by the police. As a result, in 1954 the British Government commissioned an investigation into redefining the law on homosexuality (and prostitution). Evidence for the investigation was provided from a number of interested parties, including representatives from the police, magistrates, lawyers, prison officers, doctors, psychologists, church representatives and, interestingly, several homosexual men of reputable social standing. The inclusion of these particular social groups (criminal justice, medicine, faith organisations) reaffirmed the notion that homosexuality in some way impacted on people in these areas and thus warranted their opinions. In 1957, the resulting '*Wolfenden Report*' concluded that homosexuality was a condition which should not be subjected to criminal sanctions but instead required a more liberal legal approach (Home Office and Scottish Home Department, 1957). Based on the recommendations of the report, 'homosexual acts' which took place in private between two men aged over 21 years in England and Wales were decriminalised in the Sexual Offences Act 1967. Exceptions to this included men who were merchant seamen, members of the armed forces, and mental health patients.[1]

Towards 'Sex Positive' Political Recognition

Although attitudes towards homosexuality were liberalising generally, some authors of the 1967 Act were eager to stress that it was not a 'stamp of approval' and that decorum regarding sexual behaviour was still to be expected (Wilson 1993: 175). It was not anticipated that attitudes would change overnight, but this begrudging tolerance of homosexuality was seen by some to mar what would otherwise have been a significant victory; 'tolerance' as rarely a positive sign. Wilson (1993: 174), for instance, argues that 'toleration' of homosexual acts:

> [N]ecessarily rests on a bed of disapproval. And it is this underlying theme which is most frightening. With a history so dominated by social, political and moral outrage at the very mention of homosexuality, toleration cannot be welcomed as a virtue of liberal character as much as a warning of eventual unrest.

---

1   The Act was not automatically extended to Scotland, so in 1980 Robin Cook MP tabled an amendment to the Criminal Justice Act which resulted in the decriminalisation of homosexuality in Scotland.

Nonetheless, the legislation proved an important step for the burgeoning 'gay rights' movement in the West. Events in America had also reinforced the politicisation of sexual identities. In 1969, a protest was held by LGB&T patrons of the Stonewall Inn in New York against perceived police harassment (D'Emilio 1992, Carter 2005). This venue was subjected to repeated police raids with its patrons routinely humiliated and placed in fear of exposure. This protest, which has subsequently become an internationally celebrated occasion consisting of annual gay pride parades in many Western countries, lasted for three days in total. Nardi et al. (1994) outline the acts of resistance demonstrated by those in attendance:

> Puerto Rican drag queens, lesbians, effeminate men, and young street people resisted a police raid and fought back. Two more nights of fires, hurled bottles and stones, and demonstrations followed. By Sunday, the Stonewall Inn was burned, 'Gay Power" graffiti appeared and within months, Gay Liberation Front groups [started] forming throughout the country.

Traditionally persecuted minorities began to fight back, using their sexual identities as a platform for resistance. After decades of negativity, positive images and discourses regarding LGB&T communities were beginning to emerge. In some cases, previously negative labels and language were employed as tools of resistance. Furthermore, the burgeoning LGB&T movement was important for illustrating the vast sexual diversity contained within the umbrella term 'homosexuality'. This had previously been overlooked (or dominated by white, middle class gay men) as Butler (1991: 16) notes:

> If it is already true that 'lesbians" and 'gay men" have been traditionally designated as impossible identities, errors of classification, unnatural disasters within juridicio–medical discourses ... then perhaps these sites of disruption, error, confusion and trouble can be the very rallying points for a certain resistance to classification and to identity as such.

These riots indicated the vital importance of reclaiming identity and using this as a strategic site of resistance against persecution, victimisation and social exclusion. Inspired by this ideological culture of social mobility, campaigners for equality and freedom from legal and social prejudice began to emerge in Northern Ireland, organising under their shared experiences of oppression.

Mobilising for Legal and Social Change

The failure to automatically extend the 1967 Sexual Offences Act to Northern Ireland meant that the 1861 Offences Against the Person Act and the 1885 Criminal Law (Amendment) Act remained in force. In the early 1970s, the Gay Liberation Movement (GLM) was formally established in Northern Ireland with several GLM members creating a more political wing, the Campaign for Homosexual Law Reform (Northern Ireland).[2] They lobbied the Northern Ireland Office (NIO) – which had been established at Westminster while the Assembly was suspended – to decriminalise homosexuality. At this point, no Northern Irish political party supported the extension of the 1967 Act, despite the clear inequality and discrimination promoted through its absence.

As political decisions regarding Northern Ireland were being made by Westminster (known as 'direct rule'), the decriminalisation campaign suddenly seemed more feasible. In 1976, the Secretary of State for Northern Ireland announced that he would be assessing areas of potential law reform, namely homosexuality and divorce, in light of ongoing direct rule. However, he realised that there may be potential difficulties in implementing such reforms given Northern Ireland's strong adherence to morally conservative ideologies. Therefore, the NIO consulted the Standing Advisory Committee on Human Rights (SACHR). This was a committee established under the 1973 Constitution Act to monitor the effect of anti–discrimination laws and regulations on Northern Irish society. SACHR conducted an assessment of public opinions regarding homosexual decriminalisation. Upon completion, SACHR recommended extending the 1967 Act but warned that overall public support for this move in Northern Ireland would be unlikely. Furthermore, they recommended only implementing the existing legislation, as it stood in England and Wales. In other words, they advised against enacting any measures to automatically apply future amendments without prior consultation with the people of Northern Ireland (NIGRA 1976b).

In 1978 the Westminster Government published a proposal for a draft Homosexual Offences (Northern Ireland) Order. If successful, this would have brought Northern Ireland into line with England and Wales in decriminalizing private homosexual acts between two consenting males over the age of 21. These recommendations were supported by the Social Democratic and Labour Party (SDLP) and in part by the Church of Ireland (Dudgeon 1980). However, none of the 12 elected Northern Irish MPs publicly supported the proposed reform and several openly voiced their opposition to it (Dudgeon 1980). In the end, the Democratic Unionist Party (DUP) held off the Order of Council by abstaining from voting at Westminster. Furthermore, the minister for Law Reform, James Dunn, made two additional independent assessments of public opinion which led the Standing Advisory Commission on Human Rights SACHR to rescind their input as representing social views on homosexual decriminalisation (NIGRA 1976b). As a result, this first attempt at decriminalisation failed and homosexual acts continued to be illegal in Northern Ireland.

---

2   These efforts were matched in the Republic of Ireland where Senator David Norris began his campaign to have the British law criminalising homosexuality repealed in 1974 (Norris v. Ireland – 10581/83 European Court of Human Rights). Decriminalisation was eventually enacted two decades later in 1993 after a 1988 ruling by the European Court of Human Rights.

The Northern Ireland Gay Rights Association (NIGRA), established in the 1970s, focused heavily on campaigning for the extension of decriminalisation legislation in Northern Ireland. As part of their strategy, NIGRA began recording gay men's accounts of harassment by the RUC, as well as offering help and advice for men detained for questioning by police officers (NIGRA 1976d). The pro–active approach taken by the RUC in cracking down on homosexual activity in Northern Ireland led to a number of gay men having their houses raided under the pretext of alternative behaviours, such using drugs (*Sunday News* 9 May 1976 in NIGRA 1976b, *THES* 14 May 1976 in NIGRA 1976c, Dudgeon 1980). Several of these men were involved in the law reform campaign, a factor which led to the *Belfast Telegraph* (19 May 1976 in NIGRA 1976a) also documenting this harassment. The paper indicated that despite seemingly searching for drugs, correspondence relating to the political campaign for decriminalisation had been amongst the items confiscated by the police:

> Leaders of the [law reform] committee who have made themselves known to the public allege that they have been suffering police harassment and have had all their organisational papers taken away by police.

As a result of the raids, twenty–two men were arrested, including all the male members of NIGRA (*Sunday News* 9 May 1976 in NIGRA 1976b). As well as questioning the men and threatening them with exposure to family and employers if they did not comply, the police also subjected the men to forced medical examinations as part of their enquiries (Dudgeon 1980). Furthermore, several men were reportedly questioned in front of their parents, leading to uncomfortable questions from family members upon their release. None of the men were prosecuted, yet none of their complaints about their continued harassment and unfair treatment were upheld either. Despite this, the British government appeared ready to take steps to enact decriminalisation although they realised that the proposed changes would incur hostile opposition. As a result, the government actively invited public comment on the draft proposal, an invitation taken up in the press by members of three key Churches in Northern Ireland (NIGRA 1979b, 1979c, 1979d). Although none of the main faith organisations were willing to accept homosexuality as a natural orientation, few publicly decreed that homosexuals should be illegal. Therefore, most did little more than state their general opposition to the matter.

Nevertheless, the DUP actively and vociferously campaigned against extending the 1967 Sexual Offences Act to Northern Ireland, exacerbating and utilising the moral mandate they had through their affiliation with the Free Presbyterian Church. However, it was a campaign which would eventually lead to the very thing they tried to avoid: homosexual decriminalisation in Northern Ireland.

Saving Ulster from Sodomy

In the early 1970s, the DUP made their active opposition against the proposed decriminalisation a prioritised campaign, unusually garnering the support of Catholic churches where possible, regardless of the ongoing sectarian divisions (NIGRA 1979d). The DUP campaign was visibly led by the Reverend Dr. Ian Paisley. His highly publicised 'Save Ulster from Sodomy' crusade involved a large advertisement taken out in national newspapers stating that such a change in the law 'can only bring God's curse down upon our people' (McKittrick 1977). Heavily invoking doctrinal ideologies of doom and destruction, primarily the destruction of Northern Ireland's 'moral fabric', Dr. Paisley's campaign targeted Sunday worshippers. This tactic resulted in more than 70,000 Northern Irish residents (at that point 5 per cent of the population) signing a petition opposing decriminalisation. Support was also garnered through the distribution of pamphlets, documented by NIGRA, which focused heavily upon the fear that such a law would adversely impact on social values:

> We oppose the legalising of Homosexuality as we believe the practice is contrary to the Word of God and the moral standards of the people of Northern Ireland. HOMOSEXUALITY DEMANDS NOT ACCEPTANCE BUT A CURE. The legalising of homosexuality would open the floodgates of immorality, with countless other vices demanding acceptance. The consequences of such a deluge would be grim... (NIGRA 1979c)

Invoking the key tenets of Northern Irish identity – faith and family – as well as the fear of chaos, DUP councillor Alan Kane ensured that his pamphlet left no doubt as to the potential destruction legalised homosexuality would bring:

> Homosexuality should not be regarded as a disease but as a sin which debases individuals, degrades society and which is outrightly condemned in the Bible in the strongest possible terms. ... The deviance of homosexuality is a direct attack on the family – the microcosm and vital basic unit of society. The demands for the legislation of homosexuality represent a serious threat to the social order and another attempt to undermine the basic tenets of morality which are held by the vast majority of decent people in Northern Ireland. ... The law must act as a deterrent otherwise a society totally devoid of any form of legal control would be created, where mass murder, rapes and incestuous relationships would take place. (NIGRA 1979d)

This clear recourse to deeply held fears of serious and violent assaults may have been hyperbole to those with a rational take on sexuality, but to the morally–driven majority in Northern Ireland it went to the very heart of what they sought to avoid: a challenge to family instability.

In case the message was still unclear, Kane went on in his propaganda to cast aspersions regarding potential links between homosexuals and the Paedophile Information Exchange group (NIGRA 1979d). In effect, Kane was juxtaposing homosexuals' liberties with the protection of children. The implication that vulnerable children need protection from homosexuals reverts back to a powerful negative imagery of predatory deviants. What is ironic is that at the time of this campaign in the 1970s, a large–scale investigation into allegations of child sex abuse was ongoing which strongly implicated members of the DUP and Free Presbyterian Church (Dillon 1999). The Kincora Boys Home was subject to investigation for allegations of child sexual abuse which had not been reported as a result of the statuses of many of the men involved. These were alleged to include senior political figures, state agents and Church members, many of whom were later condemned for failing to act on information regarding this abuse (Greer 2003). Dillon (1999) claims that a report by Colin Wallace of MI5 regarding a paedophile network was overlooked due to wider security concerns involving some of the affected parties. The home was run by William McGrath who was part of a paramilitary organisation called Tara and a member of Ian Paisley's Free Presbyterian Church. Dillon (1999: 183) claims that it was McGrath's inside knowledge on the Loyalist community which granted him immunity, initially from social persecution and later from legal prosecution. It would appear that reverting back to the 'stranger danger' fear of homosexuals may have been a convenient way of deflecting attention from the threats of those with power and influence in society.

The DUP presented their petition against the decriminalisation of homosexuality at Parliament Buildings, Stormont, where the Northern Ireland Assembly was ordinarily located. This presentation came complete with a convoy of more than 60 vehicles, guaranteeing a great deal of media coverage (Jeffrey–Poulter 1991). Their tactics worked; in 1979 the Government announced its decision not to pursue the proposed reform to enact decriminalisation. Although the law against homosexuality remained in Northern Ireland, public assurances were made that no prosecutions would actually be brought against gay men. Although none technically were, several men claimed to be continually harassed by the police for other misdemeanours which, the men asserted, were used in place of prosecutions for same–sex activities. The arrest of one such man, NIGRA secretary Jeffrey Dudgeon, proved pivotal to the Northern Ireland homosexual decriminalisation campaign.

Winning the Battle but Starting the War

During one of the aforementioned RUC drugs raids, Dudgeon was arrested following the discovery of marijuana at his home (McLoughlin 1996). The police also confiscated personal diaries which indicated his engagement in homosexual acts and he was interrogated about this at the police station. Although Dudgeon was threatened with a charge of 'gross indecency', the prosecution service decided not to take the case any further. NIGRA used the opportunity to advance their decriminalisation efforts on the basis of police harassment and discrimination. In 1975, the case went to the European Commission of Human Rights to be screened for admissibility and to see if the claims had any merit. In 1978, the Commission found the claim to be admissible, deciding by nine votes to one that 'the legal prohibition of such [homosexual] acts between male persons over 21 years of age breached the applicant's right to respect for his private life'. Following this, in 1980, the Commission (10 judges) found no violation of art 8 where the applicant was under 21 years old (8 judges to 2); violation of art 8 when he was over 21 (9 judges to 1); and chose not to examine the issue of gender discrimination (9 judges to 1). The Commission referred the case to the European Court of Human Rights for clarification of the law, who in turn decided to take the decision in plenary as they do with important legal matters so they could make an authoritative decision. On 22 October 1981 the Court in plenary (19 judges) agreed with the Commission's position by 15 votes to 4, ordering that decriminalisation be applied to homosexual acts in private in Northern Ireland.

Dudgeon's success was slightly marred through judicial comments which alluded several times to the perceived majority disapproval of homosexuality in Northern Ireland. Given the publicity sought by, and granted to, the ongoing DUP campaign against decriminalisation, it would have been hard for the judges to miss this moral battle. Although the effects of continued criminalisation upon homosexuals were taken into consideration, so too was the fact that changes in law did not necessarily reflect changes in morality. In some cases, the dissenting opinions of the judges in disagreement (and the one judge who partially disagreed) went further in their condemnation with closely–held religious beliefs cited in the arguments for avoiding social degeneration (McLoughlin 1996). Some of these opinions proved particularly damaging. Judge Zekia, for example, discussed homosexuality within a discourse of 'curable tendencies'. However, it was his suggestion that widespread social disorder would be a likely outcome of decriminalisation which really tapped into Northern Ireland's ongoing political battles at the time:

> A change of the law so as to legalise homosexual activities in private by adults is very likely to cause many disturbances in the country in question. The respondent Government were justified in finding it necessary to keep the relevant Acts on the statute book for the protection of morals as well as for the preservation of public peace. (ECtHR Dudgeon Case, Series A, Judge Zekia no.3)

Judge Matscher, on the other hand, initially alluded to the fact that there had been no prosecutions for engaging in homosexual acts and therefore the claims of 'fear, suffering and psychological distress' indicated by Mr Dudgeon were unfounded.[3] However, it was Judge Matscher's comments reiterating negative stereotypes of homosexuals as being engaged in paedophilia which proved potentially more dangerous:

> The reason why the police pursued their enquiries was probably also to investigate whether the applicant did not have homosexual relations with minors as well. Indeed, it is well known that this is a widespread tendency in homosexual circles and the fact that the applicant himself was engaged in a campaign for the lowering of the legal age of consent points in the same direction; furthermore, the enquiries in question took place in the context of a more extensive operation on the part of the police, the purpose of which was to trace a minor who was missing from home and believed to be associating with homosexuals. (ECtHR, Dudgeon Case, Series A, Judge Matscher, pt I)

Judge Matscher's conflation of homosexuality and paedophilia are directly linked to the oppositional discourses manifested by the DUP in their campaign against extending the 1967 Sexual Offences Act to Northern Ireland. Almost reinforcing this 'care of the child' ideology, the judges ensured that the age of consent was firmly set at 21 years of age. This was despite it being recognised that this was, at the time, four years older than the heterosexual age of consent in Northern Ireland (which remained at 17 years of age until 2006).

Furthermore, no damages were awarded following this success, possibly as a result of underlying feelings of conservatism, or through the judges not wanting to incur any further antagonism from those who opposed their final decision. This can be contrasted to the decriminalisation of homosexuality in the Republic of Ireland where a case taken by Senator David Norris (who was represented by former Irish Prime Minister Mary Robinson) warranted significant damages being awarded.

Making the Personal Political

Few instances have been comparable to the DUP/Free Presbyterian Church's campaign against decriminalisation. The fusion of religion and politics, most specifically this church and – during the 1970s – the largely Protestant Assembly, was most prominent during this 'Save Ulster from Sodomy' campaign of the 1970s. Almost overnight, the issue of homosexuality was being talked and written about

---

3   This seems to parallel Northern Irish women's access to abortion services: although they face prosecution under the Offences against the Person Act 1861, no woman has yet been charged with obtaining an abortion, yet there may well be similar forms of 'fear, suffering and psychological distress' at being discovered which cannot be displayed while such a law remains in force.

everywhere, and almost always with an overtly negative and stereotypical slant. Discussions around the campaign invoked mixed feelings, with some believing it was a genuine attempt to preserve morality and shield the people of Northern Ireland from sexual 'deviancy' and moral corruption. For others looking at this period retrospectively, it seemed like there might have been more to this agenda.

Interviewees who had been involved in the NIGRA campaign to enact homosexual decriminalisation offered an additional perspective of what may have been going on behind the scenes in the 'Sodomy' campaign. Taking on board the wider conflict situation and the battle for political recognition and support, some felt that the assault on homosexuality may have served to unify and solidify the DUP. A commonly indicated perspective was that the DUP were losing ground politically and socially at the time. In the 1970s, the period of violent conflict had intensified and the Assembly was repeatedly being dissolved (McKittrick and McVea 2001). With homosexuality not being well received in society generally, all the DUP needed to do was to capitalise on this feeling and provide a political impetus to oppose decriminalisation. In doing so, some interviewees felt that the promotion of this policy was an effective smokescreen for any internal discrepancies within the DUP that may have otherwise made it appear unstable or unsupported. Therefore, the 'outside enemy' of homosexuality may have been a useful diversion to deflect bad press away from the DUP while ensuring they stayed in the media for what they saw as the 'right' reasons.

Additionally, the campaign increased the publicity for the Free Presbyterian Church which had only recently been established as an autonomous Protestant denomination in Northern Ireland prior to the campaign. The fact that these two organisations were linked by their leader and founder, the Reverend Ian Paisley, was telling. In effect, the opposition to decriminalisation may have been the perfect opportunity to promote his Church and his Party. Pushing a moral agenda through both may have been aided by having a demarcated political 'other' to focus on as a perceived threat to the social fabric. However, the political tensions and continued reversion to direct rule provided the pockets of space needed for sexual minority groups to get their point across. Several of the interviewees realised that grass–roots activism in Northern Ireland was vital during these periods if decisions were to be taken at Westminster rather than Stormont:

> What mattered to me was that one politician could keep me illegal – that was the problem. You might have homophobia in society, but if you have it at the top in the government then it's obviously going to be more of a problem, particularly if you're talking about Northern Ireland. (John, 49, gay male)

> Fifty years ago we might have been arrested and jailed; fifty years before that we might have been hung, and there's nothing to say that 25 years from now the government might not say for some reason or another, 'Oh, it might be better if we bring homosexuality back into the criminal law because we need a few victims'. (Mack, 55, gay male)

As a result, many interviewees felt that this 'Sodomy' campaign was a major catalyst for the politicisation of sexuality in Northern Ireland. It simultaneously advanced the visibility of the gay rights movement as well as the growing opposition to homosexuality. Although Mack's comment, above, indicates the uncertainty some felt that one strategically placed politician could have a negative impact on lesbian and gay freedom, others such as Pat saw the positives in politics:

> Just with one stroke of the pen, this great campaign to save Ulster from sodomy was smashed or, as we like to say, the big pink hand slapped him across the face and left its mark! But we've felt it too – he's never let up on us. Although [the Rev. Ian Paisley] never took us on publicly like that again, he's made sure we've had to work for everything we've got. (Pat, 61, gay male)

It appears as if the failure of the DUP campaign had both positive and negative implications for those on both sides of the debate. However, an unexpected result appeared to be the informative element it had for some gay male interviewees who indicated that prior to this 'Sodomy' debate, they had little idea of what it was that they were 'meant to do' as a homosexual. They commented that it appeared as if heterosexuals such as the Rev. Ian Paisley understood better than they did about how to interact sexually with other men. While they were aware of the 'evils' and wrongfulness of homosexuality, such discourses often failed to elaborate on exactly *what* it was that was wrong. In other words, many of the male interviewees admitted having no idea as to how to intimately engage with another man prior to the 'Sodomy' campaign, as Rob outlined:

> For me, it was all about the closeness and the nearness of being near a man. It was much later before I realised you could have sex with a man. I think I eventually found that out because of what was going on at the time, that campaign. (Rob, 58, gay male)

For these interviewees, Rev. Paisley inadvertently advanced their (and most likely a lot of other men's) understandings of homosexuality for the better. Ironically, given the absence of sexual education, literature or media exposure, this was the first time they had come across the concept of men engaging physically and sexually with other men.

LGB&T Visibility within the 'Ring of Steel'

During this period, the various campaigns mounted by political and social groups meant that lesbian and gay visibility was slowly increasing in Northern Ireland. This was an important development to combat the ideologies propagated by some that homosexuality in Northern Ireland was little more than a temporary aberration. While increased visibility was encouraging, this also placed enormous pressure on the limited resources established to aid lesbians and gay men seeking advice, information and social outlets (Dudgeon 1980). Between 1974 and 1978, over 2,000 men and women from all over Northern Ireland contacted Cara–Friend, a lesbian and gay organisation based in Belfast. Dudgeon (1980) illustrates how a selection of letters archived by NIGRA demonstrate the isolation, loneliness, frustration and fear people felt at being 'the only one' before seeing Cara–Friend's advertisement in the *Belfast Telegraph* for support and advice and contacting them. This level of interaction and the backgrounds of the people coming forward to get involved with the burgeoning LGB&T movement were integral to getting the community up and running while the battle for legitimacy waged on.

Space, Subversion and Safety

Under the threat of criminalisation, inventive uses and subversions of space greatly aided the lesbians' and gay men's social and political development. Northern Ireland's metaphorical and physical 'gay scene' had for years been truly subcultural, but slowly began to grow in visibility during the 1970s. Despite progressing more slowly than in comparable areas of the UK, the development of this 'scene' was both helped and hindered by the ongoing conflict and continued criminalisation of homosexuality. Paradoxical situations arose in relation to lesbians' and gay men's use of city centre spaces during the height of the Troubles. For example, spaces rendered empty by security fears could become spaces of safety for those who feared general discrimination on the basis of their sexuality. However, use of such space also brought with it increased visibility and regulation. Tales of social and political resistance to varied forms of homophobia involved negotiating social and sexual policing.

As the Troubles in Northern Ireland heightened, bomb threats (particularly in urban areas) became more frequent. In addition to enhanced security measures such as added troops being deployed in and around Belfast city centre, curfews were imposed and people voluntarily restricted their social mobility. In the evenings, as well as on public holidays and Sundays, very few people were out in the city centre as shops were not permitted to open. Many chose to spend time at church or with families. Some of the interviewees made the most of these opportunities with public displays of affection or intimacy with a partner. Mack recalled one particular event that stood out for him:

> On those days you can't believe just how *empty* the city was. This is a nice story, I'd met Rob [his partner] – we hadn't been going together that long, and it was a beautiful day, one of those gorgeous, summery, beautiful days – and I met him and I kissed him on the mouth outside the City Hall, and the reason I could do that was there was no–one, *nothing* the whole length of Donegall Avenue – that's how empty it really was. So the chances of getting beaten up were very little. (Mack, 55, gay male, his emphasis)

In Belfast, one security measure was the 'ring of steel': a fence seven feet high which ran round the inner section of the city centre. Several entry and exit points were staffed by members of the security forces who searched people going in and out of the area in addition to the searches taking place at the entrances to all major stores. As a result of this, some of the older interviewees retrospectively saw the Troubles as having a somewhat unintended, yet positive impact on their socialising, as Jane noted:

> Everything in Belfast shut in the evening as people went home to the safety of their communities. The inner bit of the city was ringed off and the Army searched you when you went through. The town was empty most nights save for the Army and those on their way to the gay disco. (Jane, 50, lesbian)

These new spaces which opened up in the evenings facilitated LGB&T community development, allowing people to engage with one another in relative safety. In the 1970s, The Chariot Rooms was a particularly important Belfast city centre venue run by a gay male couple, Ernie and Jim. Their discos on a Saturday night used to attract LGB&T people from all over Northern Ireland, many of whom went to great lengths to attend. Other bars in local hotels and Queen's University began to hold 'gay friendly' nights. Within these spaces, a 'melting pot' of sexual and gender identities were evident. Interestingly these groups were met with other 'subcultures' including groups of deaf people and those aligned by music interests, such as punk rockers. Rather than demarcating people as a result of the apparent differences, this diversity was welcomed and encouraged.

With such a varied selection of people demonstrating their abilities to interact with one another, the conflict being waged outside these venues appeared increasingly futile to some of the interviewees. The policy of leaving identity divisions almost literally at the door served to further highlight the problems around them, as John indicated:

> The contrast was amazing; outside our society was being torn apart with people killing each other because they were different, but in the discos you couldn't get more difference in one room and we welcomed it with open arms! (John, 49, gay male)

Also of note was whether people had access to their own cars and could arrive to and from events in relative safety. Although small in comparison to the Republic of Ireland and England, Northern Ireland's geography means that larger cities are located some distance from one another. Even today, public transport is less well developed compared to England. Owning private means of transport is vital to people's independence, particularly if they are frequenting social venues which they would rather not tell friends and family about. Safety was also paramount, as Mark explained:

> Gay people weren't going to get on a heterosexual bus service like Ulsterbus
> to get beaten up and nothing be done about it. Their security is paramount, and
> they've years of experience of clamming up, not speaking, keeping themselves
> safe, so they're not going to put themselves through that. (Mark, 32, gay male)

For those who did venture out, there were still fears around leaving these spaces
as they were situated in the middle of an ongoing conflict. Additionally, the visible
and numerous security personnel deployed to Northern Ireland, particularly
Belfast, during the 1970s – 1980s may have meant a greater risk of being caught
up in conflict. This was due to members of the RUC and British Army routinely
being targeted for violence.

Imposed curfews meant that most people were not meant to be out after a
certain time in the evening; anyone who was incurred suspicion. Jane articulated
this general feeling of fear that she attributed to her sexual identity but which
could easily have been an extension of the wider fears of being alone on the streets
in Northern Ireland during the Troubles:

> Sometimes after the discos you'd feel pretty unsafe if you weren't heading on
> somewhere else. The streets were deserted, funnily enough because of all the
> ongoing violence, but that didn't always make you feel safe if you thought they
> knew it was [the gay bar] you were heading from. (Jane, 50, lesbian)

These feelings of fear and trepidation were not only felt by lesbians and gay men in
Northern Ireland but also those who had travelled up from the Republic. 'Antonia',
a contributor to the anonymously compiled anthology *Threads* (which documents
lesbian lives in 1970s and 80s Northern Ireland) reiterated these feelings from an
outsider's perspective when she'd visited Belfast:

> I felt distinctly unsafe on the streets after the Disco. I remember when I worked
> across the north going to visit in North Belfast and staying in a friend's house
> while driving through Ballymena and Londonderry the streets would be dark
> and empty. When leaving the light and warmth of her house, it was as if life went
> out. Life and vibrancy was alive in the houses in Belfast but not on the streets.
> The contrast was striking on the way home, as I drove to Dundalk, there were
> lights and people out on the streets enjoying themselves, drinking and talking,
> laughing and walking. ('Antonia' cited in *Threads* 2008: 58)

As soon as the problems and fears associated with the Troubles started to abate,
lesbians and gay men found themselves without the familiar regular venues in
which to congregate. As hotels and bars started attracting a more diverse evening
trade, LGB&T custom became less vital. The seemingly temporary nature of their
welcome in the city centre venues led some interviewees to assume that they had
not been accepted as much as they had thought:

We got discos in place that, had there been no Troubles, we wouldn't have got them, because the hotels were empty in the centre of town; nobody was coming in to town – we were prepared to go into town. ... There were certain bars that began to understand that the only trade they were getting was from gay men coming into town ... and they made a lot of money out of it, because there was a need. But I reckon had we been in what you could call, more 'normal' times, we would've found it very difficult in the early days to be able to hire these things, because businesses wouldn't have wanted to be associated with the pink pound. (Scott, 49, gay male)

Other spaces outside of Belfast appeared to fare slightly better: discos in Derry/ Londonderry were being held in the University by representatives of Cara–friend, providing a vital social outlet for LGB&T people located in the west and north– western parts of Northern Ireland. This scene thrived throughout the 1970s and 1980s thanks to a committed group of lesbians and gay men who were working together to make the city as vibrant as possible. In Dublin too, where the scene had women–only discos and themed nights, many people found that they could escape the culture of the Troubles and revel in the anonymity the larger city offered.

LGB&T Interactions with the Security Forces

While the city centre space in Belfast had opened up to LGB&T communities as a result of the Troubles, the overt security presence of domestic police, the British police and the army led to a heightened level of scrutiny levied at those using these spaces. Some of the more problematic interactions the lesbian and gay interviewees had with the police involved the RUC's targeting of venues which had quickly become known as 'gay friendly'. These discos were seen by the people who attended them as safe havens from social prejudice and potential victimisation. Yet the very people who were meant to be protecting them from one form of victimisation were inflicting another type in its place. The frequency and certainty of police raids led some of the patrons to believe that perhaps the police were less concerned with lesbians' and gay men's security and more concerned with intimidating them:

Aye, the disco was frequently interrupted by the RUC. They'd come in and they'd turn on all the lights so they could get a good look at you. Some of us were used to that, but for the newer ones it was always a bit nerve–racking so you really felt for them, you know? It was just intimidation; we were hardly a threat compared to what they were really stationed there for. (Mary, 58, lesbian)

The intimidation evident here can be read in a variety of ways. For those not used to this form of exposure (turning the lights on, getting a good look at who was in there) it may have put them off returning to the venue again. If enough people did this, then it would ultimately impact on the venue's income and possibly result in it closing down. For those more used to this form of interruption, it put them in a situation where they were aware of the reasons behind such actions but were unable to do anything about them. In addition, given the wider security issue going on at the time, this form of policing may have been an indication of the powerlessness some members of the security forces felt in relation to their role in the ongoing conflict. Indeed, several interviewees pointed out the irony of policing LGB&T establishments in the middle of such violent instability:

> Most gay people were amazed; people were getting arms and legs blown off and people were getting shot and tortured and still the police found time to harass gay people. (James, 60, gay male)

Connor, a retired police officer, served in the RUC/PSNI. As he was a married man and a father, his colleagues were unaware of his true sexuality until he decided to come out later into his career. Connor was concerned about the treatment of identified lesbians and gay men by his colleagues. Describing how the police interacted with patrons of gay friendly venues he observed how the language used illustrated the negative sentiments directed towards them:

> I suppose because I was gay I thought I should keep an eye on how the police were responding to the gay community. ... Sometimes [when on patrol] there'd be 10 or 15 police cars all sitting round watching what was going on and when questioned, my sergeant would say, 'Well, they're here to watch the freak show, you know, all the queers'. Any police officer knows there is titillation within the police service about gays so they cruise round bars to see if there's any stuff to laugh at, or to see if there's anybody they know, and there was a lot of anxiety around that. (Connor, 46, gay male)

Some of the male interviewees, particularly those who were older, appeared to still hold a level of suspicion towards members of the criminal justice system in Northern Ireland. Those who had been targeted by police officers prior to decriminalisation while the campaigns to extend the legislation were ongoing claimed to have been harassed despite assurances to the contrary. Pat, the oldest of the gay male interviewees, believed that the continued criminalisation of homosexuality in Northern Ireland, coupled with the more openly displayed culture of intolerance gave licence to officers to demonstrate their distaste with impunity:

> We assumed that once they got decriminalisation in England, [the police] weren't supposed to be so heavy handed in Northern Ireland, but I think if you talk to a lot of guys you'll see that that wasn't the case. (Pat, 61, gay male)

This policing was not limited to gay friendly venues but appeared to some interviewees to feed into a wider culture of harassment occurring at the time:

> [The police] would be chasing us rather than the IRA, because we were easier targets. They'd go on about how they'd need all the manpower they could get to chase the criminals yet they'd still have police officers at toilets and things like that, just in case a guy got his dick out or something like that. And you'd think, 'There are more important things going on in Ulster than this!' But we just seemed to be easy targets at the time I suppose. (Rob, 58, gay male)

The fear that it was the victimised person who would incur the full weight of the law was also pressing for some gay men who had to weigh up the full implications of reporting any negative treatment they incurred:

> There was no way you could go to the police if you were attacked because you yourself were a criminal. In that sense, you didn't actually belong within the community, the community was rejecting you and indeed the powers that were being employed to protect you weren't protecting you; they were there to persecute you along with everyone else. (David, 43, gay male)

As this mentality was often coupled with an internalised feeling that what they were doing was bad or wrong anyway (see Chapters 4 and 6), reporting their instances of victimisation, may have meant incurring blame for the assault. Worse – as David outlined – they could have been charged with some criminal offence themselves. Some interviewees felt that they were unlikely to garner sympathy or support from family, friends or other members of their community, so contacting the police would be of little benefit to them and might incur greater harm.

Another potential reason for these repeated police raids may have been to expose and embarrass the members of the security services, including British soldiers and off duty policemen who frequented LGB&T venues. Soldiers who had recently been posted to Northern Ireland attended several of the gay discos without fear of causing a security alert because these spaces were not seen to be divided along sectarian lines or subject to threats as part of the ongoing conflict. Still, some interviewees viewed the presence of British soldiers at LGB&T events as potentially compromising the safety of all the patrons. The reality of such fears was illustrated in one incident involving a member of the RUC in such a venue. Darren Bradshaw, a young, off duty RUC police officer was shot by IRA paramilitaries while in a popular city centre gay bar in 1994. This event was viewed by some interviewees to have ended assumptions that gay venues were 'neutral zones'. Despite their best efforts, lesbians and gay men living in Northern Ireland could not fully escape the wider social and political events taking place all around them.

Interrogating Sexuality and Sectarianism

The inclusivity evident within facets of LGB&T communities in Northern Ireland significantly contrasted with the wider culture of sectarianism that was dividing societies during the Troubles. Dudgeon (1980) recognised the harmonising properties of shared persecution and the ability to overlook other differences in identity:

> It is also very heartening that in a province where religious differences divide most of the community, the gay social scene has never been sectarian. The labels 'Protestant' and 'Catholic' do not apply: people develop relationships and friendships with each other as individuals and not as representatives of either community. The bond of a common sexuality is far stronger than adherence to sectarian differences. Heterosexual society in Ulster could well take a lesson from the homosexual minority in its midst.

However, this view was not shared by everyone. The issue of sectarianism in LGB&T communities in Northern Ireland has been addressed from different perspectives over the past three decades. Several lesbians and gay men have spoken publicly about their sexual identities whilst also defining themselves in largely sectarian political terms. Since the mid–1990s, a number of narratives have emerged which have sought to locate individual lesbians' and gay men's perspectives within Northern Ireland's wider socio–political history.

Nell McCafferty, a journalist and writer from Derry/Londonderry, depicts in her autobiography the similarities between the nationalist struggle for rights, equality and justice with those of lesbian and gay communities in Northern Ireland (2004). She describes how her personal sexual, national and gender identities were, at times, in conflict with one another when she was involved in exposing and campaigning against civil rights abuses and injustices in Northern Ireland. This was similarly the case for Cherry Smyth, also a lesbian journalist, who saw her sexual identity as allowing her fluidity to identify with those she may otherwise not have engaged with:

> My coming out as a lesbian paralleled and informed my emergence as a post–Prod [sic: Protestant] Nationalist. Common sexuality allowed me to identify with Republican lesbians and gay men in a new way, just as feminism had given me the opportunity to forge new links with women across different backgrounds of class, nationality and race. (Smyth 1994: 224)

Other lesbians describe a process of rejecting either side of the socio–political divide in Northern Ireland. In this case, an alternative community which harmonises identities may be preferable to a political one which divides them. Illustrating this position, Grainne Close (2003: 9) outlines the cultural ostracism faced by those in Northern Ireland who felt they could not reconcile their national and sexual identities, even within their own communities:

> In the north of Ireland, identity and religion are so intermingled it is hard for queers to be accepted within their own Catholic and Protestant communities. A Catholic dyke living in a Nationalist/Republican community is not safe and a Protestant dyke living in a Unionist/Loyalist community is not safe.

Such a reading infers that there are few options available to lesbians and gay men who are 'out' within their communities. Therefore, an alternative space is needed for the formation of a cohesive community which incorporates alternative sexual identities. Close states that in Northern Ireland, 'the queer community must maintain a space neutral to both religions so we can organise together' (2003: 9). This direct call to eschew politically constructed divisions sets LGB&T organising in Northern Ireland apart from similar developments in the UK.

These ethno–political histories could not be overlooked by all; some felt that the denial of and struggle for civil rights by Catholic and/or nationalist communities, regardless of sexuality, may have led to a greater propensity for lesbians in particular from this side of the traditional divide to be more politicised in Northern Ireland than in comparable areas of the UK:

> It didn't surprise me to see more [lesbian] Catholics up there fighting for rights. Catholics are more used to a civil rights idea, they're more tolerant … take the politics out of it and they're simply into civil rights. (Smythie, 39, lesbian)

This visibility of Catholic lesbians was also addressed in relation to the apparent invisibility of Protestant lesbians:

> Why were there so many 'out' Republican or Catholic lesbians and so few Protestant women? They say that sectarianism had no place in the LGB&T community, but I think people are too preoccupied to distance themselves from being tarred with that brush and so they have just refused to recognise it for what it is. (Mary, 58, lesbian)

The topic of traditional divides in LGB&T communities in Northern Ireland proved to be a thorny issue for most of the interviewees and one which resulted in immensely varied responses. While some – like Mary, above – believed that there may have been an underlying sectarian issue amongst some of members of the burgeoning LGB&T communities, almost as many others were keen to state the opposite. How much this opinion varied proved to be dependent on how the person viewed these divisions as functioning. On the one hand, when depicting the development of LGB&T communities during the early years of the Troubles, lesbians and gay men were described as already being in a marginalised minority and therefore could not afford any further divisions. For people who saw the situation in this way, the Troubles were seen to have harmonised the LGB&T community to a degree:

> During the Troubles, the queer community was the only place Catholics and Protestants came together as they were not always safe in their communities. But then everyone who lived here was affected significantly, it didn't matter what your sexuality was, you were affected. (Ryan, 35, gay male)

Some people with this perspective, who attended LGB&T events during the Troubles, felt that religious or political identity was rarely ever an issue amongst attendees. This may have been because LGB&T communities and spaces were so few and far between in Northern Ireland in the early years of the conflict that gathering together was inevitable. It may also have been necessary to ensure the continuation of what limited social outlets and support networks existed. However, this was not necessarily a unanimous view.

Others saw the LGB&T community during the Troubles as far from exempt from the wider socio–political issues affecting Northern Ireland at the time, particularly in urban areas. It appeared that the wider ethno–political tensions had more of an impact through subtle means than may have been recognised at the time. These divides were not just limited to religion or nationality as Mary was keen to point out, but also gendered and, to a degree, classed:

> I genuinely feel that the sectarianism in Northern Irish society was reflected in the LGBT community. The few who were visible and out organising on behalf of the community – and it was mostly men – were largely from a Protestant or Unionist background ... Most of the lesbians, on the other hand, were from Catholic or nationalist backgrounds. Lesbians who were organising tended to relate to networks in the South [of Ireland] and the men to British networks. In that sense the LGBT movement was split and tended to reflect the concerns of gay men and be promoted in the context of an acceptance of the Unionist position. There were few, if any, links with the more radical politics emerging in the Republican community. Many also felt that social venues were not safe places for people from Republican communities. (Mary, 58, lesbian)

Contrastingly, outside of Belfast the reverse situation may have been occurring. One interviewee, Mark, grew up Derry/Londonderry in a sectioned off Protestant area known locally as the 'Waterside'. This area was separated from the rest of the city centre by the river Foyle; a physical and mental divide which was very evident to him:

> I grew up in a small place called New Buildings, in a very perceived Protestant area, where UDA would have been written all over the place and 'Catholics out' and things like that ... I never liked that. It was bred into me that [the city side] was IRA territory and it was violent ... that was the Catholic side and that I lived

in the Protestant side and I wasn't to mix. There was this unknown boundary,
even though we lived so close to the border. (Mark, 32, gay male)

During the latter years of the Troubles, an LGB&T 'scene' and several support
groups began to emerge in this city, although these were located within the
'Catholic' area. For Protestant lesbians or gay men, this internalised territoriality
may have made accessing these LGB&T venues more difficult. Therefore,
the developing Derry/Londonderry LGB&T community was seen as being
predominantly Catholic. As few Protestant lesbians or gay men accessed this
space, it may have reinforced this perceived divide within the burgeoning LGB&T
community in the city:

> In Derry, because the gay community tended to be on the city side we always
> had a problem with fewer Protestants coming over [from the Waterside]. We
> constantly noticed that there were more out gay Catholics than there were
> Protestants. I don't know about Belfast but it's been noticeable here. (David,
> 43, gay male)

> I think as a result of everything that's gone on, the LGB&T community is
> predominantly Catholic, or at least is perceived to be Catholic – particularly
> outside of Belfast. If you haven't dealt with religious prejudices then you could
> find this intimidating which beggars the question, 'Where are all these other
> groups of people?' (Philomena, 49, lesbian)

Internalising traditional divisions in terms of space and community may have led
Protestant lesbians and gay men to perceive some LGB&T communities as being
dominated by Catholics. If they were less willing to engage with these communities
(or venues) as a result of this, then the cyclical nature of how this invisibility may
have been reinforced becomes clear.

Paramilitary Accounts of Sexual Struggles

The suppression of homosexual politics in Northern Ireland must also have
affected people embroiled in paramilitary activities who identified as homosexual.
While homosexuality may be seen as suspect within hyper–masculine paramilitary
organisations (McDonald 2008), less is known about this phenomenon, particularly
in Northern Ireland. Therefore, a unique insight is provided via the first–hand
accounts of two men, one Republican and one Loyalist, who have documented
their experiences of being a gay paramilitary member during the Troubles.

Writing about his experiences as a gay Republican prisoner incarcerated in
Long Kesh prison for his role the Troubles, Brendí McClengahan claims that his
position was 'one that is common to many – I hid, lied and pretended. I felt unable

to deal with the consequences of coming out within the Republican struggle' (McClengahan 1994: 124). These negative outcomes, which he describes as homophobia, ostracism from his 'comrades' and depression, materialised once others became aware of his sexuality. The year 1969 was a pivotal moment both in the gay/lesbian and Republican social movements. Recognizing this, McClengahan's desire to 'discover and articulate the relevance of gay/lesbian liberations within the struggle for Irish/national liberation' eventually led to his coming out (McClengahan 1994: 126). McClenaghan's analysis of the failure of political parties such as Sinn Féin to engage with his sexual identity alongside his nationality suggests the cultural importance of strong gender roles reinforced by the Republican image: Catholic, nationalist and an upholder of Christian influenced 'traditional family values' (McClengahan 1994: 124). The family, he notes, was of primary importance in upholding these social constructions. Families, large families in particular, were vital in terms of support, community and numbers. This observation alludes to the claims made by Republican activist and former prisoner Bernadette Devlin McAliskey who also located the importance of the family in what she perceived as the 'numbers game' element of the conflict:

> Unionists must ensure that nationalists don't outnumber them. On the other side what are we confined to do – outbreeding [sic] them? What are our choices? Either we shoot them or we outbreed them. There's no politics here. It's a numbers game. (quoted in Conrad 2004: 70)

McClenaghan notes how Sinn Féin was slow to lend their support to equality discourses for sexual minorities. Conrad (1999) illustrates how the party's reluctance to recognise the important parallels between their struggle and sexual minority efforts for equal treatment may have been fuelled by a larger fear of alienating more conservative constituency members. Over a decade after civil rights events in America, with which Sinn Féin aligned their struggle, they eventually put forth a motion at their annual party conference in Belfast, the Ard Fheis, supporting lesbians and gay men in 1980. Sinn Féin's foundations lay in this recognition of discrimination and the disadvantages faced by minority groups. The Party was also more familiar with equality dialogues than their unionist/Loyalist opponents. Yet they appeared to take a long time to recognise having lesbian and gay members and supporters within their ranks (McClenaghan 1994).

On the other side of the political divide, former Ulster Defence Association (UDA) C Company member, Sam McCrory, became the first Loyalist paramilitary member to come out publicly in a newspaper interview (McDonald 2008). Like McClengahan, he too spoke of having to hide his sexuality from his cohort due to the 'macho, homophobic culture' which led him to sustain a charade of heterosexuality (McDonald 2008). When speaking of his relationship (with a male RUC police officer) amongst colleagues, he described the police officer as female so as not to arouse suspicions. Acknowledging the historical treason and blackmail claims associated with homosexuality, McCrory reiterated in the interview that the relationship was not for, or did not yield, intelligence relating to the conflict. McCrory relocated to Great Britain where he claimed he could be 'himself' in a more accepting environment. His decision to speak out about his sexuality may not have been a surprise to those who knew him. However, he stated that enemies within his former UDA Company group appeared to have known about his sexuality for some time but had not confronted him about it.

Ultimately for McCrory, it was his image and the masculinity of his culture which both silenced his sexuality and protected him from potential reprisal (McDonald 2008). Neither McClenaghan nor McCrory divulged much detail as to why they chose to tell their stories, or why they chose to do so when they did. It appears that to some degree, an extension of the 'family cell' – in their case their individual organisations – regulated them to such an extent that they felt confined by silence when they were an active part of their individual groups. Perhaps, following a certain period of distance from the Troubles, they felt more comfortable in indicating that gay men (and lesbians) were, and are, part of Northern Ireland's varied tapestry.

Plus ça Change… Contemporary Political Responses to Homosexuality

The progress made by lesbians and gay men in Northern Ireland with regards to the recognition of their civil, human and legal rights may be significant, but the battle to be politically accepted wages on. The continued public denigration of homosexuality by prominent Northern Irish politicians, often through recourse to biblical discourses or ideologies, ensures that there is always something for activists to rally against. Problematically, it appears that such public denigration of lesbians and gay men is permitted without fear of disciplinary or criminal repercussions. Following Iris Robinson's comments, not only was she found to have done nothing wrong criminally, but the Ombudsman declared that she had also not breached Assembly protocol. Nevertheless, over 16,000 people signed an online Downing Street petition urging that she be reprimanded for her part in condoning homophobia. This was refuted by Prime Minister Gordon Brown who through a Downing Street statement claimed that MPs were 'accountable to their electorate for their own comments' (*BBC News* 2008). As this section of the exploration will demonstrate, Mrs Robinson's comments did not arise in a vacuum, nor were they the first to court controversy over the apparent ineffectiveness of ministerial accountability when the issue in question is the expression of homophobic ideologies.

The Rev. Ian Paisley's public condemnation of homosexuality may have abated with the 1982 ruling in favour of decriminalisation, but his sentiments live on in his son, DUP Minister Ian Paisley Jr. In 2007, Mr Paisley Jr was interviewed in *Hot Press* magazine (O'Toole 2007) stating:

I am, unsurprisingly, a straight person. I am pretty repulsed by gay and
lesbianism. I think it is wrong. I think that those people harm themselves and –
without caring about it – harm society. That doesn't mean to say that I hate them.
I mean, I hate what they do.

Unsurprisingly, these claims sparked severe criticism, not only for their
inflammatory accusations but because at the time Mr Paisley Jr's department was
responsible for overseeing equality. The ability for the minister to adequately
represent sexual minorities in his role was called into question by the public,
but not the Assembly. Mr Paisley Jr was investigated by the Stormont Assembly
Ombudsman but found not to have violated the ministerial Code of Conduct
with his comments. His aversion to homosexuality was nothing new however;
these comments came just two years after he had been reprimanded for making
homophobic comments about the Canadian marriage of Stephen King, an advisor
to David Trimble at the time, to his male partner (*RTE News* 2005). On this
occasion, his depiction of homosexual relationships as 'immoral, offensive and
obnoxious' led to a formal censorship from the Northern Ireland Policing Board,
of which he was a member.

Other members of the DUP have similarly been quite open about their strong
aversion to homosexuality, with some convinced of the potential devastation
attributable to this deviant sexual orientation. In 2005, DUP councillor Maurice
Mills indicated that Hurricane Katrina, which devastated New Orleans and killed
over 1,300 people, was a message from God against lesbian and gay men, stating:

> The media failed to report that the hurricane occurred just two days prior to
> the annual homosexual event called the Southern Decadence Festival, which
> the previous year had attracted an estimated 125,000 people. Surely, this is
> a warning to nations where such wickedness is increasingly promoted and
> practised. (quoted in Chrisafis *The Guardian* 19 November 2005)

Mr Mills refused to apologise claiming that he had the support of his constituency
regarding such a perspective, although he did not present any statistical data or
research to confirm this. Mr Mills was also cleared after an investigation by the
Assembly Ombudsman. Had action been taken, then these cases could potentially
have delivered a symbolic message that hateful words are as serious and as
damaging as actions. The amendment provided by article 3 of the Criminal Justice
(No 2) (Northern Ireland) Order 2004 to the Public Order (Northern Ireland) Order
1987 may have applied in these cases but they were not followed up, possibly as
proving hatred may have been difficult. Nonetheless, it was clear via newspaper
comments, letters pages and online discussion forums following the above
incidents that the nature of these comments are instigating fears among some
members of the LGB&T community in Northern Ireland.

Condemnatory attitudes toward members of LGB&T communities appear to be
widespread within the DUP's ministerial ranks. During sexual orientation equality

implementation talks, DUP MLA Bert Johnston made his feelings clear in a letter obtained by the Impartial Reporter (2004) to the former Prime Minister Tony Blair regarding the proposals prior to the implementation of sexual orientation and gender recognition laws:

> I don't think God made a mistake when he made us male and female and these people who call themselves gays and the like are essentially perverts. I believe their problems exist only in their minds. ... the people who are most often this way inclined are mostly Godless people with reprobate minds.

Similarly, DUP MLA Edwin Poots publicly spoke out against the use of a public venue in Lisburn for civil partnership ceremonies, denouncing the civil partnership law as 'wrong and immoral and sticks in the throat' (Dudgeon 2005). At the same meeting Councillor Ronnie Crawford of the Ulster Unionist Party (UUP) attacked homosexuality stating that gay marriage was an 'ideology of evil' and that homosexuality was 'intrinsically disordered' (Dudgeon 2005). DUP MLA Jim Wells commented publicly on the funding secured for the LGB&T sector between 2006 and 2009 by former Northern Ireland Secretary of state Peter Hain prior to his departure from office:

> I am appalled that this level of money was committed to homosexual support groups behind our backs before devolution. … I would much prefer that any young person were not encouraged to seek advice from Government funded homosexuality groups. People in their early teens often go through a period of confusion but the vast majority come through these difficult periods, marry and have children. (*News Letter* 30 November 2007)

Mr Wells' use of the term 'our' indicates that he believes others are in agreement with him, regardless of whether they are or not. This type of assumption is not unusual within such anti–homosexual statements.

Those within the DUP whose sexual orientations have been challenged have also experienced difficulties. In 2005, for instance, former DUP MLA Paul Berry was accused by a Sunday tabloid of engaging with a gay male escort in a Belfast hotel, a claim he strongly denied (*BBC News* 2005). The escort at the centre of the row stated that his reasons for speaking out were allegedly to expose the DUP and Free Presbyterian Church's 'hypocrisy' towards gay people. Mr Berry subsequently failed to secure his constituency selection and was ejected from the party.

One of the only DUP councillors to be officially charged for misconduct was Arthur Templeton who was sacked from his position on the Newtownabbey District Policing Partnership after being found guilty of harassing a gay colleague (*BBC News* 2004a). Mr Templeton was fined £250 for harassing John Blair in a manner which he had described as 'intimidating and threatening' during local government electioneering (*BBC News* 2004b). As well as the fine, Mr Templeton was also suspended from the DUP following the incident. What makes this event different from the others is unclear, but the fact that action was taken by the DUP is unlikely to have been symbolic of their failure to tolerate prejudice but rather politically motivated instead.

These attitudes cannot be generalised to all the political parties in the Northern Ireland Assembly. In particular, politicians from a Catholic and/or nationalist background do not typically object to homosexuality with such public ferocity. In many cases, in fact, these parties have slowly come round to actively promoting equality, rights and freedom from discrimination (Conrad 2004, Porter et al. 2006). At the same time, nationalist parties cannot be said to have prioritised or championed LGB&T equality issues to the same extent as other civil rights issues. For many years nationalist parties failed to recognise LGB&T communities within their drive for equality and recognition of social persecution. Many interviewees felt that such Northern Irish political parties could have done more to assist lesbians and gay men during the struggle for decriminalisation. The low status afforded to this cause – an important starting point for achieving equality – meant that grass–roots activism had to become stronger and more coherent within Northern Ireland. As a result, this was seen by some to work in favour of the burgeoning activist LGB&T community:

> I don't believe that many political parties were prepared to take [LGB&T issues] on as part of their agenda. However, the LGBT community itself felt stronger then as they were working for own issues. (Carmel, 43, lesbian)

Nevertheless, many interviewees were incensed at the political rhetoric still being used against them. Furthermore, many were fearful of the harmful ideologies these comments could spawn as a result of going unchallenged by other government ministers. The Assembly's failure to take action against these comments was as damaging as the statements themselves. Inferences could be made that other party or Assembly members believed there was indeed something 'repulsive' or 'nauseating' about homosexuality. One of the interviewees, Connor, took it upon himself to confront Ian Paisley Jr about his notorious comments:

> I asked him if he thought there was any correlation between what he said and people feeling like it's ok to smash my windows and damage my car because one of our most senior politicians says I'm repulsive. (Connor, 46, gay male)

Needless to say, Connor received no reply to his inquiry, but he felt it imperative that if politicians were not to be held accountable for their statements, then they should be at the very least made aware of the wider social problems facing those they so publically denigrated.

Liberal Democrat MP David Heath was one of the few British MPs to question the anomalous situation whereby disparaging political comments continue to go unchallenged by those in power. Referring to the law regarding incitement to homophobic hatred, Mr Heath aligned the comments made by politicians in Northern Ireland to homophobic lyrics in some forms of popular music:

> The slight concern that I have is that the legislation which is already in place in Northern Ireland hasn't yet been used and there is an argument that is repeatedly raised by Stonewall and others about extreme homophobic lyrics. Why has that not been addressed in Northern Ireland? It may be something to do with the particular political situation in Northern Ireland. My worry is once it's on the statute it just stays on the statute book rather than being used in the circumstances where it should properly be used. (Grew 2008)

Mr Heath's allusion to the 'particular political situation in Northern Ireland' somewhat glosses over a deeper problematic issue. The politically sensitive nature of Northern Ireland's history may be the central issue in this failure adequately to address homophobic hostility. A key issue may well be the geographical and social climate in which such discussions are occurring, but whether or not this should be a concessionary issue is open for debate. The intersectionality of religion and politics in Northern Ireland is so entrenched that routinely it dominates legal and political decision making. The fact that various changes made to sexual orientation equality legislation and the enhancing of LGB&T rights purposefully occurred outside of Northern Ireland's political remit illustrates this. So too does the ongoing campaign for a woman's right to choose following the failure to extend the 1967 Abortion Act to Northern Ireland (Fegan and Rebouche 2003).

As well as not engaging with incitement to hatred legislation due to perceived political sensitivity, there is also the issue that so many comments have been made that it could be problematic to start investigating them all. Commenting on this issue during debates on the English and Welsh legislation in 2007, Mr Don Horrocks, head of public affairs at the Evangelical Alliance, illustrated a potential problem of setting a precedent in this area:

> My observation about Northern Ireland, why that has been the case and why the precedents are not necessarily compelling, is that there is a different religious and cultural situation over there. Northern Ireland and the mainland are very different. The police over there are very, very sensitive and concerned about protecting freedom of speech, precisely because of community tensions. The feeling that I get from over there, certainly from what I have been told, is that if any of those laws were used, floodgates could open. There has therefore been a keenness not to use those laws.[4]

---

4   Written evidence to be reported to the House, Criminal Justice and Immigration Bill, Public Bill Committees, 18 October 2007, available at www.parliament.the–stationery–office.com/pa/cm200607/cmpublic/criminal/ 071018/pm/71018s01.htm.

Perhaps this comment goes to the heart of why the implementation of laws protecting and enhancing equality on the basis of sexual orientation in Northern Ireland are viewed by some to be tokenistic. Abatement of tensions is the sole focus in Northern Ireland politics, a place where economic prosperity is dependent upon such 'community tensions' being kept to the peripheries of society. But this is a society with a deeply entrenched history of segregation, difference and a visible, opposed 'other'; a position seemingly now being filled by LGB&T communities, minority ethnic communities and, increasingly, people from the disabled community.

An important distinction setting homophobia apart from other prejudices in Northern Ireland is the response given by politicians to acts of hate crime or prejudicial violence. There is a clear discrepancy between political representatives' willingness to condemn sectarian, religious, racist or other forms of prejudice based violence but not homophobically motivated violence. Indeed, MLAs are almost compelled to denounce sectarian acts of violence in case they are seen to be tacitly complying with the objectives of the aggressors (*BBC News* 2009a). Yet when the targets are lesbians and gay men these same politicians are often adding fuel to the fire. Furthermore, ingrained cultural stereotypes informed by moral conservatism have proved effective enough to be replicated in the European Court judgements which similarly fail to condemn the condemners (McLoughlin 1996). If it remains the case that such political perspectives go unchallenged by those in power, then LGB&T communities and activists have a constant battle on their hands for continued access to rights, freedoms and equality, as John indicated:

> [Ian] Paisley's comment, that was a value judgement and ought to have been properly challenged. If he'd said that [gay people] are sinners, well, that's a religious view but he didn't, he said we're repugnant. And that thing about spreading illness, that's a very dangerous thing to say because that's getting into queer bashing but nothing was done. (John, 60, gay male)

LGB&T activists, therefore, must continue to engage with political representatives if they are to challenge the label of being 'acceptable' targets of hostility, victimisation and violence. Instead, LGB&T communities need to be seen as acceptable organisations in need of funding to address cultural stereotypes and prejudices. However, if this funding is to come from a government who remains opposed to the most fundamental rights being extended to lesbians and gay men, then fresh challenges are bound to arise over time.

Summary

Lesbians and gay men in Northern Ireland have demonstrated that among their communities, the 'traditional' sectarian divides seen to permeate all facets of Northern Irish life could be overcome, set aside or ignored in their pursuit of recognition, equality and freedom from persecution. LGB&T communities indicated the way in which identity politics outside of the 'national question' were trivialised. Yet lesbians and gay men still found space in this political and social ostracism to organise together and use the measures available to them as a result of this politically sensitive time (curfews, direct rule and economic uncertainty) to challenge sexual suppression.

The political hurdles lesbians and gay men have had to negotiate and overcome set Northern Ireland apart from comparable areas of the UK. The continual resort by a politically powerful moral minority strategically functions to keep homosexuality in the public domain but is rarely addressed in terms of representation. Not all politicians agree with the comments of the few, and not all of those opposed speak on behalf of those whom they have been elected to represent. It is perhaps telling that more politicians in Northern Ireland do not speak up for LGB&T communities when they are subjected to degradation and denouncement; similar minority or identity persecution necessarily warrants a swift and public response so that inferences of acceptance are not tacitly assumed.

In the following chapter, the foundations for some of this political prejudice are explored in an analysis of the ways in which morality and religious rhetoric is used to set homosexuality apart as deviant, unnatural and harmful. The obsession with sexual repression demonstrated by a vocal minority of politicians is mirrored by an ongoing moral condemnation which routinely keeps LGB&T issues alive in Northern Irish society. Within this investigation, a clearer divide is drawn between Catholic and Protestant perspectives towards homosexuality which, in part, accounts for the differing approaches taken by unionist and nationalist politicians in this chapter.

Also of note is the development of the gay pride parade in Northern Ireland. This event, which celebrates its 21st anniversary in 2011, has had to contend with sustained moral opposition since its inception. Nevertheless, it continues to grow in popularity each year, indicating the potential discrepancies between political and social attitudes towards homosexuality in contemporary Northern Ireland.

Chapter 4

The Moral Maze: Negotiating Sexual and Spiritual Selves

The aforementioned NILT study and the political composition of the Northern Ireland Assembly are just two of the ways in which religion is shown to be an important and constant factor in Northern Irish people's lives. In the 2001 census, over 85 per cent of respondents in Northern Ireland indicated having a Christian background or belief, a figure which is consistent with the 1991 census results. This proportion is higher than in England and Wales where 71 per cent of census respondents identified as Christian. Thus, Northern Ireland can be seen as an example of a society whereby Christianity underpins the language within which morality (even the morality of non–believers) is commonly articulated, and in some examples, imposed (Weeks 1989). This particularly orthodox religiosity is often entwined with public policy to refute proposed legislative changes relating to matters of sexual morals or rights. Contemporary examples of this include the severe restrictions placed upon women's access to full reproductive rights (Fegan and Rebouche 2003, Rossiter 2009). In addition, for many years divorce was unavailable to couples married for less than two years and the age of consent stood at 17 years of age for heterosexuals and homosexuals until the Sexual Offences (Northern Ireland) Order 2008 lowered this to 16 years of age in parity with Great Britain.

In this chapter, an exploration of the predominance of religious rhetoric denouncing homosexuality as dangerous and corrupting illustrates how these harmful ideologies inform and sustain homophobic prejudices. This analysis is largely facilitated through an exploration of the interviewees' experiences: from enduring powerful sermons denigrating the perceived evils of homosexuality through to confrontations with evangelical Christians opposed to the annual Belfast gay pride parade. Several pressing problems are evident in the chapter, which link under the theme of viewing homosexuality as a 'lifestyle choice'. The evangelical Christian perspective that homosexuality is something from which a person can be 'reorientated' suggests that heterosexuality is the original state and homosexuality is a temporary aberration. It also casts the homosexual as complicit in choosing a sexual identity which they know has been constructed as undesirable and problematic within their society. Similarly, this 'choice' assertion works to cast lesbians and gay men as corruptors of others who may be labelled as having been led astray into a deviant lifestyle.

It is apparent from the interviewees' experiences that those who took on board the idea that they had subconsciously chosen a lifestyle were none the wiser as to how they had done this, subsequently making it difficult to 'undo'. In such cases, the measures taken to manage different aspects of their identities indicate the restrictions with which they had to contend. Examples of decisions made as a result of cultural constraints included choosing whether or not to live with a partner, whether or not to move from the family home or area and whether or not to keep up the pretence of heterosexuality in the workplace. The decisions taken indicate the manner in which the interviewees found, forged and maintained interpersonal relationships with others as a lesbian or gay man in Northern Ireland.

The morally–informed construction of lesbian and gay identities as frivolous and uncommitted and the allusion to 'stranger danger' discourses was seen as feeding directly into perceptions that homosexuals (in particular, men) constituted acceptable targets of victimisation in society. Many of the interviewees cited awareness of the links between negative interpretations of religious doctrine and the impact of these on hostile attitudes towards homosexuality. In some cases, interviewees recalled attempts to engage with local Christian representatives in order to address some of these harmful misconceptions which they saw as impacting on the victimisation they faced. More importantly perhaps, others recognise the value that can come from engaging with doctrinal discourses. This not only benefits society, but LGB&T Christians too. Therefore, the chapter ends with an evaluation of the importance of groups such as Changing Attitude Ireland: an organisation of lay and ordained LGB&T and heterosexual people whose aim is to provide positive sexual and spiritual guidance to LGB&T people and their families.

Christian Teachings on Sexuality

The importance of religion in Northern Ireland spans across society but can be seen clearest within modes of stifling sexuality, from regulating reproductive rights and the age of consent through to censoring sexual education in schools. Rolston et al. (2005) and Mitchell (2006) indicate the silencing power of the churches on issues surrounding sex, morality, conservatism and tradition. The role Christianity plays in the education sector means that these moral ideologies are imparted from a fairly young age. Schools in Northern Ireland are generally controlled by the Catholic Church, although some integrated institutions may be informed by a Protestant ethos. A 1996 survey conducted by the Health Promotion Agency for Northern Ireland found that parents from either denomination were most likely to want the topics of abortion and homosexuality excluded from the curriculum (Rolston et al. 2005). Simpson's (2001, cited in Rolston et al. 2005) research illustrated how in Catholic controlled schools the topic of abortion was strongly informed and underpinned by powerful moral, Christian ideologies which framed this particular act within a discourse and ideology of 'murder'. Discussions regarding homosexuality, however, were avoided where possible. In Protestant controlled schools, issues such as homosexuality and abortion were less emotively engaged with as they were largely ignored (Simpson 2001, cited in Rolston et al. 2005). Only a third of all types of schools in Rolston et al.'s (2005) study appeared to cover the topic of homosexuality at least once as part of sex or relationship education. The researchers also indicate how one young gay male respondent was expelled for three days following his query to his teacher during a sexual education class about how gay people have sex. This draconian response to a legitimate question indicates the level of conservatism surrounding homosexuality (and abortion) and the difficulties young people may have in accessing vital, unbiased and correct information. Nonetheless, compared to the interviewees' experiences of school and sex education (or lack of), contemporary efforts can be seen as progressive, if still lacking.

Homosexuality was not an issue commonly alluded to within the general remit of the interviewees' schooling. This led to cultural barriers whereby the absence of necessary vocabulary was a significant hurdle in understanding their burgeoning feelings. There appeared to be a greater culture of talking about sexuality earlier and more frequently in boys' schools than in the girls', where the emphasis was to abstain from any sexual conduct at all. The focus on 'holy purity' and not 'defiling' yourself were indications that engaging in sexual practices would inevitably lead to a state whereby the young people would find themselves beyond redemption and destined for lives of solitude. For many women, lesbian or otherwise, it was assumed they would just know 'what to do' upon marriage. Until that point, they were, for the most part, only advised to ensure they did not get into any precarious situations with boys. For example, one interviewee, Mags, recalled a nun suggesting to the girls in her Catholic school that if they should ever find themselves sitting on a boy's lap to make sure that there was a piece of paper wedged between them 'just in case'. Whether this comment showed a naïve understanding of conception or was designed to put girls in such a state of fear that they stayed well away from boys is unclear but illuminating nonetheless.

The culture of reluctance to engage with the topic of sexuality meant that, in a manner similar to Rolston et al.'s (2005) findings, genuine queries posed to authority figures were usually met with stock responses which offered little insight:

> We had immense debates around sexuality: what exactly was a sin and what wasn't and so forth. However, when it was something out of the ordinary, so to speak, rather than answering our questions they just retreated to authority: 'because the Bible says so', that sort of a thing so we never really learnt anything useful. For all our constant chatter about it I doubt we learnt anything at all, actually. And that, unfortunately, has bedevilled our education system to the present day. (Pat, 61, gay male)

The dominant religious ethos of the educational system and the staff (often priests or nuns) involved created a knowledge barrier which was particularly acute for several interviewees who were unable to find the language to name their feelings of difference. Language surrounding homosexuality (pejoratively or otherwise) was not part of popular discourse when many of the older interviewees were growing up. For those who had come to recognise what their feelings of difference might mean, often through discussions with other students or the marked aversion of discussion by their teachers, the outcome was fairly similar. This usually involved praying to God or Jesus to rid the person of their sin and to make them 'normal', like everyone else appeared to be.

Resorting to their faith was a common route taken by several of the older male interviewees. Although some sought condolence in prayer, others felt that a more involved approach was needed. Mack, for example, joined the priesthood straight from school in an attempt to avoid dealing with his feelings. However, this was short–lived when his reasons for being there became apparent to those in charge of his vocational training. For many of the interviewees who sought solace in their faith, it did not occur to them that, to some extent, it was the teachings of this faith that might be causing them distress in the first place. Biblical and moral conceptualisations of sex, sexuality and deviance were so interwoven in Northern Irish cultures, that understanding one without the other was practically impossible. As a result, this compounded the culture of silence for many people and led to further social and personal problems. Choosing not to be part of a religious community was not really a viable option for many of the interviewees, thus forcing them into a situation where opposing identity characteristics needed to be managed:

> One of the main problems is people still have this belief that you can't be Christian and be gay or lesbian. So you have to keep saying to people, 'Well actually, you're wrong' .. though I'd say that there'd be very few people who'd be in their churches, sitting there with their Gay Pride t–shirts out! (Philomena, 49, lesbian)

This fundamental premise was an important theme in the interviewees' conceptualisations of how sexuality and spirituality could be reconciled. Whilst attitudes towards homosexuality from Christian groups have been well documented, less is known about lesbians' and gay men's negotiations of these doctrines.

Christian Responses to Homosexuality

The differences between Catholic and Protestant perceptions of, and responses to, homosexuality had a significant bearing on the decisions taken by many lesbians and gay men with regards to the disclosure of their sexuality and forming intimate relationships with others. Catholicism and Protestantism are both doctrinally opposed to homosexuality, but differ somewhat in their practical responses to homosexual identities. Most Catholic teaching understands homosexuality through a natural law perspective and papal direction. Homosexuality is specifically condemned through the perceived 'homogential expression' which it is seen to encompass. In other words, notions of homosexuality focus largely on the same–sex sexual acts perceived to be involved (Nugent and Gramick 1989). Catholicism therefore generally welcomes the person so long as they abstain from engaging in 'homosexual acts'. Some facets of less orthodox Protestant faiths, such as Anglicanism and the Church of Ireland, have demonstrated a more liberal attitude towards homosexuality in recent times. These approaches, however, are less developed in Northern Ireland, where evangelical Protestantism, usually the most vociferously opposed to homosexuality, dominates political denunciations of homosexuality.

Evangelical Protestant perspectives rely more heavily on biblical testimony and classify homosexuality as part of a person's whole being. Here, biological, psychological or social explanations for homosexuality are presumed to exist, so are sought out and addressed as part of the 'recovery' process. This rigid strategy fits within the general ethos of orthodox Protestantism where the Bible is held as the sole source of faith and a vital tool of guidance and information. Homosexuality forms one of the most serious sins which people are born into; repentance is integral and is often visibly (or audibly) reinforced through powerful sermons. For many interviewees with a Protestant upbringing, images conflating the 'sin' and the 'sinner' led to assumptions that a person who was homosexual was by default engaging in sexual activities strongly prohibited by the Bible, even if the person in question was not at that point, or had ever been, sexually active. Kitchin and Lysaght (2004) claimed that this rigidity was a reason why many people in their research perceived Protestantism as being the more difficult faith in which to be homosexual.

This notion was certainly supported by the interviewees, some of whom suggested that the differences which existed between Catholic and Protestant responses to homosexuality were strongly felt by themselves and others they knew:

> There's a huge visibility difference between my gay Catholic friends and my gay Protestant friends and I think it's because in this country politics is wrapped up in religion and it has been for years. (Smythie, 39, lesbian)

> I don't have a lot of Protestant gay friends, for some reason I am surrounded by Catholic gay friends. Protestants seemed very secluded – a lot more so than their Catholic counterparts. (Matthew, 56, gay male)

These differing approaches can be seen as impacting on the choices made by people according to what they viewed their options as being. Subsequently, differences emerged between the interviewees' stories about how they overcame personal sexual and spiritual struggles according to their religious background. For example, many of the lesbian and gay Catholics felt able to reconcile their conflicting sexual and spiritual identities. This is not to detract from difficulties they encountered, but comparing their positions to lesbian and gay Protestants meant that they saw flexibility in their religion where it was lacking elsewhere.

The strong biblical language used to disparage homosexuality was experienced first–hand by several of the interviewees on a regular basis, having a profound impact on many from a relatively young age. As Scott outlines below, the platform from which this negativity was being delivered, in his case during sermons in his Church, held weight. This was due to the religious 'expert' or authority decreeing the information:

> Somehow you learnt that the sin that you are a homosexual was the worst sin in the book. You heard this quite often from the pulpit about the abomination and the evil and all that and you'd know that on some subconscious level people were taking that in and not really thinking about it at the time, but it was powerful stuff you know? It certainly stuck with me, for obvious reasons! (Scott, 49, gay male)

Interestingly, the tacit assumption of homosexuality being a male sexuality or activity imparted similar apprehensions with the female interviewees, albeit towards male homosexuality. Mags's statement below indicates that, in her mind at least, homosexuals were another form of dangerous male:

> Well now, we wouldn't have known too much about them [homosexuals], but what I did know what that they weren't to be trusted – there was something not quite right about them so you were to stay well away. (Mags, 59, lesbian)

Given this implicit, and at times explicit, gendering of homosexuality through political oppression and religious denigration, it is understandable that lesbianism went largely unchallenged (and unnoticed) in Northern Ireland. It appeared that these ideologies were painting a uniform picture of the homosexual: he was male, older, a solitary individual, unfulfilled in life and ultimately dangerous – almost like the archetypal bogeyman. Also of issue for some interviewees was the potential impact of such religious fundamentalism on other people's perceptions of homosexuals. The lack of visibility to refute defamatory allegations meant that it was possible that some people felt very strongly against homosexuality per se, not necessarily individual lesbians or gay men, to a point where they may have been blinded by their faith. The basis for these feelings led some interviewees, such as Pat, to see such indoctrination as informing opinions which could potentially become dangerous acts:

> It worries me how much influence very religious households may have sometimes. I mean, quite a lot of serial killers have shown quite a crazy attitude towards religion as well, for example, Peter Sutcliffe, killing all those prostitutes because they were occasions of sin to him. (Pat, 61, gay male)

Although this may have been an extreme example, the fact that such dangers were being considered indicates the recognition that lesbian and gay men were aware of the potential dangers with which they could be presented. Nonetheless, towards the latter half of the 20th century, representations of gay men began to filter through to Northern Ireland via a selection of popular television shows and within music cultures. The previously promoted 'stranger danger' homosexual persona was soon replaced with the image of the hedonist who engaged in a wanton 'lifestyle'. This lifestyle was understood as being frivolous, promiscuous and uncommitted, ultimately threatening the moral fabric of society through being the antithesis of the heterosexual ideal: family, stability, longevity.

Challenging 'Lifestyle Choices'

Many interviewees had been confronted with ideologies and attitudes which sought to condemn them as wicked, sinful and engaging in a form of behaviour that was unnatural. The 'lifestyle choice' argument is a theme which still predominates in Northern Ireland today. This notion suggests that people have chosen a lifestyle which incurs greater exposure to harm and victimisation and is reminiscent of victim–blaming in its approach. In 2009 *Daily Mail* journalist Jan Moir sparked controversy by appearing to infer that Irish boy band singer Stephen Gately's death was in part caused by his being gay and the presumed lifestyle that she attributed to this orientation (Brook 2009). After an investigation by the Crown Prosecution Service in England, no charges were brought against Moir, but the furore surrounding her willingness to cite a 'gay lifestyle' as existing and as contributing to the death of a young gay man indicates the continued dominance of this 'lifestyle choice' argument. For some of the interviewees who were used to dealing with this 'choice' discourse, several found it hard to contain their frustration towards those who failed to see it as a valid aspect of their identities:

> Anybody who has the audacity to say that you choose to be gay, please let my hands go round their neck! (Philomena, 49, lesbian)

> The Presbyterians, some of them, are still insisting that being gay is a choice. Are you honestly, seriously thinking that some child who is getting kicked around at school, as if that's not bad enough, thinks, 'I know what I'll do, I'll become a queer and really get kicked around for the rest of my life'. Are you saying that somebody really, honestly chooses that? (Pat, 61, gay male)

Hearing religious rhetoric insisting that homosexuality was a rationally decided 'choice' impacted heavily on many lesbians and gay men, as well as those around them. The benchmarking of heterosexuality as the desired norm led to a culture of blame shifting towards those deemed outside of this framework. Long before it was recognised that heterosexist societies were negatively impacting on the social, mental and emotional health of lesbians and gay men growing up in them, any problems incurred were attributed to the sexual orientation 'chosen' by that person.

By the time some of the male interviewees (and others they knew of) felt comfortable accessing sexual partners or relationships without fear of reprisal, they were usually already adults. Therefore, many felt that they had a significant proportion of 'catching up' to do in comparison to their heterosexual counterparts as a result of not undergoing similar sexual experiences in their teenage years. Most recognised this period of delayed sexual adolescence as being a result of moral messages they had absorbed, as well as not knowing other lesbians or gay men, or fearing violent reprisals if they showed an interest in the wrong person. The depth to which some had internalised this regulation was recognised only when they had freed themselves from it. Mack's discussion of how hiding his sexuality caused him severe stress, although leaving Northern Ireland to escape this proved advantageous as it brought him into contact with other gay men. His initial response, however, was illustrative of the attitudes with which he had previously been surrounded:

> I got to a point where it was making me mentally ill. I couldn't stay [in Northern Ireland] so I left, I went to England and that's when I started going out with other boys. … I remember the first time it stunningly hit me .. I was walking up the stairs [of a gay bar] and I remember seeing two guys about my own age kissing each other … I was quite taken aback – for the first second or two it was like, 'That's really vile, really disgusting – they shouldn't be doing that' because that's what I had been taught to think and then it was afterwards my own side clicked in saying, 'No, this is great, this is how it should be'. (Mack, 55, gay male)

Mack had failed to realise the depths to which he had absorbed such negativity about homosexuality until presented with visual representations of the very thing he had been taught to despise. Luckily for him he was able to successfully integrate with other gay men; for others this process may have taken far longer, or not have been an option at all.

The 'lifestyle' argument is an interesting one to levy at homosexuality from a religious perspective given that religion itself provides a better example of a 'lifestyle'. Organised religions rely heavily upon children either being born into a specific faith or converting later into adulthood. Children are not born with a particular religious identity (it is inferred as a result of their family's beliefs or actions) in the same way that many lesbians and gay men indicate that they were born with their sexual orientation. One interviewee, David, took this issue up with several representatives from his local churches in order to show them the discrepancy in their arguments. His attempts to educate them about lesbians and gay men proved futile, leaving him more frustrated at their failure to recognise this basic contradiction:

> They started talking about gay lifestyles and I said, 'Now, which gay lifestyle exactly are you talking about? I've a friend who's a bin man, very hard working

man, doesn't socialise a wild lot, he works and he has a partner and that's it. Is that the lifestyle you're talking about or is it the 16 year old student who is delaying a social life and a sex life? As far as I'm concerned, you're the people with the actual lifestyle that can change." … So what they are talking about when they are talking about 'our lifestyle' is they are talking about people [personality]; they're the ones with the 'lifestyle'. (David, 43, gay male)

David's argument that there is a specific order to a religious lifestyle, comprising of routines, practices, interactions, language and ongoing stages of affirmation is a valid one. For many religions, sustenance is also guaranteed though rules and regulations, for example restricting marriage to partners from the same belief or denomination. For decades in the Republic of Ireland, the Catholic Church permitted a mixed Catholic/Protestant marriage only on the understanding that any resulting children were baptised as Catholic. This religious lifestyle requires structure, the engagement in rituals and the adherence to a template of living. In a sense, as David argues, religious lifestyles are more homogenous, recognisable and enforceable than the so called 'homosexual lifestyle'.

Many lesbians and gay men are aware that their potential exposure to victimisation is enhanced by the 'lifestyle choices' they are seen to have made. Another interviewee, Matthew, felt strongly enough to challenge this mentality by taking an active stance in his local community, coming out as a gay teacher in the process. His interaction with lesbians and gay men in his area led him to draw direct correlations between religious fundamentalist discourse and people's problems with low self–esteem. As a result, he frequently spoke out about and challenged these discourses in his capacity as someone well known in his area. The repercussions of this fazed him less and less over the years as he gradually withdrew from his own religious background:

Religious fundamentalists are not really very nice people. They have targeted me, but I sort of set myself up for it as I am very public. Within our local Free Presbyterian Church apparently it was quite common for them to discuss me and [insult] me in their little circle. I know that some of the Free Presbyterians, Church of Ireland and the Catholics have all had either covert or more obvious references to my corrupting influences in sermons, so I'm not very friendly with Christians for that reason. (Matthew, 56, gay male)

His experience of being a direct target for abuse from Christian fundamentalists was an unusual one amongst the interviewees as he was located in a rural area and, as he mentions, quite open about his sexuality. For others, like Pat, this problem was not limited to rural parishes, but could be seen as affecting lesbians and gay men from a more powerful, bureaucratic position:

We are one of the very few minorities which has an equal opposite minority sitting there, watching our every move like a hawk, and are determined to thwart us at every opportunity. The Christian Institute are determined to destroy us, and they'll do that by lies, they'll say everything they can think of. (Pat, 61, gay male)

Of particular note to Pat and several of the interviewees was the morally–informed 'reorientation' response to homosexuality and the impact this could have on people, LGB&T or heterosexual.

Reorientation Responses to Homosexuality

For some, the moral denigration of homosexuality as involving choice brought with it ideologies of 'contagion'. That is, if someone could be seen to choose to be homosexual, then they may seek to influence or convert others. The inaccurate and potentially harmful notion that homosexuals can 'make people gay' was a powerful theme which imparted on some of the interviewees' lives in significant ways, particularly in relation to disclosure of sexual identities. Furthermore, given the virtual absence of openly lesbian and gay people in Northern Irish society, often there was usually no indication of exactly *who* had prompted this 'conversion'. This was an issue that resonated with Mary, who recalled being seen as having 'turned' lesbian as a result of being in a heterosexual marriage for a lengthy period of time:

> That's how they would have referred to me, as one who *turned* lesbian. I'm always going to be 'that one who *turned* lesbian', never the one who is, or was a lesbian. They refuse to accept that I might have been gay all along. (Mary, 58, lesbian, her emphasis)

Until Mary came out, she was unfamiliar with other lesbians. In other words, there was no discernable person who 'converted' her. However, to those around Mary, her apparent switching from a heterosexual marriage with children to a same–sex partner potentially reinforced the notion that sexuality was a choice. It was not considered that prior to coming out, Mary had felt too stifled to express her true feelings, or had not been given the opportunity to do so. This was evident in several of the women's stories when, in a similar situation to Mary, the initial hostility they encountered from family members was centred on the apparent delay in converting to, or 'choosing', lesbianism. There was a need to attribute blame if a person's sexuality could not be effectively ignored. If there was a partner visible and available to hold responsible, then this was often employed as a tactic by disapproving family members, thereby imparting the conversion ideology once more:

> I had constant abuse from my partner's father, just about every day. He didn't accept us and claimed that I'm to blame for it all and that I turned her into a lesbian. He made my life hell for years. (Alice, 44, lesbian)

If a person is seen as being able to convert, or be converted, then it follows that this conversion can be reversed. Indeed, Christian adoption agencies in the UK generally have used this argument to deny offering their services to lesbians and gay men who wish to adopt, stating that children will 'become' lesbian or gay as a result of having lesbian or gay parents. Using faith based arguments to avoid wholly complying with laws designed to protect sexual minorities from discrimination means that religious perspectives cannot be as effectively challenged as other forms of prejudice (Mitchell and Tilley 2004). Christian adoption organisations in Northern Ireland have stated their supposed inability to comply with the Equality Act (Sexual Orientation) Regulations (Northern Ireland) 2006 whereby they would be required to accept lesbians and gay men as potential adopters. Though such conversion claims are unfounded (and misguided as lesbian and gay children can clearly come from heterosexual parents) these claims also allude to the 'lifestyle choice' perspective postulated by moral opponents to homosexuality:

> That's the fear that the religious right is still praying on, that we can make you gay somehow. Conversion is their business; if it wasn't possible to convert people between religions then their business is done. I've never heard of anybody convert from gay to straight, even after major things like aversion therapy, electric shocks, or years of therapy with warped psychiatrists, I've never heard of a successful conversion. (David, 43, gay male)

A 'successful conversion' in this instance may mean different things to different people. David was aware of several male friends who underwent such treatment and later married women, yet he maintained that these men could not be described as heterosexual. On the other hand, for the psychiatrists and others in the community, this adoption of a heterosexual persona would indeed be considered a success. Similarly, Pat recalled interactions with representatives of organisations promoting 'ex–gay' therapies which were operating in Belfast. In some sessions clergy acted as counsellors, focusing on biblical teaching and heterosexual ideals to 'reorientate' the person's desires towards heterosexuality. Pat regarded these efforts to be largely amateurish in relation to larger scale psychiatric programmes promoting such practices. In most cases, these ideologies and treatments were promoted amongst men as opposed to women:

> They've been saying it for years over here – this tiny minority within the psychiatric profession who insist that you can cure gayness. This has been jumped on by the Religious Right who've made a huge amount of publicity about it, parading the smiling person with his wife and family. (Pat, 61, gay male)

In 2010, a conference held in Belfast by Christian group Core Issues, whose leader Reverend Mario Bergner routinely states that he can convert homosexuals back to heterosexuality, attracted criticism for upholding misguided notions that homosexuality is a condition which can be reversed or changed. In a move which marked a turn of events, members of the Stop Conversion Therapy Taskforce (SCOTT) picketed the church where the conference was being held. However, their targets were not the therapists inside, but the lesbians and gay men in attendance who felt that their sexuality, and not the wider homophobic society, was the problem (Green 2010). SCOTT aimed to interact with these people in order to illustrate that it was their wider environment, not their inherent sexuality, which had the problem.

Not all conversion ideologies were rooted in psychological practice. Another interviewee, Mark, was a qualified counsellor whose interaction with one such man was a result of his largely unsuccessful attempts to 'reorientate' his sexuality. He had come to Mark following a disastrous conversation with his Protestant faith leader which had left this young man feeling more isolated and fearful that his disclosure would become known in his community. As Mark recalls:

> His religious leader said, 'You must stop this sin at once – go home and read your bible and get out there and find a good Christian woman.' He got married and unfortunately he's got this huge burden of guilt to bear. It's a lie; he's as gay as I am, but he forced heterosexuality on himself because that's what his faith told him he should do. (Mark, 32, gay male)

Of course, this is a smokescreen of heterosexuality. People still have sexual desires. How they chose to act upon them given the constraints of their religious and social community was illustrative of the covertness forced upon them by these constraints. Seeking guidance from faith leaders may have been a way of unburdening some of the guilt harboured by those uncomfortable with what their sexuality had come to mean through doctrinal denigration. Other reasons may have included people believing that homosexual feelings deserved additional punishment, feeling that they would be humiliated out of such behaviour; wanting to save their family's reputation in the community before others found out about them; or trying to block out any sexual feelings being experienced. The more popular response was to effectively bury such desires, rather than confront them, and to engage in a heterosexual relationship. This led to two common outcomes amongst the participants. Either the relationship broke down, freeing up the person to 'come out' and face up to these issues from a stronger emotional position, or they continued to live a form of 'double life'.

'Lavender Liaisons'

This focus on the sexual aspect had an interesting impact on some Protestant gay male social interactions. As well as keeping their behaviours hidden, some took great measures not to be discovered during periods of intimacy with other men, or went where they thought they would be more accepted by those around them.

Several interviewees suspected that Protestants were less willing to reveal their sexual identities or orientations. This seemed reinforced by claims made during conversations with Protestants who indicated that if they were gay, they would lie about their sexuality or else try to hide it. Reasons for this centred on the widely perceived unwillingness of Protestant family or community members to accept homosexuality, as well as the desire to live a 'quiet life' – avoiding any unnecessary aggravation within their families or communities.

The term 'men who have sex with men' (MSM) is generally used to describe men who engage in sexual activity with other men, but do not ascribe to a 'gay' or 'homosexual' social identity. In some ways this 'MSM' description is a misnomer as the activity can be on a continuum from masturbating in front of one another to full penetrative sex. In a form of self–fulfilling prophecy, the presumed sexual liaisons used to denounce homosexuality proved an outlet for some men. Some of the male interviewees were aware of, or had interactions with, married men who engaged in clandestine sexual behaviours in secluded public spaces. Amongst the interviewees who discussed their experiences of this issue and the cultural reasons for its existence – particularly in rural areas of Northern Ireland – the term 'lavender' was used, not MSM. When questioned about this, it emerged that the term was preferred to MSM because lavender seekers encompassed a wider, non–definitive, spectrum of sexual activity which may not include penetration:

> The expression MSM is rejected by a lot of men I know who observe that practice, they prefer to call it 'lavender'. It's something I hear quite a lot and is something that is widespread among Northern Ireland and, from talking to [a friend of his], among that group of men. And it covers a wide range of behaviours, not just sex. (Mark, 32, gay male)

A strong theme of guilt was attributed to men engaging in these 'lavender liaisons' by the interviewees; a guilt that was often directly attributed to a strict Protestant upbringing. Management of this guilt required a separation of the sexual from the emotional; occasional indulgence in homosexual acts was offset with a largely heterosexual public lifestyle. This may have been an acceptable middle ground for some and kept them feeling in some control of the situation.

While there may be a degree of control over their physical engagement in sexual acts, for some men the psychological battles they underwent were more difficult to reconcile. Their long–held associations of homosexuality with 'dirtiness' and 'uncleanliness' had significantly adverse mental and physical effects on some men, particularly during interpersonal sexual encounters with other men. Sometimes, this impacted on their ability to sexually perform with a male partner as they were engaging in the acts they had been brought up to despise as 'abominable'. Others felt, or encountered, hostile responses to the situation they felt they had 'succumbed' to against all their teachings. James' experience demonstrated this. Growing up exposed to this type of ideology led to an indoctrination that was so deeply ingrained in his psyche that he (and, he noted, several of his partners) were

physically unable to engage in sexual activity until they had shed themselves of
the guilt and self–loathing:

> It took me a long time to come to terms with certain aspects of my own sexuality
> but that wasn't to do with the gay bit, it was more to do with the physical side
> of sex. I had trouble with it because I'd subdued it for so long. (James, 60, gay
> male)

James indicated the depth to which he absorbed the 'sin/sinner' ideology and the
resultant physiological impact it had on him. This was also the case for several of
the other male interviewees who reported feeling nauseous or being physically
sick after their first sexual encounters because of the revulsion they had come to
associate with male same–sex sexual activities.

This 'lavender' situation may, in part, have been facilitated by vociferous
moral condemnation. The notion of homosexuality as constituting a 'lifestyle'
possibly allowed some men to act on their same–sex desires without ascribing to
the homosexual label. Therefore, it could be that judgmental religious ideologies
provided a form of 'loophole' for some men who were able to tolerate their actions
so long as they could emotionally disassociate themselves from what it was they
were taught was bad and wrong. In other words, they could privately atone for the
acts (as Protestants do not confess via a priest in the way that Catholics do) so long
as they did not see themselves as labelled by these same acts.

As well as guilt, there are further reaching implications for people involved
these sorts of clandestine scenarios. In some cases, these men are not only living
'heterosexual' lives, but also have partners and children at home who are unaware
of these indiscretions. However, herein lies a further problem in that all parties
may be at risk of contracting and passing on sexually transmitted diseases, but
information and support around testing for these is generally limited to identifiable
'gay' communities and spaces. Therefore, these 'lavender' men comprise a grey
area within public health as they are unlikely to disclose their actions and, if seen
to be in a heterosexual marriage, may be fearful of raising suspicion should they
access sexual health screening. The health risks they pose to the gay and bisexual
men they interact with is also an important reason to find ways of making sure
safer sex information reaches this hidden population.

A degree of sympathy was felt for these men among several of the interviewees
who recognised their plight as being testament to the fact that being gay was
indeed not a choice and not always something that could be switched off. John in
particular indicated towards the constraints of social stigmas around homosexuality
in Northern Ireland:

> Guys would go into the toilets or woods because they'd know that the gay men
> went into them for sex. It's seedy but it wasn't really the men's faults. They'd go
> there because they couldn't get it anywhere else, at gay bars and the like. They'd

often be businessmen with a wife and family at home or whatever. I think a lot of
them were left alone [by the police] because of that. (John, 49, gay male)

This final point is an interesting one. Although the issue of class and status did
not arise in the interviewees' narrative to the scale that national, religious and
gender identity did, John's statement indicates that there may have been a degree
of diplomacy regarding some men's ability to remain 'closeted' at the expense of
others. This position was corroborated by Connor who, in his role as a patrolling
police officer earlier in his career, sometimes came across situations similar to
those described by John:

> In the past, when a number of the old–style policing operations were conducted
> in cruising areas, you were finding police, solicitors, doctors, professionals who
> were professionally at risk if their sexual orientation had become known so
> you'd have to tread carefully sometimes. (Connor, 46, gay male)

It would appear that in these cases, the better known (and respected) a man was
in his local community, the more likely he was to escape any form of police
intervention, investigation or charge. This was not the case for men whose
interactions with criminal justice representatives resulted in less favourable
outcomes. The unfortunate ones, perhaps those holding a less prestigious status
role in society, seemed to suffer greater consequences, especially when compared
to heterosexual couples engaging in similar public sex acts:

> There's a difference when it's gay men [who are] caught out. You've seen how
> their names, photos, all their details are splashed across the paper and you're
> targeted by the small–minded members of your community. Horrendous stuff
> happens to them and it's just not fair. (Scott, 49, gay male)

A number of news reports of men being fined for engaging in sexual activity in
public toilets in and around the north–east coastal area of Northern Ireland indicated
that this is an ongoing issue with cause for concern on both sides (Smyth 2007).
On the one hand, members of the public most likely do not want to be suddenly
confronted with people engaged in acts of intimacy. On the other, publishing these
men's names in national newspapers serves to stigmatise them further and, it could
be argued, make an example of the wider LGB&T community. Either way, the
rationales as to why some men may feel compelled to meet others in such a covert
and, to a degree dangerous (as they could become victims of crime) manner may be
indicative of how some men manage their desires in sexually oppressive cultures.

Recognizing Relationships

Focusing on sexual activity as opposed to companionship, love or spiritual intimacy with another person of the same sex fits into the general Christian obsession with sex and suppressing sexuality. As Foucault (1976) notes, the more often that sexuality is repressed by moral discourses, the more it is thrust into the social imagination: it is literally brought into being. The DUP's 'Sodomy' campaign illustrated this in practice, highlighting issues relating to homosexuality to those who otherwise would have been none the wiser. The power of doctrinal denigration may bring many lesbians and gay men to a point whereby they must decide how their sexual and spiritual lives can be reconciled. Men may be more visibly affected by this due to the focus on male homosexuality, whereas female same–sex desire was generally absent from discourse or ideology (as a result of not being explicitly outlawed). As a result, many interviewees found their choices limited to silence, migration or facing confrontation.

Recognising the impact religious doctrine had on their lives and the lives of others led some to question the humanity of a faith which denigrated them for loving their partner, refused to accept the relationship as valid, or saw them as culpable when victimised through homophobia. Although those who challenged their religious representatives may have intended to engage in dialogue, what often followed were feelings of increased anger, betrayal and a desire to cut oneself off completely from the church. One interviewee, Jennifer, spoke to her minister about her partner. Upon doing so, Jennifer realised that despite knowing her minister for years, the aversion towards her sexual identity had been prioritised. Similarly, she felt her position as a member of her church and the wider community had also changed. In describing the situation, she explained how the response from her minister made her realise that she was in effect being made to choose between her partner and her faith. As their commitment to one another would not be declared valid, issues which were brought to the fore for her included the protocols which come with being religious and in a relationship, such as the recognition of a partner during times of ill–health, or upon bereavement.

This clearly indicated the ongoing battle some lesbians and gay men have, not only recognizing their relationship on a daily basis, but at important events such as how much support they can expect, or input they will have, when a partner becomes ill or dies. There are very significant rituals that many, regardless of their distance from their church as an institution, may feel necessary to undergo as a result of lifelong indoctrination regarding rites of passage. The trauma which could ensue from not being able to give a proper burial to a partner, or not having their grief validated is a pressing issue given the increasing ageing population of lesbians and gay men in Northern Ireland. Although the recent legal developments, particularly the enactment of civil partnership legislation, had relaxed some interviewees' fears, the potential refusal of a person's local church to recognise their partner was still a concern for some. In such cases, it appeared that the choice was one made for the individual by those focused on the 'sin' rather than the person.

Using Relationships as a Platform for Discussion

For those who openly engaged in lesbian or gay partnerships, the impact of exposure to religious doctrine was experienced in a number of other ways. Several interviewees were involved in long–term relationships and some had subsequently entered into civil partnerships when the legislation was passed in Northern Ireland allowing them to do so. Some expressed regret that civil partnerships remained secular and could not be held in churches, regardless of how spiritual or devoted the person or people involved were. Changes announced by the Coalition government to look into remedying this in England and Wales as part of the recommendations in the Equality Act 2010 are not currently intended to be extended to Northern Ireland, but could signal an important message about recognizing sexual and spiritual identities. Lesbian and gay couples can, and do, receive blessings from some more liberal minded members of the clergy but many have stated that they wish to have their relationship recognised not only by the state, but in the eyes of God too through a religious ceremony. This is significant in Northern Ireland as there is likely to be a considerable proportion of lesbians and gay men who practise their faith regardless of what religious leaders might say of their sexuality. Additionally, for those who do not, it may make family, friends and colleagues more aware of the commitment they have made to a partner if they are able to demonstrate this within such a 'Christian currency'.

Many interviewees recognised the symbolic potential of demonstrating commitment in a society where the 'family' is of great significance. As a result, some saw their civil partnerships as working tactically to denounce philosophies which perceived homosexuality as frivolous, promiscuous and uncommitted. Colette commented on the importance of recognizing this:

> I was ambivalent about [civil partnerships] at first but I can see their value in changing our society for the better. Family is very important here, and although that's a source of conservatism, it's also about the links that brings. Whole groups of heterosexual people have been exposed to lesbian and gay couples where they wouldn't have been before, and that to me is where true change needs to begin. (Colette, 48, lesbian)

Civil partnership statistics also offer a possible indication of how the sanctity of marriage ideology has filtered through to lesbians and gay men in Northern Ireland. As of 2009, 40,237 civil partnerships were registered in the UK, with 421 taking place in Northern Ireland. Between 2007 and 2009, 572 dissolutions (similar to a divorce) took place between people to end their civil partnership, although none of these were in Northern Ireland (Office for National Statistics 2009).

This is not to say that applications for dissolutions will not happen, but rather that the wider culture of lifetime partnerships appears particularly important to lesbians and gay men in Northern Ireland. This is perhaps a factor less recognised and potentially important in challenging negative ideologies regarding homosexuality.

Being open about lesbian and gay relationships may also have proved beneficial for several other reasons, such as exposing gay relationships to heterosexual family members less used to interacting with lesbians and gay men on a regular basis. Civil partnerships have also facilitated greater visibility into all facets of lesbian and gay life, indicating how similar they can be to heterosexual relationships (such as parenting). This was not the case for everyone, however. Following his civil partnership, Mack's colleagues signed a card for him and his new partner. However, one person in particular had difficulty expressing his good wishes due to his religious views. Mack spoke to him about it and realised the implications for those trying to do what is right by all people concerned:

> He was in such a state, he said, 'I like you, and I want the best for you, but I can't – my religion won't let me approve of what you are doing. This idea that two men are going to be married, be having sex together, it's not right." He was in this quandary of, 'Do I support my colleague, a person who I like, or do I take the other route of the church? My soul or my friendship?' (Mack, 55, gay male)

This colleague's dilemma reinforces the previous point that Christian teachings around homosexuality have led people to focus on the primacy of sexual activity whilst overshadowing all other aspects of the committed relationship. Religious depictions of male homosexuality concentrate predominantly on the act of sodomy and how this is apparently outlawed in some interpretations of biblical passages. It is this issue which the colleague appeared to pick up on and which caused him most angst in being asked to celebrate the partnership. This scenario illustrates the problems which can arise for those who cannot condone a homosexual relationship because of their faith, but simultaneously do not know how to respond when placed in such a situation. Similarly, it presents problems for people who cannot deal with this situation when it involves their own children, leading in some cases to a greater feeling of betrayal and a need for ostracism from the family in lieu of any other available response.

Paradoxically for some lesbians and gay men living in Northern Ireland, the doctrine of marriage worked in their favour. Catholic policy dictates that homosexuality, fornication and adultery are all equally sinful, but the emphasis placed on marriage and the failure of the Church to allow persons of the same sex to marry resulted in a form of 'loophole'. In cases where heterosexual siblings were forbidden to allow their partners to spend the night at the family home, lesbians' and gay men's partners were shown more leniency. Initially, this appeared to be due to a denial that anything sexual could or would happen due to the context of oppression surrounding homosexuality. However, in some of the interviewees' cases, the justification for having their partners stay was based upon the fact that although the heterosexual siblings could marry their partners, the homosexual family members could not. Therefore, they were seen as being 'as good as married' if that was as close they and their partners could get under the church's guidelines.

Variations of this theme were corroborated in a number of the stories, whereby the 'life–long partner' belief was transferred onto their relationships and eventually facilitated acceptance. This perspective of working within the limitations of Christian regulations indicated the ways in which some Catholic families sought to accommodate their families within the boundaries of their faith. Importantly too, this indicated a vital chink in doctrinal condemnations of homosexuality as frivolous and uncommitted. Several of the lesbians' and gay men's families were prepared to treat their homosexual family member in the same way as the heterosexual siblings or relatives. In several of the lesbian and gay Catholics' families where there had been a marital breakdown or a divorce, more tolerance was shown to same–sex partners where there seemed to be a genuine relationship bond and prospective longevity. It was here that the person really was being separated from the condemned act, on the basis of being judged for their commitment to another, regardless of that other person's gender.

Parading Perversion: The Pride Debate

One of the most important developments for lesbians and gay men in Northern Ireland was decriminalisation. So too was the decision to hold the first gay pride parade in 1990. This now annual event celebrates its 21st anniversary in 2011 and is a symbol of LGB&T progress and inclusion. It is this event, also, where evangelical Christian condemnation of homosexuality is at its most visible, vocal and vociferous.

Parades in Northern Ireland have a specific and contentious history. Although they date back to the 18th century, modern day parades in Northern Ireland tend to be symbols of remembrance of key historical events. The parade season runs from April to September with almost 4000 events held annually (Jarman and Bryan 1996). The vast majority of these are hosted by the Protestant/unionist community and are most contentious when they involve routes through primarily Catholic/nationalist areas. The violent clashes and subsequent restructuring of parade routes have contributed to the association of fear, violence and hostility with some of the more notorious parades in Northern Ireland (Jarman and Bryan 1996). Due to such disturbances, and the heated disputes over chosen routes, the Parades Commission was established in 1997 and its powers and duties codified in the Public Processions (Northern Ireland) Act 1998. This independent, quasi–judicial body ensures the adherence to the rules and regulations governing the approval and undertaking of parades.

The gay pride parade was developed to recognize the historical legal and social persecution of lesbians and gay men and celebrates progress and positive change (Johnston 2004). Gay pride is a community celebration open to people of all sexual orientations. As well as the parade itself, a number of social, political

and informative events are held in the week leading up to this in which key
stakeholders are given the discursive space to air their issues, highlight problems
or advertise new initiatives. The parade itself proceeds through the main city
centre, around the City Hall and back up to the Cathedral Quarter; and area which
constitutes Belfast's unofficial 'gay space' by virtue of its gay–friendly clubs,
bars and saunas, all within close proximity of one another. Once it leaves the
Cathedral Quarter, the gay pride parade leaves the safety of this 'gay space' and
seeks to bring a message to wider public space (Moran et al. 2001). So–called
'heterosexual space', which may previously have been only tentatively negotiated
by LGB&T groups, is engaged with in a more public manner by the display of
sexual identities ordinarily regulated through imposed invisibility (Carbado 2000,
Corteen 2002). Because the gay pride parade utilizes and subverts space in this
way, those involved in the parade can be deemed to be 'flaunting' their sexuality
(Valentine 1996). Unlike everyday heterosexual displays of sexuality, affection
or relationships – which occur with such frequency and regularity that they are
rendered for the most part invisible – this mass display of sexual difference, so
visibly subverting the 'normal', is seen to epitomise and typify sexual 'deviance'.
As Mason (2001: 24) outlines, this transgression is not mirrored by heterosexual
displays:

> We need look no further than the popular and longstanding refrain against
> those who 'flaunt' their homosexuality to realise that the very suggestion that
> homosexuality *can* be flaunted is itself the product of the social and the political
> hush that has historically enveloped the subject of same sex sexuality.

'Negotiating space' in this way is rendered important by the fact that it is 'constantly
produced and remade within complex relations of culture, power and difference'
(Hubbard 2001: 51). Lesbians and gay men are likely to form the minority in
public space as it is 'commonly assumed to be 'naturally' or 'authentically'
heterosexual' (Valentine 1996: 146). This hetero–authenticity is indicated through
'heterosexual couples kissing and holding hands as they make their way down the
street, to advertisements and window displays which present images of contented
'nuclear' families' (Valentine 1996: 146). Therefore, challenges to the subversion
of this space are almost to be expected in Northern Ireland.

Moral Opposition to the Parade

A now–defunct website managed by a group called 'Stop the Parade' (STP) was
created in 2006 with the aim of 'reaching out to sodomites taking part in the
parade to show them that there is an alternative and that they can be delivered from

the bondage of sodomy by repentance from sin and faith in Jesus Christ alone'.[1] This assimilation of a homosexual identity with engagement in 'deviant' sexual activities goes towards the legitimate construction of such identities as not natural or desirable. Additionally, the interchangeability of 'homosexual" with 'sodomite' omitted the recognition of women as anything other than heterosexual. The decision taken by STP to single out gay pride over the 4000 other, less peaceful, less inclusive and less cross–community parades was defended on the basis that more people living in Northern Ireland were offended by the gay pride parade than any other march, although no evidence was provided to support this claim. In describing the gay pride parade as 'contentious', the Parades Commission were compelled to investigate as it was within its role to examine and potentially ban 'contentious' parades in Northern Ireland. In a 2005 meeting between representatives of STP, gay pride parade organisers and the Parades Commission, several guidelines were set ensuring that verbal abuse and harassment would be avoided by both parties towards the other. While verbal abuse was ruled out, other forms of getting the moral message across were not.

STP organizers hired an advertising lorry emblazoned with pictures of same–sex couples accompanied with moral messages against homosexuality. They displayed the vehicle outside several popular gay venues in Belfast to 'assist in conveying God's message of repentance to Belfast's sodomite community' (*Gay Belfast* 7 August 2005). When challenged about their need to remonstrate against the pride parade, Jonathan Larner from STP claimed that the group was being 'pigeon–holed as hateful and homophobic' but chose to make its presence known as 'the far greater hate would be shown by staying at home and doing nothing' (Jackson 2005). This message seems to have reached others with similarly opposing views as the numbers of people protesting against the parade appear to have increased in recent years. There are now two identifiable sites of protest along the parade route: the traditional spot outside the City Hall and more recently outside St Anne's Cathedral, both in Belfast city centre. The protestors are largely silent and in most cases turn their backs on the gay pride marchers as they pass by. Many hold large placards emblazoned with biblical passages alluding to the sinfulness of homosexuality and, in some cases, other perceived sins such as adultery (although in light of Iris Robinson's extra–marital indiscretions it will be interesting to see if these are revised). In most cases, 'sodomites' are told in no uncertain terms that they are destined to 'Hell' if they choose not to repent.

Many of the banners and placards can be perceived as offensive in nature and likely to instill fear of hostility, yet are not dealt with in such a way. Some proclaim that 'Homosexuality is Sin' and 'The wages of Sin is [sic] Death', so are quite directive in their condemnation. LGB&T people in attendance may fear that such condemnation can resonate with homophobic people who may feel justified acting on their prejudices. Given the media attention garnered at the annual parade, the

---

1   This site was available at http://www.stoptheparade.com/ (accessed 8th May 2008) but no longer exists.

protestors' decision to display their sentiments in written as opposed to oral format may also be tactical. Again, these passages relate mainly to male homosexuality as a result of less being written about female homosexuality in biblical passages.

However, it was the suggestion by one pride marcher in the 2007 parade that Jesus may have been homosexual that demonstrated the double standards held about claims which could or could not be made. The matter which ended up being debated in the House of Commons centred around a placard reading 'Jesus is a fag'. This particular placard incurred heavy criticism from many Northern Irish politicians and clergy. North Belfast DUP MLA Nigel Dodds lambasted the claim as 'offensive and blasphemous (*News Letter* 2007a). East Belfast council member May Campbell also seized this opportunity to call for an end to future gay pride parades being held in Northern Ireland. She remarked that 'Christians all over the province, and indeed, the world will be disgusted by this slur. If such provocative claims were made against Mohammad, Muslims would rightly be up in arms' (*Metro Eireann* 2007). However, it was chaplain Ian Hall (*Irish News* 2007) who was perhaps the most vociferous, stating:

> This event . . . was in fact a parade of perversion. The reality is that the behaviour of the sodomites is totally unacceptable. The Scriptures condemn the homosexual lifestyle in the most strident language. The Bible not only calls homosexual practices sinful but uses terms like 'reprobate mind", 'vile affections" and 'abominations" . . . Saturday's parade brought shame and disgrace to the good name of our nation's capital . . . The vast majority of Ulster people regard homosexual practices as depraved and disgusting and certainly would not give their approval to this tiny minority blighting their capital city with their monstrous march.

The language used by Hall demonstrates the focus on sexual activity which remains at the forefront of some Christians' minds. They also indicate their willingness to speak for the community without supporting these claims with any form of evidence. If they do feel that they represent the general sentiments held by members of their community, then they are most likely the ones instigating these ideas in the first place. Interestingly, judgments made about the placard centred upon the perceived attack on religious morality rather than seeing them as a personal opinion or one person's own religious perspective (that Jesus existed and possibly was homosexual). The author's use of the verb 'is", rather than 'was", may be interpreted to show religious adherence to a particular belief, regardless of how contentious it was. Nevertheless, the row served to highlight the growing propensity for community and political leaders to comment with relative impunity against homosexuality in Northern Ireland.

This oppositional stance against the gay pride parade appears to be a platform from which to test the legality of Christian opposition to homosexuality. In 2008, the Sandown branch of the Free Presbyterian Church, established by the Reverend Ian Paisley and led by him until his recent retirement, took out a full page advert in the *News Letter* in the days leading up to the gay pride parade. Headlined 'The word of God against sodomy' it promoted a gospel witness meeting against the 'abominable' act and was quickly held up as a homophobic tactic against pride by those involved with the parade (Moulton 2008). Such an action could not be overlooked by pride organisers as a result of the links between the members of this church and the political Assembly.

A ruling by the Advertising Standards Authority (ASA) initially decreed that the advertisement was homophobic and in breach of its code of practice. However, this decision was overturned following a judicial review in 2011. The appeal won on the basis that the ASA's original decision disproportionately interfered with the church's right to freedom of expression. Mr Justice Treacy stated that:

> The applicant's religious views and the Biblical scripture which underpins those views no doubt cause offence, even serious offence, to those of a certain sexual orientation. Likewise, the practice of homosexuality may have a similar effect on those of a particular religious faith. But Article 10 (of the European Convention on Human Rights) protects expressive rights which offend, shock or disturb. Moreover, Article 10 protects not only the content and substance of information but also the means of dissemination, since any restriction on the means necessarily interferes with the right to receive and impart information. (*BBC News* 2011)

It is likely that for this same reason the claims made on placards held by opponents to the parade also go unchallenged. Religious condemnation of sexuality is permissible but sexual speculation about religious figures is clearly not.

Recently, Derry/Londonderry has developed a smaller gay pride festival recognizing LGB&T communities in the north-west area of Ulster. This too has been targeted for opposition, albeit to a lesser extent. Nonetheless, Christian opposition to the perceived immorality of homosexuality has been evident in other facets of community life in the city. Two Protestant ministers protesting against the opening of a gay sauna in Derry/Londonderry in 2011 founded their objection on what they perceived to take place inside such venues (Deeney 2011). Ian Brown, from the Free Presbyterian Church along with Mark Bradford, a minister with the Bethnal Baptist Church tried to have the sauna shut down. Bradford gave his reasons for this as follows:

> I know from 15 years in ministry with the Bethnal Baptist Church and 20 as a Christian that the kind of debauched behaviour that goes on in these so–called sling rooms is detrimental to everyone who follows this kind of lifestyle. This is killer behaviour and is not how the city of Derry needs to be portrayed in the run up to the City of Culture title year. Make no mistake, we will oppose this sordid, sinful carbuncle on the face of Derry in every way we can. (Deeney 2011)

Seemingly, Bradford is going straight for the jugular and inferring that such venues incite members to engage in unprotected sexual intercourse and thus risk contracting potentially fatal sexually transmitted infections such as HIV/AIDS. This is no different to heterosexual interactions which take place on a weekly basis across the UK in pubs and clubs, yet very little condemnation of that particular 'heterosexual lifestyle' is demonstrated by these same religious leaders.

The HIV/AIDS panic that took hold of England in the 1980s failed to make a significant impact in Northern Ireland. This may have been as a result of moral condemnation being so entrenched in society that further reasons for homosexual persecution were redundant. Nevertheless, it appears from these ministers' actions and comments that stereotypes of disease, danger and death are still used where possible to cast aspersions on the gay community. Looking at the evidence around this issue, a more complex matter is evident. The HIV transmission figures for 2009 suggest that of the 68 new cases identified that year, 'out' gay men accounted for half of these (Public Health Agency 2010). However, they are more likely to interact with safer sex literature and information in a venue such as a sauna (which are often targeted by safer sex advocates from the LGB&T community) than closeted men in a secluded, remote area. Recognizing this, the Public Health Agency differentiate between gay men and 'men who have sex with men' (MSM), citing the latter group as being particularly at risk of contracting infection but not accessing the necessary information designed to target men. Therefore, it could be argued that in trying to close down venues such as the sauna in Derry/ Londonderry, these ministers may be exacerbating the public health issue, rather than challenging it.

Changing Attitudes

As indicated earlier in the chapter, some lesbians and gay men may also identify as Christian (or another denomination), so set about living in a manner which recognises and harmonises their sexual and spiritual selves. This may be facilitated by organisations such as Changing Attitude Ireland (CAI). This is a network of people aligned by their faith who work towards the full affirmation of lesbian and gay people within the Churches in Ireland. Taking a more inclusive approach towards diversity of identity, CAI see sexual difference as God's work and LGB&T people as expressing a form of God's message that must be acknowledged, not repressed or expelled. Representatives from CAI march in Northern Ireland's gay pride parades, give blessings to lesbian and gay couples who enter into civil partnerships and provide the space for Christian lesbians and gay men to live the spiritual lifestyle that they desire. CAI is perhaps aided by the fact that they are based within the Anglican community, however as a template for inclusion and spreading God's word their Christian ethos transcends individual doctrines, demonstrating the true message of God's love that so many of the interviewees grew up learning, believing and investing in.

CAI were also involved in campaigning to enact civil partnership legislation in the Republic of Ireland, recognizing the benefits this can bring to LGB&T visibility, acceptance and social integration. The fact that this group of people are able to live openly as LGB&T Christians and spread the word of God to others in Ireland, north and south, is significantly progressive when viewed against the backdrop of Northern Ireland's general ethos of moral conservatism. As ostracised as lesbians and gay men may feel from society, the difficulties faced by lesbian and gay Christians remains an under–researched area and one which may prove insightful in terms of sexual and spiritual reconciliation.

Summary

In Northern Ireland, recognizing and engaging with moral discourses and ideologies is fundamental to understanding social and political responses to homosexuality. This is particularly so given that the opinion of a small minority appears to dominate what is construed as consensus of public thought. There are other perspectives in Northern Ireland which must not be suppressed by this minority view. Similarly, there are measures being employed by some lesbians and gay men which indicate that resistance and resilience is working for them, but there are others still afflicted by the negative images concerning homosexuality which have been absorbed over a lengthy period of time.

Much of this chapter related to the experiences of the gay male interviewees as a result of women's sexuality being more generally regulated, ignored or overlooked. In the following chapter the focus is specifically on women's experiences of homophobia, sexual regulation and resistance, illustrating the gendered dynamics of homophobia that often go unnoticed within a wider culture of sexism or gender inequality.

Chapter 5
A Woman's Worth: Lesbian Lives in Northern Ireland

As with many studies into victimisation incurred by lesbians and gay men, there are reasons why official figures may not show the true picture for the persecution incurred by lesbian and bisexual women specifically. Accessing lesbian respondents is more of a problem in LGB&T studies as research suggests that lesbian women are less visible in society (Kitzinger 1987, John and Patrick 1999). Particularly in Northern Ireland, women may fear being 'out' about their sexuality if they have children, are in jobs where homosexuality has traditionally been treated with suspicion (such as youth work, nursing or teaching) or if they encounter hostility from openly prejudiced friends, family and work colleagues (Quiery 2002, 2007). The fact that these fears still remain challenges assumptions that it is now 'easier' for lesbian women to be open about their sexuality to others around them.

Within the chapter's focus on lesbian women's experiences, a nuanced view is also provided of the gendered dimension to homophobia. This is illustrated through acts seemingly motivated by the victim's perceived sexual and gender deviancy. Although lesbian women have not been legally persecuted in the same way as homosexual men, there are other ways in which legal regulation has affected their lives. For many women, this has involved considerations around child care and how their identity as a mother is juxtaposed with their identity as a lesbian woman. While social homophobia can be psychologically and physically damaging, legal and political homophobia can destroy family units and cause women significant distress and alarm.

Importantly within the chapter, there is a focus on women's pro–active engagement in politics. Northern Ireland is a culture where women are still under–represented in the political environment. Therefore, the political insight shown by the interviewees indicates how women worked within the wider socio–political structure to make their voices heard and their needs known. The importance of the women's movement in shaping and progressing lesbian development in Northern Ireland proved as integral as the wider civil rights issues occurring at the time.

Gendering Lesbian Victimisation

Fuss (1989: 110) describes lesbianism as often constituting a 'footnote to gay male history' in mainstream literature, only occasionally studied in order to physically and psychologically differentiate lesbians from heterosexual women. Lesbian terminology, alluding to reduced femininity or heightened masculine traits, has a history of being used to silence strong or assertive heterosexual women. In addition, affiliating feminism with lesbianism has also been used to scare women away from discovering what feminism is and what it might mean for them.

As literature on homosexuality has traditionally been biased towards male same–sex desire, theorising on female same–sex desire has been situated within feminist and/or lesbian–specific studies (Kitzinger 1987, Robson 1992, Wilton 1995). This indicates that lesbians and gay men may have little else in common other than not being heterosexual. While they may share a stigmatised existence of the 'sexual outlaw', women additionally incur 'the oppressed existence of the sexually subordinated' (Wilton 1995: 42). Although the perceived invisibility of lesbian existence may have shielded women from excessive legal persecution, Rich (1980: 649) outlines how lesbian history:

> has, of course, included isolation, self–hatred, breakdown, alcoholism, suicide and intrawoman violence; we romanticize at our peril what it means to love and act against the grain, and under heavy penalties; and lesbian existence has been lived (unlike, say, Jewish or Catholic existence) without access to any knowledge of a tradition, a community, a social underpinning.

The inclusion of gender dynamics displayed in acts of homophobia towards lesbians has been described by some as more properly constituting a terminology of its own, namely 'lesbophobia' (Treblicot 1994, Jay 1999). While this is a useful concept to theorise violence towards lesbian women within the wider spectrum of female suppression generally, it also indicates the importance of recognising differences when gender and sexuality biases appear blurred. Western cultures with patriarchal histories complicate the assessment of violence towards lesbians as victimisation may be predicated on the victim's sexuality, or gender, or both as Mason (1993: 4) illustrates:

> Documenting anti–lesbian violence is more difficult because there are many instances where lesbian women are unable to tell whether violence they experience is due to their particular status as a lesbian or forms a part of more general violence against women as a whole.

Ruthchild (1997: 3) suggests that there may not necessarily be a separation between the two, but that homophobic violence towards lesbians may be at the far end of a continuum of sexist violence: 'it is likely that lesbians' sexual autonomy and independence is perceived as a threat to male hegemony and control of women. As such, lesbians are seen to warrant a particularly vicious response.' This intersectionality of gender and sexuality is also depicted by Mason as illustrating the 'double positioning' which lesbian women occupy as victims of violence (1997: 22). Mason also offers a number of scenarios to exemplify the links between gender–based and sexuality–based victimisation. These include violence occurring in the private domain, the likelihood of an acquaintance as the perpetrator and the on–going nature of the hostility or victimisation, which is rarely limited to a single encounter. The likelihood of lesbian women experiencing violence from family members and of being sexually rather than physically assaulted reaffirms repressive, patriarchal ideologies of male property and ownership rights over the female body (Comstock 1991, Berrill 1992, von Schulthess 1992). In addition, similar to many women's experiences of violence, the harassment may become normalised to the victim and reporting is not usually considered to be a viable recourse. Incidents of 'low level' victimisation, such as verbal harassment, become part of the fabric of everyday life and may not be taken seriously or seen as causing significant harm.

Quiery's (2002) study of 160 lesbian and bisexual women's experiences of victimisation in Northern Ireland showed that nearly half had experienced varying forms of discrimination, with 20 per cent experiencing at least one violent assault. In addition to these more serious incidents, virtually all of the women recounted experiences of 'lower level' harassment and abuse, some indicating that this had become a regular occurrence. Examples of this type of persecution, which impacted negatively on the women despite being depicted as 'low level', included harassment, ostracism and isolation at work as well as homophobia incurred from strangers, family members and healthcare professionals. More significantly, despite many experiences potentially counting as crimes, none of these women said they had reported their incidents to the police. Instead, Quiery (2002: 18) argued that these women internalised these feelings and adapted their identities until a point where they felt they had a greater level of freedom (or invisibility):

> Women reported that they are seen as freaks who are vilified or, at best, tolerated by mainstream society. It is hardly surprising then that a large proportion of lesbians and bisexual women take the line of least resistance, conform to society's stereotypes of women and enter into marriage and child–rearing before eventually coming out as lesbian.

The 20 per cent of women who experienced violent assaults in Quiery's study recognised that in some cases they were unsure whether the violence was wholly based on their sexuality or also invoked misogynistic prejudices. This intersectionality of gender and sexual deviation is a common factor in violence towards lesbians and in the women's reluctance to report their experiences to the police (Comstock 1991, Mason 2002). Taking a general overview of anti–lesbian violence, Berrill (1992) notes that lower reporting rates may be a result of lesbian women's reduced visibility or the complexity in distinguishing homophobic violence which is specifically anti–lesbian from misogynistic violence which is generally anti-woman.

In addition to this culture of non–reporting is the relationship between the perpetrator and victim. While many of the more widely reported incidents of identity–based victimisation in the media document assaults perpetrated by people unknown to the victim, the vast majority of events involve someone who is not necessarily known to the victim, but is not an absolute stranger either (Mason 2005a). An exploration of this gives rise to the dichotomy of whether the violence is directed at the person for what they are known to be (if familiar), or is more symbolic of what they are seen to represent (if stranger). Either way, the hatred displayed towards the identity which is being attacked is most likely to be informed by a retributive ideology invoking both sexual and gender deviations (Mason and Tomsen 2001).

Regulating Lesbian Sexualities

The types of victimisation and violence depicted by some of the lesbian interviewees consisted of intimidation, verbal abuse, physical bullying and sexual assault. In a similar guise to the male interviewees, experiences of 'reorientation' efforts were evident for some women. These were not necessarily psychiatric or spiritual in nature, but rather involved threatened or attempted sexual assaults which appeared motivated by the male perpetrator's belief that he could 'straighten' the woman out. Some of the verbal abuse recalled by the interviewees also alluded to this ideology, particularly if the woman was out with her partner when the abuse took place. This can be seen reflecting the failure to accept women's sexuality as autonomous from men, and lesbians' sexual autonomy perhaps even less so. In Smythie's case, however, her lesbianism was seen as an outcome of supposed sexual abuse she must have encountered as a child:

> To this day there are members of my family that are still absolutely adamant that some man did something to me when I was [young] because to them that *has* to be the reason why I'm gay. (Smythie, 39, lesbian, her emphasis)

This perception was slightly different to several of the other female interviewees' stories of being told that they were lesbian because they had *not* 'found the right man' nor had a proper (heterosexual) sexual experience. Although no such abuse had taken place, the presupposition of this as a cause of lesbianism again illustrates the failure to perceive non–heterosexual orientations as naturally occurring among some people.

Many of the lesbian interviewees grew up at a time when women's sexuality was heavily regulated and under particularly close scrutiny compared to men's. This was based on their ability to conceive, a factor which – if done out of wedlock – was more of a socially stigmatising issue than for men. The difficulties in accessing contraception meant that pregnancy was harder for women to avoid before the introduction of the contraceptive pill or the increased accessibility of condoms. Some women cited this reproductive issue as being a possible reason why their sexual behaviour was noted more than their male siblings, particularly by male family members. Therefore, as they were being closely watched in terms of what they did with boys, the fact that they might be more interested in girls was largely overlooked. However, where this same–sex attraction came to light, it may also have accounted for the angry and violent responses some of the female interviewees experienced. In some cases, victimisation on the basis of women's sexual orientation was overlooked by other family members who were aware that the abuse was taking place. Negative perceptions of lesbianism may have led to this reluctance to become involved or challenge such behaviour.

Sexual assault against lesbian women in Northern Ireland was not always about reorientation, regulation or repression. In some cases, it appeared to be rooted in ideologies of 'punishment' or seeing the woman as precipitating her victimisation. This was highlighted by the interviewees who, either through personal experience or having counselled close friends, encountered a greater insight into such traumatic events. However, they were also aware that such assaults were less likely to come to the attention of the police as a result of fears held by victims which indicated the vulnerability they felt as women and as sexual minorities:

> [Lesbian] women won't report sexual attacks for the same reason [heterosexual] women generally don't report rape: because they fear reprisal especially if it's someone they know, which it usually is. They're terrified of it happening again. It's doubly so with lesbians as they fear being outed as well as attacked again. (Carmel, 43, lesbian)

Women's experiences of victimisation did not always involve an overt sexual component. One interviewee, Smythie, grew up in a rural area characterised by a strongly conservative Protestant identity. Describing how she came out as lesbian at 16 years old, she recalled how messages were posted through her letterbox which informed her that she was 'evil' and was going to 'Hell'. Eventually this escalated into a campaign of abuse which gradually worsened until it reached a point where she felt she had to move out for her own physical safety:

> I had to leave fairly soon after; I pretty much had my suitcase packed for me. There was no way they were going to let me be. The threats started getting more personal and the language was terrifying for someone only 16 years old. So I got out and I'll never go back. (Smythie, 39, lesbian)

In smaller and more rural towns, although lesbianism was virtually unheard of, negative ideologies of 'homosexuality' were evident. Any characterisation of lesbian sexuality was mostly likely framed within these ideologies of male sexual deviancy. As demonstrated in Smythie's experience, the language used against her indicates the origin of these harmful notions. As a result, fears that lesbian women were an evil or corrupting influence may have cast them as acceptable targets for abuse. The resultant effect was to regulate women's lives so that they remained 'under the radar' as much as possible, or moved away to escape persecution.

Women's needs and wants in relation to avoiding, managing or challenging violence and victimisation may be different to men's as a result of both their gender and their sexual identity. In Northern Ireland, an additional cultural pressure may exist in the form of the small and close–knit nature of some communities in Northern Ireland. Philomena, who grew up in a rural community, recalled a story which made her aware of the fact that wherever a person may be in Northern Ireland, they were never really far from home:

> I remember in the 70s, when a friend of my sister's came out, she'd been having difficulties coming to terms with her sexuality so was undergoing treatment in a clinic in Belfast. A nurse in the clinic was from our wee town and didn't she just come back and spread the word about this girl! [The girl] ended up leaving for England in the end for her family's and her own sake. (Philomena, 49, lesbian)

Community gossip might also have meant a simple police report of assault leading to speculation on the person's private life filtering back to their hometown. Therefore, hesitations about accessing the police or pursuing redress through the criminal justice system were founded on fears that such disclosures may filter out to others in the community. Where this had occurred, interviewees indicated that people who were previously unaware of the victim's sexuality had subsequently found out about this 'on the grapevine'. Once it was out there, they had no way of knowing what the implications might be for themselves or their families.[1] Women did not want to be identified as engaging in deviant or immoral activities.

Lesbians as Wives, Mothers and Carers

For women coming out in later life, added complications arose if they were, or had been, married and if there were children to consider. The interviewees who were mothers and/or grandmothers spoke of fears over the possible implications for the children in their families, and the ways in which they regulated or modified their identities to accommodate this. For some interviewees, this meant waiting until their children were at a certain age (usually in their teens or older) before the women explored their lesbian identities. Lesbian parents (and, some noted, gay male parents) were rarely considered in a positive light – if at all – in Northern Ireland. Therefore, coming out as lesbian while the children were younger meant that they faced the risk of losing custody or access to them. Using a woman's lesbianism to deprive her of access to her children was a real threat to those who had gone through an acrimonious split:

---

1   Similar concerns were cited in other gendered areas, such as preventing women accessing the contraceptive pill, condoms or seeking clandestine abortion advice.

Women would be terrified of losing their children as there's a lot of anecdotal evidence of judges being obviously homophobic. I remember cases where the father was patently unsuitable to be looking after the children yet he would be awarded custody despite being an alcoholic or violent, just because he told the judge that his wife had gone with another woman. Northern Ireland has to catch up with its legislation in practical terms as well as having it on paper. (Carmel, 43, lesbian)

It was here that several of the burgeoning LGB&T organisations, such as Lesbian Line (a telephone service which operated as part of the 'Cara–Friend' LGB&T organisation) proved vital for providing information and support to these women. Interviewees involved in Lesbian Line spoke of the high numbers of callers who revealed that they had contemplated suicide as their secret felt too great a burden to bear. The despair these women recounted indicated the immense service Lesbian Line provided as it was the only time they were able to talk to another person without fear of being judged or exposed. Discussing the Line in relation to women who were also wives and/or mothers, Philomena, depicted the secrecy and confidentiality needed to alleviate women's fears of being 'found out':

I started working on [Lesbian] Line and for a long time I spoke to so many women who were married and had children but who had never told a soul about their feelings before me. They were just so scared of what might happen to them or the kids if people knew. These women led lonely, lonely lives and didn't even have the option of attending the gay discos or days out for fear that they'd be seen and they'd lose everything. (Philomena, 49, lesbian)

Feelings of reassurance in the knowledge that there were others 'like them' out there tended to make the women feel more stable and confident and, perhaps most importantly, visible to some degree at least. For women who had more freedom (who were perhaps not married or not mothers) or were more willing to explore the social side of LGB&T culture, they were directed to the 'Lavender Links' monthly drop–in afternoons. Occasionally, these events included picnics or days out and were an important alternative to women not comfortable with accessing a pub–based venue or evening scene.

In some ways, Lesbian Line broke new ground through being established during a period of significant sexual – particularly homosexual – repression. Including the word 'lesbian' in the name of the helpline was an important step in raising visibility in Northern Ireland. It was also a measure which involved careful consideration beforehand. Many of the female interviewees alluded to the fact that the word 'lesbian' appeared to be far more political than 'gay'. It was suggested that this was perhaps a result of the strong women's and feminist movements and the association of these with lesbianism due to the perceived ethos of womanhood. Recognizing the potential this word had to discourage women from calling, steps were taken to make the callers feel more comfortable about using the Line or staying on the phone. For example, those on the Line were careful to use the language that the callers used, so that they were not labelled as lesbians, gay women or bisexuals. Advertising the service was also rendered difficult as a result of the taboo surrounding the use of the word 'lesbian':

> There was this enormous taboo around it, around being lesbian, actually using the word 'lesbian' in public. It said so much, that one word. It felt so much more political than saying 'gay woman'. (Julie, 48, lesbian)

When I think of that period, there was such a level of conservatism in this society. I remember women struggling to say the word 'lesbian' – I remember struggling to say it myself that first phone call! But advertising it, getting a bank account, all this took so much time and effort as no–one would go near anything with the word 'lesbian' in it. (Colette, 48, lesbian)

Nonetheless, the importance of the Line, and the impact it had on lesbian women in Northern Ireland was socially and politically progressive and a major step towards greater recognition of LGB&T communities.

Putting Lesbians on the Map

Lesbian visibility in Northern Ireland was gradually aided through adverts for Lesbian Line in community magazines such as *Women's News* and, perhaps more importantly, the prominent Northern Irish newspaper, the *Belfast Telegraph*. However, a late night television advertisement on Ulster Television (UTV) proved a significant breakthrough as were similar developments which were being made in the Republic with regards to lesbian visibility. In 1980, the *Late Late Show* in the Republic of Ireland featured an interview with Joni Crone, whose declaration: 'I am Lesbian and I am proud' made her the first openly lesbian woman to be interviewed on Irish television to an audience of over one million viewers.

Visibility was also facilitated through political organising around gender and sexuality rights. Although lesbians and gay men united to further political aims in the midst of the gay rights movement of the 1970s, the underlying patriarchal structures privileging masculinity were evident for several of the female interviewees even in this social movement. Gay men's oppression (through criminalisation) rendered them more visible than lesbians in society. However, women soon realised that the focus on the legal status of male sexuality was impacting negatively on lesbianism which was largely silenced in the wake of female sexual suppression generally. Thus women faced internal and external barriers to their coming out, accessing information or enabling visibility in Northern Ireland. Gay men had more of an idea of what they were campaigning for, given that specific laws applied to them. The gay man was constructed through negativity, but constructed nonetheless. Women were absent. Their wants, needs and desires were not recognised so were not sanctioned, but they were also not visible to the women who were unaware that they needed exposure to this discourse. Although this was not necessarily always a bad thing, it also meant that for some of the interviewees a defined identity or separation from general gender oppression was more difficult to discern.

For some of the female interviewees, the enhanced conservatism of their environment meant that they felt uncomfortable being seen in gay friendly venues which may have marked them as lesbian. Therefore, engagement in women's groups or ringing a confidential helpline were useful ways of meeting with, or talking to, other lesbian women without being so open about their sexual identities. This was particularly so for women who were geographically or socially isolated.

Progressing Women's Rights

Growing up during the ethno–political conflict and in a post-colonial society may render Northern Irish lesbians' experiences slightly different to those of women in Great Britain (and potentially the Republic of Ireland). The developing women's movement in Northern Ireland during the Troubles meant that several of the interviewees were involved in various different socio–political campaigns. Many women joined the campaign for contraception and equal rights, recognizing shared patterns of oppression and resistance. Several interviewees met and became good friends with women who also campaigning against the wider culture of gender oppression occurring in Northern Ireland. Part of this political battle also included highlighting misogyny within the burgeoning LGB&T community:

> A lot of women felt that they were invisible, that they didn't have a voice. The LGBT community is often a microcosm of minor societies so you would've had as much patriarchy in the LGBT community as you did in society. (Carmel, 43, lesbian)

Therefore, finding separate space to organise proved vital to develop and progress lesbian visibility in Northern Ireland. For some of the female interviewees, engagement in political ventures aided interaction with other lesbian women for the first time. This proved to be immensely important given the general invisibility of lesbian women in Northern Ireland during the 1970s and 1980s:

> I had been active in feminist politics before I identified as lesbian. This brought me into contact with a wide range of women activists, including lesbians and this meant that I had a safe space to be me. (Julie, 48, lesbian)

> At one meeting, a woman I was talking to was telling me about herself and used the term 'lesbian'. It was the first time I had heard this word, never mind it being used by someone who claimed to be one. As it turned out, there were far more

women there who would have been lesbian than I realised at the time. (Mary, 58, lesbian)

I started to get interested in the women's movement and that was my first experience of encountering lesbian women. ... I felt like that was somewhere I was at home. So that led me to think that this must be where my sexuality lies. (Colette, 48, lesbian)

This interaction proved to be a major turning point in these interviewees' lives, harmonising their sexual and political identities with other likeminded women. For some, there was an immediate solidarity. However, others noted the impact of Northern Ireland's socio–political environment even within organisations such as these. It was recognised that inclusivity could be both positively and negatively received, as Philomena outlined:

During the Troubles it was difficult to thrive as it was such a repressive society. Also [individual or alternative] political opinions of any kind were often frowned upon as a hindrance to the unity of the [women's groups], which meant that there was not an atmosphere of openness. For example, groups like Women's News or the International Women's Day Committee had connections both with the lesbian community and women's groups but also with anti–imperialist women, so it was often a difficult position to have. (Philomena, 49, lesbian)

Linking activism to wider socio–political issues proved beneficial for some of the interviewees directly as a result of their sexual identity. One event involved women who were part of the demonstration at Armagh prison against the treatment of female Republican prisoners. They were hosting female delegates from English groups who were there providing support. For some of the Northern Ireland contingent, they found themselves interacting with lesbians for the first time as a result of this demonstration. Colette recalled it as an inspiring moment among the women, although they were unaware of how important it was at the time:

If you can try and imagine this group of radical feminists coming into working class west Belfast which was completely militarised and completely suppressed, it was so strange but that exposure to lesbian politics was just what we needed. Many women spoke openly afterwards about that being their first exposure to lesbians in such great numbers. (Colette, 48, lesbian)

These women were not only the first real representations of lesbianism, they were also strong, positive and independent role models. Many of the female interviewees noted that these qualities were a 'big factor' in their visions for the development of lesbian politics in Northern Ireland. They saw the potential for building lesbian women's visibility in Northern Ireland although they recognised that there were certain cultural differences. While these role models were a useful template there were some factors which rendered them different from Northern Irish women's groups. For example, when attending conferences in England, some of the women from Northern Ireland began to notice the internal divisions threatening these larger women's groups. As lesbian women carved out a social presence and increased their visibility within women's groups, they became more segregated from heterosexual members of these groups. However, Colette noted that women in Northern Ireland were less likely to face this particular issue for cultural reasons:

> I remember that being fascinated by the segregation in the English women's movement because of the lesbians. Our women's movement was so small that we didn't have that luxury of splinter groups! The main thing that would have divided the women here was the constitutional issue, or the national question, which of course was something that wouldn't have applied to [the British women]. (Colette, 48, lesbian)

Despite there being fewer women's groups in Northern Ireland, the issues surrounding identity divides arose several times. Another example given by Colette occurred during an International Women's Day campaign where identity divides threatened to ostracise future members:

> There was one ferocious debate where we were trying to get all of the women's events under one banner. Some of the women felt that the Republican women and the lesbian women would put off the *normal* women. (Colette, 48, lesbian: her emphasis)

Several female interviewees commented on this internal conflict within some of the developing women's groups. Alluding to civil rights similarities between sexual minorities and Republican campaigners, some found it unsurprising that many of the women involved in women's groups were largely drawn from nationalist and/ or Republican communities. This became particularly evident when nationalist parties began taking an interest in LGB&T politics. Interviewees discussed the importance of having Sinn Féin recognise minority identities within the party. The level of engagement was not as reciprocal as they perhaps would have liked, but it was a start. For example, while many of the women engaged in pickets of prisons where political prisoners were held (as outlined above); few, if any, members of Sinn Féin accompanied the women on demonstrations for access to contraception, LGB&T or reproductive rights. There was a more distanced level of engagement, possibly so as to avoid ostracising or irritating some supporters of the political party. Nevertheless, the interviewees welcomed the eventual efforts to recognise the inequalities experienced by some lesbians and gay men in Northern Ireland:

> It was the Republican/nationalist parties who negotiated the inclusion of LGBT groups in equality measures proposed in the Belfast /Good Friday agreement –

the Unionist parties still cling to outmoded attitudes towards 'homosexuality' and have organised against the introduction of equality legislation for LGBT people. Plus, the new legitimacy of the Republican/nationalist position has allowed for the development of more radical rights–based politics. It is still early days but certainly some positive gains have been made for the LGBT community. (Jennifer, 48, lesbian)

Perhaps it was as a result of the gender dynamic to lesbian women's struggles for recognition and freedoms, but the female interviewees' narratives focused more on providing an insight into the ongoing political situation than the male interviewees.

To many of the women, the peace process was recognised as opening up spaces for discussion about wider forms of inequality. Many activists in Northern Ireland realised that procedures to enact legislation protecting minority groups from prejudice and discrimination would have to include sexual orientation regardless of the feelings of particular politicians. This was a huge boost to LGB&T visibility in Northern Ireland as not only were LGB&T communities recognised as actually existing, but they were now being considered politically and socially within law too:

> The peace process is creating room in the minds of people to think about other issues. It has also borne out the need for legislation to protect people not just from religious discrimination but other forms of discrimination. The fact of legal responsibility on departments and authorities to ensure equality of opportunity means they can no longer ignore or neglect topics they would prefer not to deal with. (Mary, 58, lesbian)

There was a pressing need to ensure that the inclusion of sexual orientation in equality, anti–discrimination and hate crime legislation was not tokenistic but instead had real relevance in combating minority victimisation and issues affecting women. Looking at gender–based initiatives designed to address violence against women and the negligible impact these have had, it is evident that the interviewees' anxieties were rooted in precedent. Concerns arose for some women that the pace at which LGB&T legal protection was being implemented in Northern Ireland was not being adequately reflected in social acceptance. Furthermore, this legislation was being imposed as part of a package of reforms aimed at addressing various types of inequality and discrimination. Glossing over problems by enacting laws or enforcing equality training was not getting to the root of the issue or addressing problematic ideologies continuing to inform hostility:

> It's a bit like the entire Troubles of Northern Ireland, we're having to go through this new phase of 'everything's wonderful' but deep, deep down prejudices still remain. … Homophobia is still there; we're all trying to be politically correct on the outside but it's still there. (Smythie, 39, lesbian)

The failure to address culturally specific issues informing homophobia during the process of rolling out legislation across the UK effectively overlooked the serious ramifications of this problem. Gulfs in relationships between those in power and those at grass–roots level were also marred by the forced interaction which came with new laws and policies regarding community cohesion. For some, strong feelings of tokenism were hard to overcome, especially amongst those who believed that homosexuality and LGB&T rights in Northern Ireland were being necessarily 'tolerated' as opposed to naturally or organically accepted:

> I'd rather have no rights than be tolerated. I'd rather fight on for full rights than be tolerated. I think in this country it's about tolerating you and I am *not* going to be tolerated. (Smythie, 39, lesbian, her emphasis)

> Some of us feel that when you're invited to go to the committees and things, is it just a case of 'are they ticking the right box'? Is it just an exercise in satisfying equal opportunities? But then again, unless you're in it, you can't have any impact, how are you going to change things? (Julie, 48, lesbian)

Most of the legal changes which had benefitted LGB&T communities came from Westminster, effectively bypassing the need for the Northern Ireland Assembly to vote on LGB&T equality laws. As a result, some interviewees described feeling 'cheated' out of a debate which could potentially have benefitted them in the long term:

> I suppose this is where I would bring in an analysis of the conflict and the effect of partition and the rest of it. If we'd had the chance to debate [the laws] here, all the parties would have had to nail their colours to the mast. As it was, it came in by stealth. In Northern Ireland you have to have political debate and argument to hear all sides. It's like the abortion issue – you realise that it has to come around again and that mobilises people, people see the consequences of repression and they react against it. So personally, I'd rather have waited and had the discussions here. (Colette, 48, lesbian)

Although such debates might have opened up the LGB&T community to increased levels of vitriol, they may also have provided the opportunity to respond. It is possible that, like the abortion issue alluded to by Colette, there was a political fear that public opinion may have shifted to a more liberal stance over time. If it had not, then many interviewees felt that it was important that such prejudicial views were aired, discussed and refuted within the public domain. This, at least, would highlight the work that needed to be done to address negative attitudes in society.

Summary

Women are often particularly marginalised during times of conflict and social instability. Similarly, within histories of homosexuality, women's experiences may also be overlooked or relegated to the margins as a result of not being specifically recognised and regulated in the criminal law. The narratives shared by the female interviewees provide an added dimension to both analyses of the Troubles and of the struggle for women's rights in the UK. Similarly, they also offer a culturally specific perspective on how women mobilised and organised themselves politically, managing different facets of their identities to their advantage, or concealing these in the wake of hostility or potential ostracism. Therefore, it can be argued that the experiences of many lesbian women in Northern Ireland, particularly those politically minded or involved in social activism, provide a unique and mostly unheard account of experiencing and resisting power from multiple perspectives.

Women generally are still struggling for social and political recognition in Northern Ireland, specifically with regards to gendered areas of law, such as campaigns to extend the Abortion Act 1967 to Ulster. Lesbian women in particular are underrepresented in all areas of Northern Irish life, leaving a large dearth with regards to positive role models, visible mothers and grandmothers and media personalities. The potential implications of fewer women (heterosexual, bisexual, lesbian, transgender and so forth) in positions of power may resonate further than experiences of violence and victimisation. Legal changes allowing lesbian women access to reproductive technologies may be hampered if hostility from healthcare professionals thwarts attempts to avail of these changes. Similarly, health issues facing lesbian women may be overlooked if misconceptions go unchallenged. Cultural heterosexism here may prove seriously debilitating if lesbian women are misguidedly omitted from routine health screening and are put at risk of developing otherwise treatable illnesses.

The following chapter continues with this theme of bringing forth personal accounts by exploring the impact of sexual disallowance on individual interviewees' lives. Though a selection of case studies, the examination indicates how cultural homophobia fed into ongoing feelings of isolation, oppression and marginalisation. This exploration forms part of the chapter's movement from repression through to resistance and eventual rebirth, finishing with a collection of accounts centred on the positive aspects of several interviewees' coming out processes.

Chapter 6
Experiencing 'Rebirth': Surviving Sexual Disallowance

The analysis thus far has illustrated lesbians' and gay men's exposure to, and resistance against, political and moral discourses condemning their sexual orientation. These experiences have painted a picture of how attitudes towards members of LGB&T communities in Northern Ireland have at times forced people into a position whereby they must defend themselves, seek legal protection from discrimination, or challenge misinformed and harmful stereotypes. Following on from assessing the collective battle, this chapter takes a more personal turn, looking at the lesbian and gay interviewees' narratives of internalising, tackling and overcoming homophobia and sexual prejudice in Northern Ireland. These experiences depict the management of homophobia and heterosexism within the interviewees' everyday lives, their coping strategies and the measures they took to live in a society which was largely unfavourable to homosexuality.

The underlying theme of 'disallowance' is evident in these stories and appears to be a fitting term which illustrates the insidious effects of living in a homophobic culture. Disallowance includes the failure to permit homosexual discourses, identities, autonomy, support, information, space, security, experiences and access to rites of passage. This can also be seen as having impacted on lesbians' and gay men's mental and physical health. To illustrate how, several case studies are presented which give a more in–depth perspective of action taken to resist sexual suppression. These focus on psychiatric responses to homosexuality, experiences of institutionalised homophobia in the police service, and seeing the coming out process as a new chapter in one's life.

The effects of cultural and internalised homophobia in the interviewees' lives are profound, but to present lesbian and gay lives solely in a negative light is to do an injustice to the resilience which was demonstrated. The interviewees' 'coming out' narratives show the inner strength, determination and spirit possessed by those who eventually managed to see a positive outcome from largely negative situations. Presenting these powerful journeys is a tool which helps to dismantles disallowance. Furthermore, it becomes evident that the increased visibility, inclusive discourse and positive representations of lesbians and gay men in a society such as Northern Ireland are vital steps to challenge the ongoing negativity surrounding homosexuality.

Internalising Homophobia

For decades, lesbians and gay men living in the UK have been told that there is something wrong with them, be it sexually, mentally, biologically or psychologically. Mental health problems in particular, from anxiety and depression through to self harm and attempted suicide, have been blamed on their abnormal 'sexual condition'. As thinking around sexual difference has progressed, it has become more apparent that the challenges lesbians and gay men in an intolerant or hostile society are extrinsic, not intrinsic. Taking such negativity on board can lead a person to loathe themselves and what they are seen to represent. This internalisation is an issue which has come to light as a result of a growing body of social research (Allen and Oleson 1999, Williamson 2000).

'Internalised homophobia' refers to way in which a person surrounded with homophobic discourses, attitudes and ideologies may start to take these on board in a negative or depreciating manner. Some studies which have sought to differentiate this from depression indicate how it is the wider negative culture surrounding a person about their sexual identity which impacts on their feelings of low self–worth (Allen and Oleson 1999). Internalised homophobia can impact on people's behaviours and actions, and can be significantly debilitating if it causes someone to see themselves as worthless. Often, they will assume that they are regarding themselves in a manner similar to others' perceptions, particularly if they do not have any positive imagery to align themselves to, or close acquaintances in which to confide. In some cases, this dislike may cause people to engage in acts designed to 'punish' or hurt themselves, or which will remove them from society temporarily (such as isolation) or permanently (such as suicide). In other cases, this anger or disgust may be externally inflicted, usually upon others through a form of 'lashing out' in a violent or aggressive manner.

Ken Plummer (1995: 9) suggests that 'the awareness of stigma that surrounds homosexuality leads the experience to become an extremely negative one; shame and secrecy, silence and self–awareness, a strong sense of differentness – and of peculiarity – pervades the consciousness.' If this state of being is left unchallenged and the person withdraws further into themselves then there is a strong chance that this stress will begin affecting them in some way. Furthermore, isolating oneself may result in a cycle of abuse where self–imposed isolation offers little chance to engage with alternative (positive) ideologies.

Common indicators such as mental health problems, eating disorders, substance abuse, homelessness and self–harm amongst some lesbians and gay men have been attributed to both cultural and internalised homophobia, as well as the fear of incurring violence (D'Augelli and Grossman 2001, Morrison and L'Heureux 2001, Rivers 2001, Cochran et al. 2004, Cull et al. 2006). Research has also indicated that internalised homophobia may be more of an issue amongst rural–dwelling gay men, who have fewer opportunities for social interaction as a result of geographical isolation (Cody and Welch 1997). Care must be taken when addressing this issue to ensure that the notion of internalised homophobia does not shift the focus away from the impact of wider social homophobic oppression on the lesbian or gay individual (Kitzinger 1987). In other words, it may not be recognised clearly enough that the effects of internalised homophobia are not a symptom of the person's sexuality, but a result of the negative ways in which their sexuality has been construed in their culture.

Victim–centred dialogues are not always productive or pro–active but may be a prerequisite of recognizing hams or having these harms taken seriously. Help and support for the LGB&T community from within the LGB&T community may serve to keep it as a perceived LGB&T problem and not a problem manifesting from, or requiring redress within, mainstream heterosexual society. The prejudice is emanating from wider society so, in effect, requires a more holistic approach. Kitzinger (1997: 211) also recognises how progress may still be constrained within the problematic medical framework applied to lesbian and gay mental health problems, suggesting that 'instead of going to heterosexual therapists to be cured of our homosexuality, now lesbians and gay men are supposed to see our lesbian and gay therapists to be cured of internalised homophobia.' This is certainly the approach taken by the Stop Conversion Therapy Taskforce (SCOTT) who sought to engage with lesbians and gay men attending the Core Issues conference (discussing psychological methods of converting homosexuals to heterosexuals) in Belfast. Problematically, such an approach serves to keep this issue within the confines of LGB&T communities when it is those in the mainstream who need to be engaged with.

Lashing Out at Others

Internalised homophobia has also been recognised in a different guise, accounting for people (usually men) acting violently towards lesbians and gay men. Certainly, this was the thinking behind the so–called 'homophobic panic defence' whereby a man, seemingly in fear of the homosexual desires stirred up within him, attacked the person perceived to be eliciting such feelings (Comstock 1992, Banks 1997). This was later redefined as the 'homophobic advance defence' to account for the fact that not all men who attacked other men (whom they perceived to be homosexual) were themselves experiencing repressed homosexual desires (Lunny 2003). Some were just affronted at the alleged sexual advance. These legal defences, used most commonly under the guise of 'provocation' in murder cases, have been criticised for reinforcing negative stereotypes (Bartlett 2007). This was less of a legal issue in Northern Ireland. However, the hostile sentiments demonstrated in such cases (and trials) were reflected in several of the interviewees' own experiences of encountering hostility from others who they suspected to be, at the very least, same–sex attracted but did who not necessarily identify as anything other than heterosexual. These people, usually men, were seemingly directing their frustrations onto the victim in order to deflect attention away from having to confront their own questions about their sexual identities. While these men may not have openly depicted themselves as bisexual or gay, the interviewees who were subjected to hostility from them appeared convinced that this was the rationale behind the attacks:

The people who gave me the worst abuse, both physical and verbal, were people who I *know* were closet gays or bisexuals. What they were doing was trying to cover their own tracks. These people … were so called happily married family men. It's a front. (James, 60, gay male, his emphasis)

I think the people who have a problem with [homosexuality] are people who have always had a problem with it; perhaps they are dealing with huge conflicts within themselves and that's why they react as strong as they do. (Connor, 46, gay male)

In cases where the perpetrator is a close friend, family member or partner, it may be more difficult for the victim to condemn the violence. This was certainly the case in Jane's experience:

He [her brother–in–law] gave me a lot of abuse: physical, sexual, harassment. I got a lot of beatings. Then I found out about him, that he was bisexual. He's married with two children. I approached him and I told him that I knew about him and he said 'Don't you dare tell anybody'. I couldn't believe it, abusing me for my sexuality when at least I was honest about it. I wasn't deceiving anyone. (Jane, 50, lesbian)

Quite possibly, an element of jealousy fuelled Jane's abuser if he felt trapped in a relationship whereby his only sexual interaction with male partners was at best covert and stressful, or at worst prohibited. By contrast, Jane lived openly in a relationship with her female partner for many years. Furthermore, she perceived the violence not only as rooted in her brother–in–law's frustration at his own repressed sexual identity, but also her vulnerability as a woman to not fight back in any threatening manner, thus incorporating elements of gender–based victimisation too.

Internalised homophobia can also affect lesbians and gay men who are in relationships or open about their identities. Violence within lesbian and gay relationships is less recognised within society, yet the reasons behind this abuse may stem from internalised homophobia. Certainly, this was seen to play a large part in the interviewees' narratives concerning knowledge about domestic abuse in lesbian and gay relationships. Many indicated that a society which failed to accept violence *against* lesbians and gay men as a serious issue was perhaps even less likely to address violence *within* such a community. The prevalence of abuse in LGB&T relationships generally was something several of the interviewees thought was not as well engaged with by wider LGB&T communities as it could be both in Northern Ireland and elsewhere. Resources for lesbian or gay victims of domestic abuse are generally limited in comparison to victims who identify as heterosexual. Recognition that LGB&T organisations may be reluctant to recognise that domestic abuse occurred in LGB&T relationships stemmed from issues ranging from such violence being seen as a specifically patriarchal heterosexual issue, through to it being a tool which may splinter burgeoning LGB&T groups. Many interviewee activists from LGB&T communities also felt that focusing on internal divisions and problems would detract from the more pressing issues of displaying a united front against heterosexism and sexual identity prejudice. Nevertheless, domestic abuse does occur in LGB&T relationships and failing to engage with this issue can not only place the victim in greater danger but may also be read by the abuser as tacitly condoning their actions.

The female interviewees who made reference to domestic abuse linked this to wider cultures of sexual repression. Although few chose to disclose much about their *own* experiences, speaking about it in general terms indicated the importance that they placed on cultural homophobia. In some cases, the interviewees saw abusive partner's failure to accept their own homosexuality as fuelling their violence. In other cases, the abused partner had internalised negative imagery about homosexuality to such a degree that they believed they had precipitated the violence in some way or were otherwise deserving of it. Interviewees were aware that there were few outlets available for them to discuss the abuse they were experiencing. Distrust of the police, coupled with a reluctance to 'come out' to medical staff or family, meant that many chose to say nothing and remained within the damaging relationship as a result of feeling otherwise trapped. Similarly, fewer avenues were open to lesbian women seeking to exit domestically abusive relationships as what services existed were equipped to deal with heterosexual relationships. Clearly, organisations such as Women's Aid need to ensure that when dealing with lesbian or bisexual women that they are dealing with the victim and not the actual abuser.

Within the context of Northern Ireland's smaller LGB&T population LGB&T community resources, acknowledging the impact of internalised homophobia on perpetrators and victims of same–sex domestic abuse is an important area which may not be prioritised when juxtaposed with challenging other, more pressing social or political forms of discrimination. As long as ideologies persist that homosexuality is wrong (and therefore any problems that lesbians and gay men are having are attributable to their sexual identity or orientation) then such difficulties will continue to exist. Strategies designed to intervene and address internalised negativity and self–loathing will also continue be fraught with difficulties if such efforts are merely perceived as tokenistic rather than focused on helping individuals.

Denying Cries for Help

For a small proportion of the interviewees unable to deal with such a hostile, oppressive environment, their feelings of responsibility, self–blame and hopelessness almost became too much and disclosures of having mental breakdowns and/or taking overdoses of prescribed medications were common. However, some indicated that whilst these may have been cries for help, the act of trying to take one's life came with an added more pressure. The issue of attempted suicide discussed by the interviewees was often referred to in light of the fact that suicide was traditionally a moral taboo in Irish society.

The Suicide Act 1961 changed the law in England and Wales so that a person who unsuccessfully tried to take his or her own life would no longer face prosecution. The provisions of this Act were extended to Northern Ireland through the Criminal Justice Act (Northern Ireland) 1966. However, in the Republic of Ireland suicide remained a criminal act for a further three decades, until the passing of the Criminal Law (Suicide) Act 1993. This difference between Northern Ireland and the Republic was noted by several interviewees, some of whom had moved to the Republic. Recognizing that the law was different south of the border, people who needed help were instead persecuted further or silenced through the fear of a criminal response.

In time, increased awareness around the factors prompting suicide attempts eventually led to legal changes which took a more liberal approach to this behaviour. Similarly, the bodies of people who had committed suicide were permitted burial in consecrated ground whereas previously this had not been allowed. Discussions and/or interventions regarding lesbian and gay suicide, however, remained at the margins of mainstream ideologies, or were overlooked altogether. In cases where an interviewee had been directly affected by the suicide of someone they knew to be struggling with issues surrounding their sexuality, concern was expressed around the handling of such deaths. Some expressed fears that coroners were reluctant to investigate whether the deceased person was lesbian or gay in case such actions caused discontent in an otherwise unaware family. Such stories indicated that both morality and heteronormativity played a large part in concealing the potential sexuality of the deceased.

Disallowance and Mental Health

Cultures of disallowance vary in Northern Ireland from failing to perceive lesbians or gay men as equal citizens, through to actively persecuting others as a direct result of their sexual identity. Along this continuum, there are various stages at which a person, their experiences or their rights may be denied or denigrated as a result of being seen as inferior, wrong or unequal. From not receiving relevant information about sexual health, intimacy and relationships at school through to not being recognised as a next of kin by medical or insurance personnel, disallowance can be seen as potentially impacting on almost every aspect of lesbian and gay lives.

A study conducted by into the mental health of young same–sex attracted men in Northern Ireland indicated the severity of disallowance and the impacts on the respondents (McNamee 2006). As well as fearing violent victimisation upon being 'outed', the study also found that frequent exposure to discourses of sin, immorality and wrongfulness in relation to homosexuality had a profound impact on the respondents' mental well–being. The suggestion that as homosexuals they were 'acceptable targets' of prejudice was seen to compound mental anguish. In some cases experiences of homophobia and negativity resulted in self–harm, as well as drug and alcohol problems to blot out feelings of low self worth (McNamee 2006). The report also demonstrated that over one quarter of the respondents had attempted suicide while over two thirds had thought about taking their own life. Similar reports into the impact of homophobia on same–sex attracted women in Northern Ireland indicated that many of the issues depicted by men applied to women (Quiery 2002, 2007).

This is not a new problem. Speaking on the topic of harms to mental health in the wake of the decriminalisation campaign, Bradley (1974: 2) noted the dominance of morally condemnatory discourses, suggesting that the internalised psychological burdens placed upon lesbians and gay men from their Christian faith may be as debilitating as the overt homophobia they experience:

> Were it not for their sense of sinfulness and rejection and their heavy burden of guilt, many homosexuals would function better in society, work more efficiently and have less tendency towards escapist behaviour, nervous breakdowns, despondency and suicide.

Such a culturally specific pressure felt by lesbians and gay men in Northern Ireland was evident to some, even then. However, as problematic as these issues may be, greater challenges faced those who were less aware of their mental anguish. One interviewee, Mark, was heavily invested in the psychological aspect of understanding, addressing and repairing mental harms inflicted on gay men through their exposure to homophobia. Drawing on experiences from across the UK, Mark spoke about clear differences he saw when comparing his friends from Derry/Londonderry to those from Manchester in England, a city known for its large, visible LGB&T community:

> The difference between my gay friends in Manchester and here – in Derry more so than in Belfast – is that a lot of people come across as, or would tell you that they're not mentally stable: that they're suicidal, that they self harm, that they don't know what their sexual identity is, that they want to commit suicide, that they are in violent relationships and somehow see it as normal, or acceptable, or that that's just the way it is, or that they can do no better. ... A lot are on antidepressants and I think that is indicative of the medical profession who are telling these people in those socially isolated areas that they are social misfits and that they are mentally not right. (Mark, 32, gay male)

In Manchester, attitudes towards lesbian and gay identities are not underpinned by the same intensity of moral conservatism that exists in Northern Ireland. The social support systems which are in place in England are less developed in Northern Ireland. There are significant discrepancies between the two areas in relation to whether or not it's 'ok to be gay'. Having lesbians and gay men in Northern Ireland resorting to prescribed medication for the same things that lesbians and gay men in Manchester would be able to talk freely about and vent anger at illustrates the problematic responses to sexual identity inherent to Northern Ireland. This also shows a dearth of understanding by doctors who may have chosen to medicate people rather than engage with the issues informing their feelings of self-worth.

Tapping into the ideology that the homosexual identity itself is in some way damaged or wrong and can be 'fixed' may result in some people taking on board a 'victim' identity. In other words, they may accept this 'damaged' label as both an explanation for their difference and a starting point to change. This response to sexual difference may appear more paternalistic, blaming forces outside the person's control for their difference. As a result, recognizing the impact of this approach helps to account for why so many people are prepared to see themselves as in need of help or intervention. They can conceive of themselves as an innocent party, so long as they wish to be changed, fixed or cured. They do not have to accept responsibility for doing wrong, or having wrong done to them, but must take steps to become more like others in society. This becomes problematic when the symptoms being treated are deemed medical or psychological but residing in the person, rather than viewed as social and residing in society's response to that person's identity. Treating the individual with spiritual intervention, drugs or therapy to address their 'issues' does nothing to address the wider culture of disallowance of that particular identity in society. If anything, it sidesteps the issues facilitating people's problems. Those involved in such religious, medical or psychological interventions are usually considered 'experts' within their fields by laypersons. Therefore, the power afforded to their judgement may outweigh that of the lesbian or gay individual, as in society knowledge is generally deferred to those deemed authorities in a particular field. In some cases, this can be very damaging.

Resorting to 'Expert' Advice

The effects of problems such as a mental or psychological breakdown, attempting suicide or battling a substance addiction may eventually bring a person into contact with healthcare professionals. Several of the interviewees had accessed health services in Northern Ireland due to such factors. In many cases, they were also told that it was their sexuality which was causing their mental distress and so it was this variable which had to be addressed or changed. Two issues arise here. The first is the perspective adopted by the healthcare professional regarding how to address the person's sexuality and its role in the issue at hand. This often reflects how homosexuality is understood in society at that particular time. This leads into the second issue of power relations and how they are played out in the client–professional relationship (Foucault 1976).

The cultural meaning take on board by the interviewees regarding their sexuality were the same messages – usually – that the healthcare professionals were exposed to. Therefore, both were starting from the perspective that the interviewee had a condition to be treated. Additionally, the more serious the condition (or its manifestations in self–harming behaviours) the greater the power imbalance between 'expert' and 'patient' was seen to be. Some interviewees even reported seeking out professional help for their sexual 'condition' themselves. As a result, the help or treatment sought may also have encompassed other afflictions, such as depression, and often resulted in being given time off work, medication or offers of therapy: all of which failed to engage with the wider environment impacting on the person's state of mind. In Rob's case, his exchanges with health workers over a decade indicate a number of misconceptions about homosexuality that were prominent among treatment professionals in Northern Ireland.

Case Study: The Patient

Rob was a 58 year old Protestant gay male from Belfast who has lived with his Catholic male partner, Mack, for over 30 years. His interactions with medical professionals in Northern Ireland illustrate both legal and medical professionals' discomfort with and attitudes towards homosexuality in Northern Ireland prior to decriminalisation. His first encounter occurred when he was in his early teens and homosexual acts were still criminalised throughout the UK. Like many of the interviewees, Rob began having feelings of 'being different' at a young age. His initial confusion soon led to feelings of low self esteem, social withdrawal and eventually depression. The first time he sought help and advice from a healthcare professional he was immediately dismissed:

> At the age of 12, 13 I took a fit of depression so went to the psychiatrist and told him that I thought I was gay, which he totally and utterly dismissed … I remember him saying to me, 'Where did you hear such words?' and I probably said at school or something. I was sent home and told to look at photographs of women and everything would be ok, just go and 'wise up', that's what I got. So I went home and suppressed it all. I remember the psychiatrist being quite irritated that I was standing there talking about this; he was quite flabbergasted that someone who was at school would know about this.

Rob's dismissal was more likely due to his youth than his sexuality. However, the psychiatrist's failure to engage with his concerns indicates a general belief that sexuality is not something that concerns children. With little other recourse for information, he took the psychiatrist's advice and tried to live as a heterosexual. This caused him many social problems at school where he repeatedly described not being able to fit in, particularly as his peers' conversations started to focus on sexual engagements with women. In an attempt to suppress his true feelings and to conform to social and family norms, he got married at 18 years old. The effect on the marriage was predictable:

It was a disaster. As much as I loved her, there was something about it …
somehow women's things annoyed me. So I had to talk to her then; it got to the
stage where I started to become mentally ill with the whole thing so I had to say
to her that by this stage I knew for definite. I knew that I was gay.

The stress of having to live a 'double life' led to his undergoing a 'full mental
breakdown' before his wife filed for divorce, citing Rob's sexuality as the cause.
Rob's second clinical engagement was ordered by the Northern Irish courts as
part of his divorce proceedings on the basis of his homosexuality. As a result, he
was referred to a mental hospital in Northern Ireland to undergo treatment. By
this point laws regulating homosexuality applied to Northern Ireland only, yet the
'medical model of homosexuality' was prominent among medical professionals
internationally. Rob noted that there were a number of other men in the same
clinic as he found himself who were there for the same treatment, but not all for
the same reason. Some were undergoing treatment to avoid criminal prosecution
while others had referred themselves.

The medical professionals told him that to enable them to begin his 'treatment'
he first had to 'admit that he was ill' – his 'illness' being homosexual identity. After
this step the 'treatment' could begin, which he described in detail:

In those days they did what they called 'aversion therapy'. You went through
two stages, one was that you went into this room and you looked at photographs
of men. When you were feeling a wee bit randy – because they suggested to
you, 'Imagine you're groping him' and you said, 'Yes, I am imagining that
now' – then you'd get an electric shock through the feet. They had wires going
into these special shoes, so it was quite a severe electric shock, and this was
supposed to make you associate it with *bad* feelings. Then you went through
to the next course where you weren't allowed to drink any water, and you were
given salt pills so that you became terribly, terribly thirsty and it was a *female*
psychologist, because it was a male who gave you the electric shocks and now
we're over to the female, and when you imagined the *right* kind of thing, then
you got a little drink of water as a *reward* for doing it! I was about 20 [years old]
when I left and apparently I was '*cured*'. (His emphasis)

Rob's experience illustrated that the medical model still held credence in Northern
Ireland despite partial decriminalisation in England and Wales. Reflecting on his
treatment by the psychiatrists, Rob was not bitter as he recognised the impact of
the wider environment in which it took place:

I don't think they'd do that anymore now, it's probably seen more as a torture!
The psychiatrists were really convinced; I think they did the same thing towards
alcoholics more or less, seeing it in the same way with rewards and denials.
You'd have thought though somewhere along the line they'd have admitted that

there was nothing they could do and that gay was gay and that was it, but they seemed to go along with this idea that they could 'fix' you.

In Rob's case, this 'fixing' created further complications for the court (who had originally ordered the treatment). Ironically, as the medical and legal experts insisted that he was 'cured', his wife was no longer allowed to file for a divorce on the grounds of his homosexuality, having to opt for alternative reasons instead. Showing true resilience, in a final postscript to the story Rob notes that the aversion therapy was not entirely fruitless:

> I had this terrible fear of electric switches; I thought I was going to get a terrible shock! I got over that, but it didn't cure me from having sex with men at all!

This case was one of the most extreme experiences recounted by the interviewees, but was indicative of the normalised attitude whereby the sexuality and not the prejudice was seen as being in need of addressing. Although Rob survived his experience and went on to engage in a loving and rewarding relationship with Mack, he was mindful that for others who had undergone similar experiences, the outcome had been less positive.

Experiences of Loneliness and Isolation

It was clear from the narratives that it was not merely being lesbian or gay that caused mental or emotional problems, but the wider culture of anti–homosexual sentiment to which the interviewees were exposed on a regular basis while growing up in Northern Ireland. Therefore, most felt pressurised into silence, denying or concealing their feelings from others without knowing if those others were experiencing similar pressures:

> There was a tremendous loneliness that went right through with me from primary school until I finally came out. (Pat, 61, gay male)

> I kind of went through it on my own, but I had a good friend... but yes, it was quite a difficult and lonely experience. (Mags, 59, lesbian)

> I'm an outgoing person and I can still tell you that it's a lonely life, so god help anyone who is shy and retiring anyway. (Smythie, 39, lesbian)

This loneliness determined a variety of coping strategies, most of which probably did more damage to people in the long term. While loneliness at first may seem largely insignificant in relation to some of the other detrimental effects of experiencing prejudice in a generally hostile environment, there are repercussions attached to this emotion. Both male and female interviewees cited the problems they experienced as resulting from their need to suppress their sexual identity altogether, or feign a heterosexual orientation. Nuala found the pressure to conform so intense that she moved away to England, returning only when she felt more secure in her sexuality. Upon returning to her rural Northern Irish town, she felt unable to go through with her plans to tell her parents. This was a major factor which adversely impacted on her mental well-being, particularly as her parents died soon after her return:

> For years I denied it, even on my parents' deathbeds, and that's where my problems stem from. I've had to have a lot of counselling. I know now that my problems aren't because I'm lesbian, but because I've been made to deny it for so long: to myself, to my family, I've had to deny it to everyone. How can that *not* mess a person up? (Nuala, 45, lesbian, her emphasis)

The counselling that she accessed was supportive of her sexual orientation, encouraging her to engage with the Belfast–based women's support group, 'Lesbian Line' in order to contact other lesbian women in Northern Ireland. This proved an important development for her as other women who had been in similar situations were able to help her address and overcome some of the guilt she described feeling as a result of not telling her parents. The link between silence, disapproval and emotional burden was something another interviewee, Carmel, recognised as affecting women in particular. She felt that the problem was more prolific than realised and was able to remain this way because of women's feelings of guilt at upsetting family members. Carmel noted that whereas men might have found it easier to move away, or have been expected to do so, the expectations placed on women meant that they were more likely to stay at home and under closer scrutiny:

> It's easier for [women] to remain silent and invisible and it's still a big problem in Northern Ireland. A lot of women may fear hurting someone in their family, or that they'll disappoint them, or [the family member] will think they've done something wrong. .. That's very damaging and it does have an impact on people's mental health because you have to make a choice whether to be visible or not and be prepared to deal with what follows. (Carmel, 43, lesbian)

The higher levels of social mobility or migration afforded to men may have resulted in more women having little choice but to remain silent whilst still in the family home. Similar opportunities of spaces were perhaps less open or available to them.

Problematic Coping Strategies

The coping strategies employed by some of the interviewees were not unusual, such as using socially acceptable outlets, for example using alcohol to 'blot out' negative feelings. In Irish cultures, particularly Catholic communities, alcohol is seen to be a socially acceptable form of intoxicant and is often a staple factor in social interactions. As alcohol is seen to constitute part of the Irish culture, higher rates of alcoholism may exist or may be normalised. As the reasons behind a person's dependency on alcohol are questioned less frequently due to the prevalence of drinking cultures, this provides a useful smokescreen to detract attention from the true issues being suppressed or avoided. Being known as a heavy drinker, particularly for some of the older male interviewees, was normalised in their culture to such a degree that this was almost part of the Irish male identity. Drinking cultures were also a gendered phenomenon; women were less likely to emulate male drinking behaviours without attracting some form of attention unless they were accompanied by men and/or other women in public houses. Although this gendered division has lessened over time with more women engaging in drinking cultures across Ireland and Northern Ireland, there is still a general failure to recognise the potential drivers behind why some people may be using alcohol as an emotional crutch, as Alice noted:

> The fact that we like a wee drink is so ingrained in our society that social provisions and social developments outside of the alcohol scene seem to have been an afterthought. I guess the possibility that half the population have a reason to be drinking is too scary a thought to contemplate. (Alice, 44, lesbian)

Public houses have proved integral to social interactions in various aspects of Western culture but within LGB&T communities there was a danger that few other options were available which did not involve alcohol. Dependence on alcohol was an issue raised in more depth by the rural interviewees as a symptom of the malaise in their communities more generally – in terms of affecting similarly hidden issues such as domestic violence and child abuse – and of particular groups specifically. John, for instance, was keen to highlight his worry about closeted or less forthcoming homosexual farmers 'drinking themselves to death' in isolation as a result of their sexuality. This group, he felt, was socially marginalised and had little knowledge of how to go about interacting with the kinds of people they needed to meet. He felt that such isolated men (as it was predominantly a male population) were in danger of exclusion from both mainstream and LGB&T communities as a result of not 'fitting in'. Despite the emergence of 'gay scenes' in Belfast and Derry/Londonderry, the fear and paranoia that they may be spotted or recognised by someone they knew kept the rural men he knew away from these bars and clubs. Their isolation from others seems significant given the current availability and general reliance upon the internet and various methods social networking which have developed in the interim period.

The largely hidden problem of drug abuse amongst lesbians and gay men may also be fuelled by an inability to confront social ostracism or prejudice. Furthermore, it was felt by the interviewees who raised this issue that such abusive behaviours may be grossly underestimated and not recognised as harming people who are exposed to cultural prejudices in their everyday lives. This was explicitly outlined by Julie and another rural interviewee (whose identity will be protected here):

> I believe that if there was a survey done on mental health issues – be it from depression, major breakdowns, suicide attempts, drugs, alcohol addiction – in the gay community I could put my hand on my heart and say at least 90 per cent of us have had, or do have, a problem. (Julie, 48, lesbian)

> I've got a bad, bad drug addiction background and big problems with my self esteem because of what happened to me when I came out as a gay woman and I'll tell you now, consequently it has led to health problems. That's how serious it can get for gay people here and I know for a fact that I'm not the only one. (Anon, lesbian)

Interviewees involved in rural LGB&T community groups were often an important point of contact for lesbians and gay men too frightened to 'come out' in their localities. Thus, the burden on them as the sole person aware of people's plights was evident. It seemed important that people in such roles should be offered support to ensure that they themselves do not end up with negative consequences, perhaps 'burning out' as a result of consciously or otherwise shouldering responsibility for those who feel they have nowhere else to turn.

An impact both of this culture of substance misuse and fear of ostracism is the tendency for some lesbians and gay men to construct new 'families' from close friends or confidants. Carving out a new 'family' may mean engaging with others through social outlets, or a 'scene', which because it normally involves licensed premises may not offer the most sound environment to those battling with addiction problems stemming from negative feelings. Many of the interviewees who raised this issue found comfort in the support of others with whom they shared similar traits – sexual orientation, ostracism (either chosen or imposed) from family members and having moved to a new, urban area from a smaller, more rural town. This was an important way of combating feelings of isolation and loneliness, but at the same time could bring with it further problems which were not realised until much later on, such as what would happen when relationships break down between relatively small groups of people.

Isolation was not just a social or family issue; for some, their chosen vocation encompassed a wider working environment where homosexuality was not just intolerable but at times condemned outright. Knowledge of this silenced people personally (to avoid hostile confrontation or singling out for abuse) and professionally (in case prejudice against their sexual identity hindered their career progression). Certainly, this was a theme most commonly alluded to in the interviewees' narratives. However, one story in particular stood out. In the following case study, Connor, a former policeman, indicates some of the constraints he experienced as a gay man within his chosen vocation as a policeman in the Royal Ulster Constabulary (RUC) and later the rebranded Police Service of Northern Ireland (PSNI).

Case Study: The Policeman

Connor was a 46 year old retired policeman in a long term relationship with his male partner at the time of interviewing. Prior to this, he had been married and he also had a son. Most of Connor's experiences related to when he was involved in the police service.

A key concern cited by Connor was the threat to his job if his true sexual identity was to be called into question. Openly homophobic attitudes were normalised to the point of being taken for granted within his working environment. Often, this was accompanied by defamatory comments towards women and racial minorities too. Speculation about a person's sexual identity was also grounds for their ostracism from social or working groups. These inferences of homosexuality rarely needed to be concretely proven for the accusations to be made and the repercussions felt by the targeted individual. However, as well as what might have been seen as 'canteen banter' (which in itself overlooks the potential seriousness of the impacts to the person being victimised) there was also the possibility that a person's career could be affected. Connor cited situations where he witnessed officers being less favourably commented about, who he perceived as being or less frequently recommended for promotion or additional responsibilities. In some cases, he regarded these individuals as being delegated tasks which could be seen as being below their rank for no discernable reason.

If these subtle exclusions were eventually recognised by those affected, such incidents occurred at a time where sexual orientation equality was not in place, therefore there was little they could do by way of remedy. In any case, to claim discrimination on the basis of sexual identity would have meant 'outing' themselves within uncertain circumstances. The option of asking for a transfer was also thwarted as it was unlikely the officer would remain anonymous at a new station. Instead, by the time the person had transferred their new colleagues were already aware of anything they thought they had left behind in the previous station. These were all reasons informing why Connor believed many gay police officers chose to stay silent (or 'closeted') about their sexuality for most of their careers.

Another issue highlighted by Connor was 'closeted' people within his workplace who were at risk of alcoholism. He emphasised how feelings of isolation among security personnel were generally to be expected and some dependence on alcohol normalised during much of the Troubles. However, Connor argued that such issues were more prevalent amongst the men he suspected or knew to be gay while serving in the police. They were marginalised from both heterosexual mainstream and police cultures and often from LGB&T communities:

> At a time when in the police service socialising in general was difficult – there was more alcoholism and we know that among gay men in particular there is more abuse and drinking – a lot of that was down to that isolation and being vulnerable. Those people were trying to live double lives, being very unhappy and also having to deal with the prejudice of being a police officer which, even today is a fairly high–pressured job, but 10 – 15 years ago it was even more so. In that context, if you have a minority within an organisation where they couldn't really be 'out' then yeah, it was difficult.

Although policing cultures are known for generally being separate to wider social groups, suspicious attitudes and the high level of risk incurred from being a police officer in Northern Ireland augmented these issues. Being gay as well had predictable effects on social interaction. During the height of the Troubles, community divisions between unionists and nationalists were evident, but separated from both of these were the police. Describing this as a 'third community', Connor indicated the emergence of this additional divide as being rooted in both suspicion (of the police against society and vice versa), and heightened security measures. As police officers, individuals were vulnerable to being targeted as symbolic casualties of the ongoing conflict. Therefore, much socialising by police officers took place in the company of other members of the police. For those trying to keep their sexual identity secret from friends and family, there was also the added pressure of also keeping it secret from colleagues. For example, care was taken in divulging personal details, or a general distance was kept from others which in some cases impacted on the perception of the officer as a 'loner' or as being odd in some way.

Connor's decision to 'come out' about his true sexuality at work towards the end of his career appeared less disruptive than he had anticipated. This could have been as a result of Connor being established in his vocation and having strong relationships with work colleagues. Also, by this point a swathe of LGB&T legislation had been implemented in Northern Ireland, plus LGB&T visibility was increasing socially in the community. Connor's decision also proved pivotal to the establishment of a support network to other gay police colleagues as took the unprecedented step of setting up a Northern Irish branch of the Gay Police Association (GPA). The GPA was established in the UK in 1990. Connor established a Northern Ireland branch in 2003, forging successful affiliations with the An Garda Siochána (the police service in the Republic of Ireland) and hosting various cross–border events for members.

Establishing a Northern Irish branch of the GPA appeared to elicit notably provocative responses towards Connor from colleagues. Having not experienced any personal maltreatment or harassment previously, this new venture brought with it a raft of emails expressing general disapproval. Resistance to the GPA centred upon what it might do to the image of the police service at such a politically sensitive and transitionary time (moving from the RUC to the PSNI). Connor was accused of wanting to break up the 'police family' and tarnish the masculine image of policing. When it appeared that he was going ahead with the project regardless, the threats became more personal in relation to the potential impact of this action on his career. Nevertheless, the moral obligation he appeared to have taken on board led him to disregard these threats and think about the greater good his actions could have for others:

> I went ahead and sent out an information email with my details for anyone who was interested. I got about 50 – 60 somewhat belligerent emails and a host of phone calls and stupid notes and things saying that I was destroying the police family and all this sort of stuff. I was told by some that it would spell the end of my career if I went ahead with it – so many people tried to stop me. I did it for personal reasons really, I'd seen how people had been treated internally and I was very much minded that that shouldn't happen.

From the response he received, it appears that the fears Connor and others held about the potential negative consequences of their disclosure were not unreasonable. Undeterred, he continued in his endeavours. Expressing the need for constant, stable and non–sexualised LGB&T visibility, Connor recognised that in order to mainstream LGB&T concerns, these needed to be addressed within the workplace (particularly the police environment) first.

He also alluded to previous comments made by interviewees who felt included in community initiatives as a result of tokenism. He stipulated that in some cases this may be true as a result of the speed at which LGB&T developments had occurred and the direct rule situation dominating Northern Irish politics for a significant amount of time:

> I think there's a big problem there; people are ticking boxes, or they're human rights champions and are seen to comply with policy documents and the training and so on. But you can tell the ones there who are thinking, 'here we go again" with another minority group. If it's not a natural change then it's forced on people, and that isn't helping.

Regardless of what equalities or diversity training officers within it may have been subjected to (or undergone voluntarily), if such prejudicial cultures continue to inform the institution as a whole then challenging and addressing homophobia in Northern Irish society remains difficult. Therefore, there is a need to consider the role of criminal justice representatives in this battle and the impact their hostility or aversion to LGB&T communities can have on positive progression. After retiring from the police service, this is exactly what Connor set out to do, taking up a key position in a Northern Irish LGB&T organisation and using his skills to harmonise relationships between LGB&T and policing communities.

Embracing the 'Coming Out' Process

Many interviewees found that once they had begun their process of coming out, the trajectory was largely out of their hands. Despite trying to employ forms of 'damage limitation' – either by requesting that the information be restricted to those told, or that the people told continue to act as if nothing had changed – it was sometimes the case that the anticipated reaction was markedly different to the actual response. For some of the interviewees', whatever fears or apprehensions they harboured about living as an openly lesbian woman or gay man paled into insignificance when they took the plunge and 'came out'. Although sometimes less than positive responses ensued, the information was not always new to those being told. Friends and family members occasionally appeared aware of the interviewees' potential sexual identity long before the interviewee themselves:

> When I finally plucked up the courage to tell my friends – I'd sat them down and got them ready and everything – I couldn't believe their response. I'd been expecting daggers but instead all I got was a kind of 'Yeah, so?' I was shocked. They were shocked it had taken me so long to tell them. (Ryan, 35, gay male)

In recounting experiences such as this, it was still somewhat surprising to the interviewees who had undergone such encounters that they had either 'given the game away' or had somehow been rumbled without them realising prior to their disclosure. It did not occur to them that their painstaking efforts may have been the behaviours that caused others to suspect in the first place, or that a notable difference surrounded them regardless of what measures they took to 'fit in' to heterosexual society.

Making Space to find Oneself

Migration proved to be an important aspect in many lesbians' and gay men's lives, allowing them the physical and mental space needed to come to terms with themselves and the potential hostility they would face as a result of their sexual identity. Finding space to embark on a personal journey of discovery was facilitated through a range of means. Migration occurred both internally, most usually from a rural community to an urban area, and externally, most commonly from Northern Ireland to England or Scotland. Perhaps unsurprisingly, many Catholic interviewees indicated their movements to have been internal while most Protestant interviewees had migrated externally. This was also noted by others among their own social groups or communities:

The Protestants I've met who've come out as gay have shed their religion completely, and if they shed their religion then they really are pariahs in their community. So they have got to get out, get away. I see that over and over again. The gay Protestants get out, they don't stay here, but the Catholics, they can do it [stay]. (Matthew, 56, gay male)

What I've found in Northern Ireland is that a lot of people will migrate internally; if they live in rural areas they'll move to Belfast and very often things like going to university or to work has been a good excuse for people to move away. (Carmel, 43, lesbian)

You had two choices: stay in the closet or get out, and a lot of people got the hell out. If the slightest rumours started at all, that was it: you were gone. (James, 60, gay male)

These patterns of migration can be seen to have altered the social geography of sexuality in Northern Ireland. The internal migration of lesbians and gay men to Belfast led to the development of an LGB&T scene there. This may have increased the isolation for those left behind in rural areas. The higher population density in urban areas afforded many people a greater level of anonymity in their daily interactions, especially in the city centre. In some cases, migrating at a fairly young age for the purposes of university or work allowed interviewees the space to come to terms, not with their sexuality, but with the implications this would have for them upon returning home (if and when they chose to):

I couldn't stay so I left for Liverpool, to find work, and met a girl. I ended up staying there with her for well over a decade. When we broke up I decided that by then I was strong enough to come back [to Northern Ireland]. But I'm glad I got away – I had to. (Nuala, 45, lesbian)

For others, university allowed them to develop a sense of individuality which in turn enabled them to address issues surrounding the negativity they anticipated or encountered towards their sexual identities. Additionally, university offered some of the female interviewees a retreat from family responsibilities and the pressures of marriage for a few years. It was here that they engaged with others who helped shape their sexual identities:

I was brought up in the country so it wasn't until I came to [Queen's] University [Belfast] that I had the freedom to engage with my sexuality for the first time. (Colette, 48, lesbian)

I started at [Queen's] University as a mature student and that's when I had my first relationship; that's when it all started for me. (Philomena: 49, lesbian)

The wider ethno–political conflict also proved to be a useful ruse under which to leave home for places free from the auspices of fear, violence or opportunity. Again England was a popular choice for some as it offered more substantive economic opportunities and better social stability compared to Northern Ireland at the time:

> When I was growing up, the Troubles were at their height and young people were told to stay at home, away from the city, so taking that step [moving to England] was a big thing for me. (John, 49, gay male)

England may have been a preferable option for some, but moving to find sexual freedom was not without its own problems. Ryan recalled a television programme he had watched which had proved memorable to him on two accounts:

> The presenter was talking about homosexuality and it was the first time I'd ever heard it mentioned on the telly. Then they went out onto the street [to interview the public] and there was this one woman they spoke to who said 'Oh no, no we don't have that sort of a thing [homosexuality] over here. England has that kind of thing but you'd not get that here." That's a popular notion among some I'd imagine, that it's an English thing. (Ryan, 35, gay male)

Some interviewees who had migrated out of Northern Ireland had to contend with combating the misguided perception that their homosexuality came as a *result* of moving away. In other words, that something or someone they had encountered had 'made' them that way. This tapped into the notion of homosexuality as being foreign and changeable. Furthermore, it was assumed that when they returned back to Northern Ireland there was no reason for them to be 'like that'. Such perceptions often resulted in the person feeling they could not remain in their home town, instead moving nearer to friends in urban areas of Northern Ireland (or migrating out altogether for another period of time).

In two of the interviewees' cases, the coming out process was more profound. For John, this was a choice made as the result of a life–changing event, whereas for Pat it was because at long last the space had opened up in his life to do so. John described how it was undergoing a heart attack which prompted him to make the decision to live the life he wanted, as life was 'too short'. Not only did he come out, but he also moved back to his rural home town in Northern Ireland as an out gay man. Some members of his community were initially hostile to this change, but he realised in the end that his happiness was more important and it was their issue to deal with. In such cases, interviewees described the process of 'coming out' as one of being 'reborn'; a positive and affirmative action. The following case study of Pat's experiences demonstrates how life–changing this process can be.

Case Study: The Teacher

At 61, Pat was the oldest interviewee in this study. His 'coming out' process was particularly complicated but highlighted many of the challenges faced by other lesbians and gay men in Northern Ireland. Unlike his cohorts, he had abstained from any form of sexual life – heterosexual, homosexual or otherwise – for a significantly lengthy period. Pat believed that this abstinence emanated from the strict religious upbringing he had from a young age which silenced any form of sexuality. His Catholic schooling was so dedicated to suppressing burgeoning heterosexual desires that homosexuality was generally overlooked. As a result, throughout his adolescence he had neither the language nor the knowledge to articulate or understand his feelings. It was not until he was at university that he encountered literature and information on homosexuality. This, he acknowledged, was a major turning point for him, but even then he failed to act on his feelings for many years to come:

> From my 20s to my 40s I sublimated like mad. I was involved in everything that was going on in the town to keep busy … that sort of took the place of any sex life. In fact, it was what eventually led to my breaking down one day.

During this time he worked as a teacher. This had a huge impact on his ability to explore or express his sexual identity. Many teachers in Northern Ireland were regulated by moral and legal conservatism, meaning that they had less freedom to discuss issues surrounding homosexuality than their contemporaries working in Great Britain. The negativity surrounding homosexuality in Northern Ireland in the 1970s, fuelled by the 'Sodomy' campaign, conflated homosexual identities with paedophilic practices. In 1986, just four years after homosexuality was decriminalised in Northern Ireland, the Conservative government enacted section 28. This curbed local authorities from 'promoting a homosexual lifestyle' but was vague enough to make people unsure of what it meant in practice. As a result, section 28 was translated into an increasingly homophobic environment in schools whereby homosexuality was not discussed (or at least not in favourable terms) and LGB&T teachers were construed as a potential threat to children. In Northern Ireland, there was little need to actively implement this policy given the already oppressive climate towards homosexuality in society.

It was this same climate which led Pat to relinquish any thoughts of engaging in an active sexual relationship for most of his working life. Instead, he described his activities in political and grass–roots movements in Northern Ireland as a 'substitute' for this part of his life, as well as a much needed distraction. Eventually, a traumatic event on a boat whereby he feared for his life convinced him to 'come out' in his forties. He perceived this event as the beginning of a new life as opposed to getting his old one back:

> [Coming out] is such a fantastic relief. Coming out is literally like a rebirth. It's
> the nearest thing in our world to the religious experience of being reborn. It's as
> world shattering and as fantastic as that.

His enthusiasm was tainted to some degree at the time by the fears which had held
him back in Northern Ireland. As a result, he began this new life by visiting the
gay friendly bars and clubs in Dublin. This allowed him to build up his confidence
and sexual experience while remaining relatively anonymous. This was important
to him as he felt the first few times he accessed such places, he was not 'doing it
right' as few people initially came to talk to him. His frequent trips to Dublin were
mirrored by many of the men he met there who held similar fears with regards
to accessing gay friendly bars in Belfast. These largely centred on being seen by
people they knew and incurring problems at work or at home. Pat had relatives in
Dublin, giving him a ready–made excuse for his increasingly frequent trips down.
Recalling one such trip, he indicates both his joy at this new lease of life and his
sadness at being unable to share it with those close to him:

> One time I was [in Dublin] and I'd met this wonderful man and I went back to
> his and it felt so *right*, and I knew then that this was right, this was me and it
> was all going to be ok. He wanted me to stay the night but I couldn't, I had to go
> back [to his relatives], which I did. In the morning it was like my whole life had
> changed through that one fantastic experience, but I could say nothing of it. No
> one was aware of this amazing thing that had happened to me. (His emphasis)

Pat found his overall journey of discovery enlightening and positive, despite the
late point in his life at which it came. It is not unusual for the 'rebirth' he spoke
of to involve physical alterations to mark the significant change that has occurred.
In Pat's case, however, these alterations were so extensive and visual that it was
almost like shedding a skin:

> Overnight I changed so radically that people didn't recognise who I was. Up
> until that time I'd taught for 20 years and I was the classic looking school
> teacher: long hair, glasses, tweed, trousers, shirt and tie with chalk everywhere,
> and overnight I got rid of the hair and beard, swopped the glasses for lenses,
> wore t-shirts, and nobody knew who the hell I was!

For Pat, this transformation signalled more than just his 'coming out' but his move
towards active engagement in LGB&T politics in Northern Ireland, around the
time of the decriminalisation decision. He realised that to be involved in such
a venture meant that he may be exposed to hostility. Indeed, after one event he
attended in which he was promoting the first gay pride event, his appearance on
television as part of the audience at the event led to a particularly tense interaction
with his father who had seen the programme and voiced his disapproval. Although
this was a difficult issue for Pat to reconcile, he felt that at that point in his life

he had personally come to a point whereby he was no longer prepared to hide his sexuality. Instead, he had reached a point where he could emotionally and mentally deal with the social repercussions of living as an openly gay man in Northern Ireland. Pat believed that the progress he others had made in making spaces for people to come out was of vital importance to those using those spaces. Yet this was an issue still largely misunderstood by many in society not privy to the difficulties faced in undergoing this process:

> You start coming out to yourself and the thing is it takes a long while for you to accept that you're going to have to put up with what society's going to throw at you. … Even now [research] will say that children are struggling with their sexuality, they're not struggling with their sexuality at all; they're struggling with society's attitude towards their sexuality, which is a totally different matter.

Pat felt that in order for attitudes to change in Northern Ireland so that people of any age coming out in contemporary society did not have to undergo such hardships, lesbian and gay visibility was paramount. He believed one of the best ways to go about this was through the increasingly popular gay pride parade, which he had been involved in organising from its origin. He claimed that had such an event been present when he was struggling with his sexuality, he may have had the courage to begin his coming out process earlier, supported by others whom he knew to be undergoing similar challenges. In effect, this would have offset the protracted periods of loneliness he described feeling and his delayed coming out process. These feelings are perhaps why he remains so active in contemporary LGB&T politics in Northern Ireland.

This need for philanthropy, reciprocity and active engagement with the burgeoning LGB&T community and voluntary sector was echoed by several of the interviewees who felt that their experiences could benefit others and show that being lesbian or gay in Northern Ireland is not 'wrong'. In effect, their efforts were designed to ensure others might not have to experience the isolation, loneliness, fear and ostracism that these interviewees went through. Either through virtue of growing up in Northern Ireland or being subjected to hostility on the basis of an inherent trait, they had recognised that advancing lesbian and gay visibility, equality and freedoms was a political battle which must be played out in full view of society, bringing on board as many diverse forms of identity as possible.

Summary

The positivity enveloping several of the coming out stories depicted in this chapter indicates the almost pious nature of this experience. Perhaps this is to be expected given the wider environment and exposure to Biblical literalism many lesbians and gay men have absorbed over the years. The experiences of rebirth, renewal and revival depicted by some LGB&T people with regards to their coming out processes mirror narratives of born again Christians. In this sense, such similarities ought to be the grounds for greater understanding, compassion and integration. Perhaps if members of the religious right were more willing to engage with members of LGB&T communities, they too would see the commonalities in both groups' experiences of discovering one's true identity or calling.

The significant progress and developments achieved by LGB&T activists, organisations and communities in Northern Ireland would suggest that there are different experiences surrounding lesbians' and gay men's coming out processes in contemporary society. It would be disingenuous to suggest that coming out is 'easier' or 'harder' for people living in Northern Ireland now, but there are still factors impacting on these experiences which need to be explored, and responded to, in the mainstream. Homophobia is not a lesbian or gay issue. It is also not necessarily an inherent characteristic, but rather founded upon social constructions, directions and insinuations. Therefore, it appears vital that lesbians and gay men are able to live openly (if they so wish) in all aspects of their lives in order to dispel harmful misconceptions and to challenge LGB&T invisibility. Although all of the interviewees involved in this research were 'out' about their sexual identities, to varying degrees, there are still many lesbians and gay men living in Northern Ireland who are yet to take this step or for whom such a decision is unthinkable. Nonetheless, in many people's cases the choice may already have been made for them by virtue of their largely hostile surroundings. For others, it may take longer to dispel the negative feelings which they have come to affiliate with their sexual identities.

In the concluding chapter, a summary of the key issues derived from the overall analysis into homophobia revisits the key findings taken from the lesbian and gay narratives explored throughout this book. These are supplemented with recommendations for adopting a more inclusive attitude towards lesbians and gay men in Northern Ireland, as well as areas identified for future research.

Conclusion

This exploration into Northern Irish lesbians' and gay men's experiences of prejudice and victimisation has been driven by the objective of discovering the ways in which homophobia has been informed and sustained in Northern Ireland. Examinations of the lesbian and gay interviewees' narratives have shed light on the complex decisions and choices confronting those who were marginalised as a result of their sexuality. It is hoped that by demonstrating these life stories, culturally specific understandings of homophobia in Northern Ireland will inform culturally relevant strategies to address this destructive and misguided form of prejudice.

The preceding chapters have assessed homophobia in a manner which illustrates Thompson's (1997) model of personal, cultural and structural oppression. At the personal level, an individual's prejudice is assessed in relation to wider cultural and structural levels. Cultural levels of oppression related to the shared values or commonalities evident about a particular group or idea. Structural levels of oppression indicate how prejudice may be woven into the fabric of society through institutions (for example, religious, social or governmental) which support both cultural norms and personal beliefs. In order to successfully identify, confront and seek to change hostile perceptions about identities or groups of people affiliated to these, all three levels must be addressed. Bearing that in mind, this concluding chapter highlights how homophobia can be challenged using political imperatives, cultural conservatism and community initiatives. A final though is given to recognising the significant achievements made by LGB&T communities in Northern Ireland and the knowledge, expertise and experience they can provide to those equally invested in harmonising what has traditionally been a deeply divided society.

Political Imperatives

At the time of writing, Northern Ireland had just elected its fourth power–sharing Assembly, historically the first one to occur after a full term of devolved government. This was perhaps more significant as it came weeks after the murder of PC Ronan Kerr, symbolically targeted by Republican dissidents for being a Catholic officer in the PSNI. The general success of the power–sharing Assembly at the polls aims to send out the message that Northern Ireland is not slipping back to the 'dark days' of the conflict. However, there are some politicians who seem to find it harder to move on: Ulster Unionist leader Tom Elliott in particular, having called Sinn Féin 'scum' during the election count (*Belfast Telegraph* 2011).

Although widely denounced among political and social commentators, it would appear that not every public figure in Northern Ireland is prepared to move on to a more progressive, integrated future.

Northern Ireland's politically sensitive situation may continue to prevent people in positions of power from being held accountable for their condemnation of homosexuality and of lesbians and gay men. However, comparable sentiments have been challenged elsewhere in the UK under similar legislation. In many cases, the attitudes displayed closely mirrored those illustrated in Northern Ireland. In England, Conservative councillor Peter Willows was found guilty of breaching the Public Order Act 1986 for equating gay people with paedophiles (*BBC News* 2006). In Bournemouth, evangelist Harry Hammond was charged under s.5 of the Public Order Act 1986 for brandishing a large double–sided sign which read 'Stop Immorality', 'Stop Homosexuality' and 'Stop Lesbianism' on each side provoking an angry reaction from some passers–by (*Pink News* 2006). In Scotland, New York preacher Shawn Holes was charged with uttering homophobic and sectarian remarks and fined £1000 for stating that 'Homosexuals are deserving of the wrath of God, and so are all other sinners, and they are going to a place called hell' (Hennessey 2010). Homophobia has been challenged in several cases in Europe too. In France, politician Christian Vanneste was the first person to be convicted under French anti–homophobia laws for his comments on the "endangerment" factor of homosexuals (Belien 2007). In Sweden, the legislation has been enforced on numerous occasions, including against a preacher who was considered to be denigrating homosexuality to an unacceptable level in sermons.[1]

There is a need for a clear message from the wider political leadership of Northern Irish society that the prejudicial attitudes of the few are not necessarily indicative of the wider population. If prominent public figures and politicians are allowed to continue to express prejudicial views with impunity, then it both reinforces the marginalised status of lesbians and gay men as not fully integrated citizens and undermines the effectiveness of supposed 'equality' legislation. Whilst the main nationalist and unionist parties continue to engage in unhelpful deviations, other parties are indicating their willingness to diversify in terms of representation and inclusion. Extending this to lesbians and gay men may prove advantageous in combating homophobia in Northern Ireland from the same political platform as those who condone it. In 2010, Andrew Muir joined the Alliance Party as a Councillor and an openly gay man. This is a small but positive step; as there are currently no openly gay MLAs or MPs in Northern Ireland, the election of Cllr Muir is a vital move in the right direction. Combating the ideologies that inform homophobia in Northern Ireland would also benefit from similar increases in visible role models in the popular media. This may be a powerful way of refuting stereotypes that to be lesbian or gay is not something 'natural' to Northern Ireland, or that lesbians and gay men are 'outsiders'.

---

1   Supreme Court of Sweden, ruling 29 November 2005 in case no. B 1050–05

Cultural Conservatism

The ramifications of personal homophobia and cultural heterosexism reach further than acts of interpersonal victimisation and violence. Lesbians and gay men may be at a disadvantage in other areas of their lives as a result of sexual prejudice. This is an issue slowly coming to the fore in Northern Ireland through research instigated by the enactment of equality laws and the need for good relations and best practice by statutory bodies to all members of society. The Northern Ireland Human Rights Commission highlighted the impact of institutionalised heterosexism on Northern Irish lesbian and gay youth as affecting their interaction with the educational and health sectors (Lourdes 2003). More specifically, the impact of homophobia on the mental and physical health of young gay men (White 1998, Toner and McIlrath 2000) and lesbian women (Quiery 2002, 2007) highlighted how members of LGB&T communities take on board the hostility of their wider environments but may feel ostracised from mainstream healthcare services.

Negotiating sexuality and religion in Northern Ireland remains an issue for many lesbians and gay men who may feel ostracised by their church or community. Some have come to terms with this by separating out religion from spirituality, recognising their faith as being valid despite the opposition demonstrated to them by their community or faith leaders. This may be experienced differently according to whether the person has been raised in a Protestant or Catholic community. Whilst the Protestant community tend to be stricter about denigrating the 'homosexual lifestyle', Northern Irish Catholics appear more flexible about what would and would not be overlooked with regards to sexuality. As such, the general consensus remains that lesbians and gay men from Catholic backgrounds seem more at ease with their sexualities than those from Protestant backgrounds. Whilst this proves useful for helping more lesbians and gay men from Catholic backgrounds challenge any negativity they may have experienced and undergo their 'coming out' processes, there is a need to recognise the specific challenges some Protestant lesbians and gay men may be experiencing.

More input from the key stakeholders in anti-homophobia and anti-hate crime initiatives, namely the lesbians and gay men themselves, is needed to give a more holistic perspective of how sexual minority prejudice is affecting people in Northern Ireland. This could start with an examination of how, when and why people choose to/not to report homophobic incidents and crimes and the impact this may have on other facets of lesbian and gay lives. Studies into the life course of hate crime reported through the Northern Irish criminal justice system may aid understanding around the various problems highlighted lesbians and gay men. Whilst several reports illustrated within this analysis outline the reasons why some Northern Irish lesbians and gay men refuse to take the initial step of reporting their experience to the police, existing research does not specifically demonstrate what happens to those incidents which are reported. Therefore, future research may be productive in showing particular problems with the system or the attitudes of those working within it. Members of LGB&T communities are best placed through their experiences to demonstrate where harms towards lesbians and gay men are currently being propagated and imparted and how best this can be engaged with and reduced.

Community Interventions

Further research into interventions designed to reduce hate crimes would also be of benefit to Northern Irish lesbians and gay men. Understanding the perspectives of others has underlined many community initiatives to reduce criminality in Northern Ireland. For example, restorative justice policies have proved to be a popular and productive means of addressing criminality with a view to confronting the causes of criminal acts as well as their consequences. For crimes of an interpersonal nature, where the victim has been targeted on the basis of their identity or what he or she is seen to represent, restorative justice policies can provide a learning opportunity for both the victim and the perpetrator to understand and express deeply held viewpoints or stereotypes about one another (Sherman and Strang 2007). Restorative justice studies conducted in Western societies have shown reductions in recidivism and victims' post–traumatic stress symptoms as well as punishment costs incurred whilst also highlighting the benefits for addressing crimes with discernable victims (Sherman and Strang 2007). While education prior to incidences of homophobia is of use, so too may be education after the event, to help the offender understand their own prejudices.

Northern Ireland's success in transitioning from a conflict–torn society to one promoting restorative justice has been aided by the interactions between members of different communities with a shared vision for the future (McEvoy and Mika 2002). A large part of this has been the sharing of truths and stories which have helped different members of society understand what others have experienced (McEvoy, 2006). A similar platform of 'truth and reconciliation' may be of benefit to members of LGB&T communities who feel that they have important stories to share within this context. However, as of yet, these communities have not had this opportunity to put forth their perspectives in a recognised and publicised manner. These stories may be of particular importance if there is, as some interviewees suggested, a shift in targets of violence for economic or political reasons in some communities. If communities are truly to move towards, and remain, within a 'post–conflict' framework, then all facets and identities must be included so as to recognise the true diversity of contemporary societies.

Perhaps what is most compelling is the threat LGB&T communities pose to Northern Irish politicians. Political sensitivity to identity difference has underpinned many major decisions regarding Northern Ireland. However, the advances made by Northern Irish LGB&T communities and organisations, both domestically and as a result of changes imposed by the British government, have indicated that the traditional divides seen as in need of careful consideration do not necessarily permeate all facets of social life. In other words, the way in which

LGB&T communities represent, and are representative of, cross–community members working together for a greater good (such as civil rights, equality, recognition, visibility, access to goods and services and so forth) indicate Northern Ireland's potential.

Furthermore, lesbians and gay men in Northern Ireland lived through the same Troubles as others, yet displayed an ability to engage with diversity in order to make changes for the better. They have shown that people do not necessarily have to be labelled, interacted with or divided along identity lines. Certainly, many activists within the LGB&T community voluntary sector have recognised that the inclusivity they strive for is a message which needs to be heard by the mainstream, not minority groups. Members of the LGB&T community have been able to organise from a grass–roots level, with minimal funding, support, advertisement and resources to become a recognised part of Northern Irish society over the past four decades. If this is the positive, inclusive vision the 'new' Northern Ireland is striving for, then perhaps it is the politicians who should be asking Northern Irish lesbians and gay men for lessons on acceptance, integration and understanding.

Bibliography

Anon. 2008. *Threads: Stories of Lesbian Life in Northern Ireland in the 1970's and 1980's* Belfast: Nova.

Association of Chief Police Officers (ACPO) 2005. *Hate Crime: Delivering A Quality Service Good Practice and Tactical Guidance* [Online]. Available at: http://www.acpo.police.uk/asp/policies/Data/Hate%20Crime.pdf [accessed: 10 April 2008].

Allen, D. and Oleson, T. 1999. Shame and internalized homophobia in gay men. *Journal of Homosexuality,* 37(3), 33 –43.

Amstutz, M. 2004. *The Healing of Nations: The Promise and Limitations of Political Forgiveness.* Oxford: Rowman and Littlefield Publishers.

Banks, K. 1997. The 'Homosexual Panic" Defence in Canadian Criminal Law. *Criminal Reports* (5th series) 371.

Bartlett, P 2007. Killing gay men: 1976 – 2001. *British Journal of Criminology,* 47(4), 573 – 595.

BBC News. 2004a. *Gay Men Targeted in Attacks.* [Online 19 May]. Available at: http://news.bbc.co.uk/1/hi/northern_ireland/3728345.stm [accessed 15 March 2011].

BBC News. 2004b. *Gay–Bashing' Killers Jailed.* [Online 1 July]. Available at: http://news.bbc.co.uk/1/hi/northern_ireland/3856839.stm [accessed 15 March 2011].

BBC News. 2004c *Gay Man Bitten in Attack.* [Online 20 July]. Available at: http://news.bbc.co.uk/1/hi/northern_ireland/3910109.stm [accessed 15 March 2011].

BBC News. 2005. *DUP Stay Tight–Lipped Over Berry.* [Online 3 May]. Available at: http://news.bbc.co.uk/1/hi/uk_politics/vote_2005/northern_ireland/4509109.stm [accessed 15 March 2011].

BBC News. 2006. *'Gay Attack' Victim May Lose Eye.* [Online 31 January]. Available at: http://news.bbc.co.uk/1/hi/northern_ireland/4664954.stm [accessed 15 March 2011].

BBC News. 2008. *No Brown Rebuke Over Gay Comment.* [Online 14 August]. Available at: http://news.bbc.co.uk/1/hi/northern_ireland/7560747.stm [accessed 15 March 2011]._

BBC News. 2009. *NI Tops Creationist Belief Survey.* [Online 2 March]. Available at: http://news.bbc.co.uk/1/hi/northern_ireland/7919180.stm [accessed 15 March 2011].

BBC News. 2009a. *Nine Held over Sectarian Murder.* 26 May. Available at: http://news.bbc.co.uk/1/hi/northern_ireland/foyle_and_west/8067742.stm [accessed 15 March 2011].

Conrad, K. 2004. *Locked in the Family Cell: Gender, Sexuality, and Political Agency in Irish National Discourse.* Wisconsin: University of Wisconsin Press.

Cooper, D. 1995. *Power in Struggle: Feminism, Sexuality and the State.* New York: New York University Press.

Corteen, K. 2002. Lesbian safety talk: problematizing definitions and experiences of violence, sexuality and space. *Sexualities,* 5(3), 259 – 280.

CPS. 2008. *Hate Crime Report.* [Online] Available at: http://www.cps.gov.uk/publications/docs/CPS_hate_crime_report_2008.pdf [accessed 15 March 2011].

Croall, H. 1998. *Crime and Society in Britain.* London: Longman.

Craig, K. 2002. Examining hate–motivated aggression: A review of the social psychological literature on hate crimes as a distinct form of aggression. *Aggression and Violent Behaviour,* 7(1), 85 – 101.

Cull, M., Platzer, H. and Ballock, S. 2006. *Out on My Own: Understanding the Experiences and Needs of Homeless Lesbian, Gay, Bisexual and Transgender Youth.* Brighton: Health and Social Policy Research Centre, University of Brighton.

D'Augelli, A. and Grossman, A. 2001. Disclosure of sexual orientation, victimization, and mental health among lesbian, gay, and bisexual older adults. *Journal of Interpersonal Violence,* 16(10), 1008–1027.

D'Emilio, J. 1992. *Making Trouble: Essays on Gay History, Politics, and the University.* New York: Routledge.

Davies, P. 1992. The role of disclosure in coming out among gay men, in *Modern Homosexualities: Fragments Of Lesbian And Gay Experience,* edited by K. Plummer. London: Routledge.

De Cecco, J. and Elia, J. 1993. *If You Seduce a Straight Person, Can You Make Them Gay?: Issues in Biological Essentialism Versus Social Constructionism in Gay and Lesbian Identities.* New York: The Haworth Press.

Deeney. D. 2011. *Fundamentalist Clerics Furious as Gay Sauna, The Cage, Opens in Derry.* [Online 16 February]. Available at: http://www.belfasttelegraph.co.uk/news/local–national/northern–ireland/fundamentalist–clerics–furious–as–gay–sauna–the–cage–opens–in–derry–15085691.html [accessed 15 March 2011].

Dillon, M. 1999. *The Dirty War: Covert Strategies and Tactics Used in Political Conflicts.* New York: Routledge.

Ditton, J., Farrall, S., Bannister, J. and Gilchrist, E. 2000. Crime surveys and the measurement problem: fear of crime, in *Doing Criminological Research,* edited by V. Jupp, P. Davies and P. Francis. London: Sage.

Dudgeon, J. 1980. *Gay Rights in Northern Ireland: A Report.* Public Records Office Northern Ireland, Ref no D/3762/1/1/11.

Dudgeon, J. 2002. *Roger Casement: The Black Diaries – With a Study of His Background, Sexuality and Irish Political Life.* Belfast: Belfast Press.

Dudgeon, J. 2005. *Lisburn's Ban on 'Gay Marriages'*, [Online] Available at: http://www.sluggerotoole.com/archives/2005/07/jeff_dudgeon_wi.php [accessed 15 March 2011].

Duggan, M. 2010a. The Politics of Pride: Representing Relegated Sexual Identities in Northern Ireland. *Northern Ireland Legal Quarterly*, 61(2), 163–78.

Duggan, M. 2010b. Homophobic Hate Crime in Northern Ireland, in *Hate Crime: Concepts, Policy, Future Directions*, edited by N. Chakraborti. Devon: Willan.

Duggan, M. 2008a. Theorising Homophobic Violence in Northern Ireland. *Papers from the British Society of Criminology Conference*, 8 [Online] Available at: http://www.britsoccrim.org/v8.htm [accessed 15 March 2011].

Duggan, M. 2008b. Hidden challenges facing lesbian women in Northern Ireland. *Women's News.* Issue 167, (May/June), Belfast.

Duggan, M. 2008c. Lesbian parenting in Northern Ireland. *Women's News.* Issue 168, (July/August), Belfast.

Duggan, M. 2008d. Gay pride, Northern Ireland Style. *Women's News,* Issue 168, (July/August), Belfast.

Duggan, M. 2008e. Hate crime in the home. *Women's News,* Issue 169, (September/October), Belfast.

Equality Commission Northern Ireland. 2009. *Equality Awareness Survey 2008.* [Online] Available at: http://www.equalityni.org/archive/pdf/ECSurvey2008.pdf [accessed 15 March 2011].

Faraday, A. and Plummer, K. 1979. Doing life histories. *Sociological Review.* 27(4)

Fay, M., Morrissey, M. and Smyth, M. 1999. *Northern Ireland's Troubles: The Human Costs.* London: Pluto Press.

Fegan, E. and Rebouche, R. 2003. Northern Ireland's abortion law: The morality of silence and the censure of agency. *Feminist Legal Studies.* 11(3), 221–254.

Feldman, A. 1991. *Formations of Violence: The Narrative of the Body and Political Terror in Northern Ireland.* Chicago: University of Chicago Press.

Foucault, M. 1976. *The History of Sexuality.* London: Penguin Books.

Fuss, D. 1989. *Essentially Speaking: Feminism, Nature and Difference.* New York: Routledge.

Gay Belfast. 2005. *Gay Pride, Another Successful Year.* [Online 7 August]. Available at: http://www.gaybelfast.net/fiveaug.htm [accessed 15 March 2011].

Goodey, J. 2005. *Victims and Victimology: Research, Policy and Practice.* Essex: Pearson Education.

Gordon, D. 2009. No Assembly Sanctions over MP's Gay Remarks. *Belfast Telegraph,* [Online 4 July]. Available at: http://www.belfasttelegraph.co.uk/news/local–national/no–assembly–sanctions–over–mprsquos–gay–remarks–14382928.html [accessed 15 March 2011].

Green, J. 2010. Anti–Gay Group to Protest Outside Christian Convention. *Pink News,* [Online 17 February]. Available at: http://www.pinknews.co.uk/2010/02/17/anti–gay–cure–group–to–protest–outside–christian–convention/ [accessed 20 May 2011].

Greer, C. 2003. *Sex Crime and the Media: Sex Offending and the Press in a Divided Society. Devon*: Willan.

Grew, T. 2008. Interview: David Heath on Incitement to Homophobic Hatred. *Pink News* [Online 3 January]. Available at: http://www.pinknews.co.uk/news/articles/2005–6446.html [accessed 15 March 2011].

Grove, V. 2005. Latest victim of a homophobia that London thought it had left behind. *The Times.* [Online 22 October]. Available at: http://www.timesonline.co.uk/tol/news/uk/article581284.ece [accessed 15 March 2011].

Hall, N. 2005. *Hate Crime.* Devon: Willan Publishing.

Hall, S., Critcher, C., Jefferson, T., Clarke, J. and Roberts, B. 1978. *Policing the Crisis: Mugging, the State and Law and Order.* New York: Holmes and Meier Publishers.

Hanafin, P. 2000. Rewriting desire: the construction of sexual identity in literary and legal discourse in postcolonial Ireland, in *Sexuality in the Legal Arena*, edited by C. Stychin and D. Herman. London: Athlone Press.

Hayes, B. and McAllister, I. 2001. Sowing dragon's teeth: public support for political violence and paramilitarism in Northern Ireland. *Political Studies.* 49, 901–922.

Henry, L. 2008. Robinson: no regrets over gay comments. *Belfast Telegraph*, [Online 10 June]. Available at: http://www.belfasttelegraph.co.uk/news/local–national/robinson–no–regrets–over–gay–comments–13507741.html [accessed 15 March 2011].

Hennessy, M. 2010. Street Preacher Fined for 'Homosexuals Going to Hell" Remark. *The Irish Times,* [Online 31 March]. Available at: http://www.irishtimes.com/newspaper/world/2010/0331/1224267399164.html [accessed 15 March 2011].

Herek, G. 1992. The social context of hate crimes: notes on cultural heterosexism, in *Hate Crimes: Confronting Violence against Lesbians and Gay Men,* edited by G. Herek and K. Berrill. London: Sage.

Herek, G.M. 2004. Beyond "homophobia": Thinking about sexual stigma and prejudice in the twenty–first century. *Sexuality Research and Social Policy,* 1(2), 6–24.

Herek, G. and Berrill, K. 1992. *Hate Crimes: Confronting Violence against Lesbians and Gay Men.* London: Sage.

Hillyard, P. 1985. Popular justice in Northern Ireland: continuities and change, in *Research in Law Deviance and Social Control*, edited by S. Spitzer and A.T. Scull. London: Jai Press.

Home Office and Scottish Home Department. 1957. *Report of the Committee on Homosexual Offences and Prostitution.* London: HMSO.

Howe, A. 1997. More folk provoke their own demise (revisiting the provocation defence debate courtesy of the homosexual advance defence). *Sydney Law Review.* 19, 366–384.

Hubbard, P. 2001. Sex zones: intimacy, citizenship and public space. *Sexualities,* 4(1), 51 – 71.

Hyde, H. M. 1955. *United in Crime.* London: William Heinemann.

Iganski, P. 2008. *Hate Crime and the City*. Bristol: The Policy Press.

Impartial Reporter. 2004. *Transsexuals and gays are perverts, says DUP Councillor*. [Online 19 February]. Available at: http://www.impartialreporter. com/archive/2004_02_19/news/story7514.html [accessed 15 March 2011].

Hall, I. 2007. Offensive march should be banned. *Irish News*. [Online 7 August]. Available at: http://www.irishnews.com/searchlog. asp?reason=denied_empty&script_name=/pageacc.asp&path_info=/pageacc. asp&tser1=ser&sid=439075 [accessed 15 March 2011].

Jackson, P. 2005. Gay Pride Weathers Belfast Storm. *BBC News.* [Online 6 August]. Available at: http://news.bbc.co.uk/2/hi/uk_news/northern_ireland/4739815. stm [accessed 15 March 2011].

Janoff, D. 2005. *Pink Blood: Homophobic Violence in Canada.* Toronto: University of Toronto Press.

Jarman, N. and Bryan, D. 1996. *Parade and Protest: A Discussion of Parading Disputes in Northern Ireland.* Coleraine: University of Ulster.

Jacobs, J. and Potter, K. 1998. *Hate Crimes: Criminal Law and Identity Politics* New York: Open University Press.

Jarman, N. and Tennant, A. 2003. *An Acceptable Prejudice? Homophobic Violence and Harassment in Northern Ireland.* Belfast: Institute for Conflict Research.

Jay, K. 1999. *Tales of the Lavender Menace.* New York: Basic Books.

Jeffrey–Poulter, S. 1991. *Peers, Queers, and Commons: The Struggle for Gay Law Reform from 1950 to the Present.* London: Routledge.

John, S. and Patrick, A. 1999. *Poverty and Social Exclusion of Lesbians and Gay Men in Glasgow.* Glasgow: Women's Library.

Johnston, L. 2004. *Queering Tourism: Paradoxical Performances at Gay Pride Parades.* London: Routledge.

Johnston, P. 1995. 'More than ordinary men gone wrong": can the law know the gay subject? *Melbourne University Law Review.* 20(1), 1152 – 1191.

Kelly, L. 1988. *Surviving Sexual Violence.* Minneapolis: University of Minnesota Press.

Kinsey, A., Pomeroy, W. and Marin, C. 1948. *Sexual Behaviour in the Human Male.* Philadelphia: Saunders.

Kinsman, G. 1996. *The Regulation of Desire: Homo and Hetero Sexualities.* Montreal: Black Rose Books.

Kitchin, R. 2002. Sexing the city: the sexual production of non–heterosexual space in Belfast, Manchester and San Francisco. *City.* 6(2), 205 – 218.

Kitchin, R. and Lysaght, K. 2003. Heterosexism and the geographies of everyday life in Belfast, Northern Ireland. *Environment and Planning A*. 35(3), 489–510.

Kitchin, R. and Lysaght, K. 2004. Sexual citizenship in Belfast, Northern Ireland. *Gender, Place & Culture*, 11(1), 83–10.

Kitzinger, C. 1987. *The Social Construction of Lesbianism.* London: Sage.

Kitzinger, C. 1997. Lesbian and gay psychology: A critical analysis, in *Critical Psychology: An Introduction*, edited by D. Fox and I. Prilleltensky. Thousand Oaks, CA, US: Sage Publications.

Knox, C. 2002. 'See no evil, hear no evil': insidious paramilitary violence in Northern

Ireland. *British Journal of Criminology*. 42(1), 164–185.

LASI (Lesbian Advocacy Services Initiative) 2006. *LASI Ipsos Mori Survey*. [Online] Ballymena: LASI. Available at: http://www.lasionline.org/research. htm [accessed 15 March 2011].

Loudes, C. 2003. *Learning to Grow Up: The Multiple Identities of Young Lesbians, Gay Men and Bisexual People in Northern Ireland*. Belfast: Northern Ireland Human Rights Commission.

Lunney, A. 2003. Provocation and 'homosexual' advance: masculinized subjects as threat, masculinised subjects under threat. *Social and Legal Studies*, 12(3), 311–333.

Martin, A.K. 1997. The practice of identity and an Irish sense of place. *Gender, Place and Culture – A Journal of Feminist Geography,* 4(1), 89–114.

Mason, G. and Palmer, A. 1996. *Queer Bashing: A National Survey of Hate Crimes against Lesbians and Gay Men.* London: Stonewall.

Mason, G. 1993. *Violence Against Lesbians and Gay Men.* Sydney: Duncan Chappell.

Mason, G. 1997. "Heterosexed violence: typicality and ambiguity" in *Homophobic Violence* edited by G. Mason and S Tomsen. Sidney: The Hawkins Press.

Mason, G. 2005a. Hate crime and the image of the stranger. *British Journal of Criminology,* 45(6), 837–859.

Mason, G. 2005b. Being hated: stranger or familiar? *Social and Legal Studies: An International Journal.* 14(4), 585–605.

Mason, G. and Tomsen, S. 1997. *Homophobic Violence.* Sydney: The Hawkins Press.

Mason, G. and Tomsen, S. 2001. Engendering homophobia: violence, sexuality and gender conformity. *Journal of Sociology*, 37(3), 257–273.

McCafferty, N. 2004. *Just Call Me Nell.* London: Penguin.

McClengahan, B. 1994. Letter from a gay republican: H–Block 5, in *Lesbian and Gay Visions of Ireland,* edited by I. O'Carroll and E. Collins. London: Cassell.

McDermott, M. 2011. *Through our Eyes: Experiences of Lesbian, Gay and Bisexual People in the Workplace.* [Online] The Rainbow Project: Belfast Available at: http://www.rainbow–project.org/assets/publications/TOE_mcd. pdf [accessed 15 March 2011].

McDonald, H. 2008. Gay UDA gunman: 'I hid my true self'. *The Guardian,* [Online 5 October]. Available at: http://www.guardian.co.uk/uk/2008/oct/05/ northernireland.gayrights [accessed 15 March 2011].

McDonald, H. 2010. Northern Ireland minister calls on Ulster Museum to promote creationism. *Belfast Telegraph*, [Online 26 May]. Available at: http://

www.guardian.co.uk/uk/2010/may/26/northern–ireland–ulster–museum–creationism [accessed 15 March 2011].

McEvoy, K. 2001. *Paramilitary Imprisonment in Northern Ireland: Resistance, Management and Release.* Oxford: Oxford University Press.

McIntosh, M. 1968. The Homosexual Role. *Social Problems,* 16(2), 182 – 192.

McKittrick, D. 1977. Paisley's power switched off. *The Irish Times,* [Online 20 October]. Available at: http://www.irishtimes.com/newspaper/archive/1977/1020/Pg007.html#Ar00702:2070E82811412471B426D1D1 19A13A21D19418C1921BC1AF2B51B42DD1D11E12E12012F627056B 29258024413D3191962EA1B532C1D129F0EA3491442771B42AC1D1-1893A61B33BB_[accessed 15 March 2011].

McKittrick, D. and McVea, D. 2001. *Making Sense of the Troubles.* Belfast: Blackstaff Press.

McKittrick, J., Kelters, S., Feeney, B. and Thornton, C. 1999. *Lost Lives: The Stories of the Men, Women and Children Who Died Through the Northern Ireland Troubles.* London: Mainstream Publishing.

McLoughlin, M. 1996. Crystal or glass?: A review of Dudgeon v. United Kingdom on the fifteenth anniversary of the decision. *Murdoch University Electronic Journal of Law,* 3(4) (Dec).

McNamee, H. 2006. *Out on Your Own: An Examination of the Mental Health of Young Same Sex Attracted Men.* Belfast: Rainbow Project.

Mehra, B. Merkel, C. and Bishop, A. 2004. The internet for empowerment of minority and marginalized users. *New Media and Society,* 6(6), 781–802.

Metro Eireann. 2007. *DUP slams gay parade over 'Jesus is a fag' sign.* [Online 16 August]. Available at: http://metroeireann.com/article/dup–slams–gay–parade–over–jesus,487_[accessed 15 March 2011].

Meyer, D. 2008. 'The intersection of gender and sexuality: homophobic violence as a social control mechanism' Paper presented at the annual meeting of the American Sociological Association Annual Meeting, Boston, MA, [Online 31 July]. Available at: http://www.allacademic.com/meta/p242094_index.html [accessed 15 March 2011].

Mison, R. 1992. Homophobia in manslaughter: the homosexual advance as insufficient provocation. *California Law Review,* 80, 133–161.

Mitchell, C. 2006. *Religion, Identity and Politics in Northern Ireland: Boundaries of Belonging and Belief.* Aldershot: Ashgate.

Mitchell, C. and Tilley, J. 2004. The moral minority: Evangelical Protestants in Northern Ireland and their political behaviour. *Political Studies,* 52(3), 585–602.

Moran, L. 2007. Invisible minorities: challenging community and neighbourhood models of policing. *Criminology and Criminal Justice,* 7(4), 417–441.

Moran, L., Skeggs, B., Tyrer, C. and Corteen, K. 2003 *Sexuality and the Politics of Violence.* London: Routledge.

Moran, L and Skeggs, B. 2004. *Sexuality and the Politics of Violence and Safety.* London: Routledge.

Moran, L., Skeggs, B., Tyrer, P. and Corteen, K. 2001. Property, Boundary, Exclusion: Making sense of hetero–violence in safer spaces. *Social and Cultural Geography*, 2(4), 407–420.

Morin, S. and Garfinkle, E. 1978. Male homophobia. *Journal of Social Issues*, 34(1), 29–47.

Morrison, L. and L'Heureux, J. 2001. Suicide and gay/lesbian/bisexual youth: implications for clinicians. *Journal of Adolescence*, 24(1), 39–49.

Moulton, E. 2008. Free Presbyterian advert ignites fresh anti–gay storm, *Belfast Telegraph*, [Online 6 August]. Available at: http://www.belfasttelegraph. co.uk/news/local–national/free–presbyterian–advert–ignites–fresh–antigay– storm–13931139.html [accessed 15 March 2011].

Mouzos, J. and Thompson, S. 2000. Gay–hate related homicides: an overview of major findings in NSW. *Trends and Issues in Crime and Criminal Justice*, June 2000, Canberra: Australian Institute of Criminology

Nardi, P. Sanders, D. and Mermor, J. 1994. *Growing up before Stonewall: Life Stories of Some Gay Men.* New York: Routledge.

News Letter, 2007. MLA "appalled" at gay support group funding. [Online 30 November]. Available at: http://www.newsletter.co.uk/news/MLA- 39appalled39-at-gay- support.354045.jp [accessed 15 March 2011].

News Letter, 2007a. Probe into 'blasphemous" Gay Pride placard. [Online 30 December]. Available at: http://www.newsletter.co.uk/news/Probe–into– 39blasphemous39–Gay–Pride.3628719.jp_[accessed 15 March 2011].

NGLTF (National Gay and Lesbian Task Force) 1999. *Anti Gay/Lesbian Violence, Victimisation and Defamation in 1998.* Washington DC: Policy Institute.

NIGRA. 1979a. *Miscellaneous Advertising Handouts and Leaflets 1975 – 1980.* Public Records Office Northern Ireland, Ref no: D/3762/1/4/4.

NIGRA. 1976b. Article from the *Sunday News*, 9 May, in *Gays in Ulster: a report of recent developments*. Public Records Office Northern Ireland D/3762/1/1/5.

NIGRA. 1976c. Article from *THES,* 14 May, in *Gays in Ulster: a report of recent developments*. Public Records Office Northern Ireland D/3762/1/1/5.

NIGRA. 1976d. *Information Sheets and Memoranda Issued by Various Gay Rights Groups, Mainly NIGRA May 1974 – October 1980.* Public Records Office Northern Ireland, Ref no: D/3762/1/4/2.

NILT (Northern Ireland Life and Times). 1998. Module Question for Religious Observance: 'And what about sexual relations between two adults of the same sex, is it?', SEXHOMO Variable. [Online] Available at: http://www.ark.ac.uk/nilt/1998/Religious_Observance/SEXHOMO.html [accessed 15 March 2011].

NILT (Northern Ireland Life and Times). 2004. Module Question for Religious Observance: 'And what about sexual relations between two adults of the same sex, is it?', SEXHOMO Variable. [Online] Available at: http://www.ark.ac.uk/nilt/2004/Religious_Observance/SEXHOMO.html [accessed 15 March 2011].

NILT (Northern Ireland Life and Times). 2008. Module Question for Religious Observance: 'And what about sexual relations between two adults of the same sex, is it?', SEXHOMO Variable. [Online] Available at:
    http://www.ark.ac.uk/nilt/2008/Religious_Observance/SEXHOMO.html
[accessed 15 March 2011].

Northern Ireland Census. 2001. *Key Statistics* [Online] Available at: http://www.nisranew.nisra.gov.uk/Census/Census2001Output/KeyStatistics/keystats.html [accessed 15 March 2011].

Nugent, R. and Gramick, J. 1989). Homosexuality: Protestant, Catholic, and Jewish issues; a fishbone tale. *Journal of Homosexuality,* 18(3–4) , 7–46.

O' Brien, K. 1941. *The Land of Spices.* New York: Doubleday, Doran & Co.

O'Doherty, J. 2009. *Through Our Eyes.* Belfast: The Rainbow Project.

O'Hearn, D. 1983. Explaining violence in Northern Ireland. *British Journal of Sociology*, 38(1), 88–93.

O'Toole, J. 2007. The Junior Minister has his say about gays. *Hot Press*, [Online 20 June]. Available at: http://www.hotpress.com/archive/2931251.html. [accessed 15 March 2011].

Office for National Statistics. 2009. *Civil Partnerships in the UK.* [Online] Available at: http://www.statistics.gov.uk/pdfdir/cpuk0810.pdf [accessed 15 March 2011].

Perry, B. 2001. *In The Name Of Hate: Understanding Hate Crime.* New York: Routledge.

Perry, B. 2003. Accounting for hate crime: doing difference, in *Hate and Bias Crime: A Reader,* editor B. Perry. New York: Routledge.

Pink News 2006. *Gay Group Supports Campaign to Clear Homophobic Preacher.* [Online 25 April]. Available at: http://www.pinknews.co.uk/news/articles/2005–1267.html/ [accessed 15 March 2011].

Plummer, K. 1975. S*exual Stigma: An Interactionist Account.* London: Routledge.

Plummer, K. 1983. *Documents of Life: An Introduction to the Problems and Literature of a Humanistic Method.* London: Allen & Unwin.

Plummer, K. 1995. *Telling Sexual Stories: Power, Change and Social Worlds.* New York: Routledge.

Porter, K and Weeks, J. 1991. *Between the Acts: Lives of Homosexual Men 1885 – 1967.* London: Routledge.

Porter, F., Hill, M., McAuley, C. and McLaughlin, E. 2006. *Eighty Years of Talking about Equality in Northern Ireland.* Working Paper 5, Equality and Social Inclusion in Ireland Project: Queen's University Belfast.

PSNI. 2008. *Statistical Report No. 3: Hate Incidents and Crime. 1ˢᵗ April 2007 – 31ˢᵗ March 2008*, [Online] Belfast: PSNI. Available at: http://www.psni.police.uk/3._hate_incidents_and_crimes–4.pdf [accessed 15 March 2011].

Public Health Agency. 2010. *HIV and STI Surveillance in Northern Ireland 2010.* [Online] Available at:
http://www.publichealth.hscni.net/sites/default/files/HIV%20and%20STI%20 report%20final%20SMK_0.pdf [accessed 15 March 2011].

Quiery, M. 2002. *A Mighty Silence: A Report on the Needs of Lesbians and Bisexual Women in Northern Ireland.* Ballymena: LASI.

Quiery, M. 2007. *Invisible Women: A Review of the Impact of Discrimination and Social Exclusion on Lesbian and Bisexual Women's Health in Northern Ireland.* Ballymena: LASI.

Radford, K., Betts, J. and Ostermeyer, M. 2006. *Policing, Accountability and the Lesbian, Gay and Bisexual Community in Northern Ireland.* Northern Ireland: ICR.

Ray, L. and Smith, D. 2002. Hate crime, violence and cultures of racism, in *The Hate Debate: Should Hate be Punished as a Crime?* edited by P. Iganski. London: Profile Books.

Rich, A. 1980. Compulsory heterosexuality and lesbian existence. *Signs*, 5(4), 631–660.

Rivers, I. 2001. The bullying of sexual minorities at school: Its nature and long–term correlates. *Educational and Child Psychology*, 18(1), 32–46.

Rolston, B., Schubotz, D. and Simpson, A. 2005. Sex education in Northern Ireland schools: a critical evaluation. *Sex Education*, 5(3), 217–234.

Rose, K. 1994. *Diverse Communities: The Evolution of Lesbian and Gay Politics in Ireland.* Cork: Cork University Press.

Rossiter, A. 2009. *Ireland's Hidden Diaspora: The 'Abortion Trail' and the Making of A London–Irish Underground, 1980–2000.* London: Iasc Publications.

RTE News. 2005. *Paisley Censured for Homophobic Comments.* [Online 3 February]. Available at: http://www.rte.ie/news/2005/0203/paisleyi.html [accessed 15 March 2011].

Ruane, J. and Todd, J. 1996. *The Dynamics of Conflict in Northern Ireland: Power, Conflict and Emancipation.* Cambridge: Cambridge University Press.

Ruthchild, R. 1997. Don't frighten the horses! A systemic perspective on violence against Lesbians and Gay Men, in *Homophobic Violence*, edited by S. Tomsen and G. Mason Sidney: The Hawkins Press.

Silke, A. 1998). Cheshire–cat logic: the recurring theme of terrorist abnormality in psychological research. *Psychology, Crime, and Law*, 4(1), 51–69.

Sluka, J. 1989. H*earts and Minds, Water and Fish: Popular Support for the IRA and INLA in a Northern Irish Ghetto.* Greenwich, Conn: JAI Press.

Smyth, C. 1994. Keeping it close: experiencing emigration in England, in *Lesbian and Gay Visions of Ireland: Towards the Twenty–First Century*, edited by I. O'Carroll and E. Collins, London: Cassell.

Smyth, L. 2007). Cottagers in Coleraine fined after police sting. *Belfast Telegraph,* [Online 12 September]. Available at: http://www.belfasttelegraph.co.uk/news/local–national/cottagers–in–coleraine–fined–after–police–sting–13475140.html [accessed 15 March 2011].

Steenkamp, C.K. 2005. The legacy of war: conceptualizing a culture of violence to explain violence after peace accords. *The Round Table*, 94(379), 253–267.

Stychin, C. 1998. *A Nation by Rights: National Cultures, Sexual Identity Politics and the Discourse of Rights.* Philadelphia: Temple University Press.

Thompson, N. 1997. *Anti-discriminatory Practice.* Basingstoke: MacMillan.

Toner, F. and McIlrath, K. 1999. *Express Yourself! An Investigation Into The Felt Counselling Needs Of Gay Men In Northern Ireland.* Belfast: Rainbow Project.

Treblicot, J. 1994. *Dyke Ideas: Politics, Process, Daily Life.* Albany: State University of New York Press.

Valentine, G. 1996. (Re)–negotiating the 'heterosexual street': lesbian productions of

Space, in *BodySpace: Destabilizing Geographies of Gender and Sexuality,* edited by N. Duncan. London: Routledge.

von Shulthess, B. 1992. Violence in the streets: anti–lesbian assault and harassment in San Francisco, in *Hate Crimes: Confronting Violence against Lesbians and Gay Men,* edited by G. Herek and K. Berrill. London: Sage.

Weeks, J. 1977. *Coming Out: Homosexual Politics in Britain from the Nineteenth Century to the Present.* London: Quartet Books.

Weeks, J. 1986. *Sexuality.* London: Ellis Horwood/Tavistock Publications.

Weeks, J. 1989. *Coming Out: Homosexual Politics in Britain from the Nineteenth Century.* London: Quartet.

Weinberg, G. 1972. S*ociety and the Healthy Homosexual.* New York: St. Martin's Press.

White, R. 1998. *How Hard Can It Be? Attempted Suicide In Gay Men, The Psychosocial Stressors And Associated Risk Factors.* Belfast: Rainbow Project.

Whyte,J. and FitzGerald, G 1991. *Interpreting Northern Ireland.* Oxford: Oxford University Press.

Williamson, I. 2000. Internalized homophobia and health issues affecting lesbians and gay men. *Health Education Research,* 15(1), 97–107.

Wilson, E. 1993. Is transgression transgressive?' in *Activating Theory: Lesbian, Gay, Bisexual Politics,* edited by J. Bristow and A. R. Wilson. London: Lawrence and Wishart.

Wilton, T. 1995. *Lesbian Studies: Setting An Agenda.* London: Routledge.

Wright, K. B. 2006. Researching internet–based populations: advantages and disadvantages of online survey research, online questionnaire authoring software packages, and web survey services. *Journal of Computer–Mediated Communication,* 10(3) Available at: http://www3.interscience.wiley.com/cgi–bin/fulltext/120837952/HTMLSTART [accessed 15 March 2011].

Young, D. 2008. Gay lifestyle is 'abomination' not a mental disorder: Iris. *Belfast Telegraph*, [Online 1 July]. Available at: http://www.belfasttelegraph.co.uk/news/local–national/gay–lifestyle–is–lsquoabominationrsquo–not–a–mental–disorder–iris–13507744.html [accessed 15 March 2011].

Index